£6-

BIOLOGICAL WARFARE IN THE 21ST CENTURY

Also from Brassey's

CDS
Brassey's Defence Yearbook

CLARKE
British Defence Choices for the Twenty-First Century

CLARKE
New Perspectives on Security

COKER
War and the 20th Century

GOW
Iraq, The Gulf Conflict and the World Community

ROGERS & DANDO
A Violent Peace: Global Security after the Cold War

TAYLOR
Terrorist Lives

BIOLOGICAL WARFARE IN THE 21ST CENTURY

Biotechnology and the Proliferation of Biological Weapons

Malcolm Dando

Brassey's (UK)
London • New York

First English edition 1994

UK editorial offices: Brassey's, 33 John Street, London WC1N 2AT
orders: Marston Book Services, PO Box 87, Oxford OX2 0DT

USA orders: Macmillan Publishing Company,
Front and Brown Streets, Riverside, NJ 08075

Distributed in North America to booksellers and wholesalers
by the Macmillan Publishing Company, NY 10022

Malcolm Dando has asserted his moral right to be identified
as author of this work

Library of Congress Cataloging in Publication Data
available

British Library Cataloguing in Publication Data
A catalogue record for this book is available
from the British Library

ISBN 1 85753 064 0 Hardback

Typeset by M Rules
Printed in Great Britain by BPC Wheatons Ltd, Exeter

CONTENTS

v

LIST OF TABLES

LIST OF FIGURES

Figure 6.1 redrawn from Weatherall, D. J. (1991), *The New Genetics and Clinical Practice* (3rd edn.), by permission of Oxford University Press. Figures 6.2 to 6.6 modified from Gerald J. Stine (1989), *The New Human Genetics*. Copyright Wm. C. Brown Communications Inc., Dubuque, Iowa. All Rights Reserved. Reprinted by permission. Figure 7.1 redrawn from Rice, C. M. *et al.* (1985), 'Nucleotide sequence of yellow fever virus: implications for flavivirus gene expression and evolution.' *Science*, **229**, 23 August, pp. 726–35. Copyright 1985 by AAAS. Reprinted by permission.

PREFACE

As the shape of international relations after the long Cold War has become clearer, the prominence accorded to the problem of proliferating weapons of mass destruction and advanced delivery systems has increased. A major objective of this book is to stress, in that context, the particular dangers that could arise from the spread of biological weapons of mass destruction, and the difficulties, but not the impossibility, of erecting an effective system of control.

During the Cold War, while biological weapons and biological arms control were overshadowed by concerns about nuclear and chemical weapons and ballistic missile proliferation, the strategic studies community was, in fact, well served by a small group of analysts who continued to publish studies on biological weapons and arms control. The Stockholm International Peace Research Institute (SIPRI), for example, published detailed material from the 1970s onwards. In addition, since the Biological Weapons Convention (BWC) was agreed in the early 1970s, an informal group of 'Friends of the Convention' and various non-governmental organisations, such as the Federation of American Scientists, have tried to assist in preserving the convention and remedying its grave defects, by publishing and lobbying, particularly around the times of the five-yearly review conferences.

The general public has also had the benefit of a series of less technical books which over the years have attempted to bring biological warfare more into the public debate. One might mention in that regard Seymour Hersh's *Chemical and Biological Warfare: America's Hidden Arsenal* from the 1960s, or Peter Williams and David Wallace's recent and distressing *Unit 731: The Japanese Army's Secret of Secrets*.

As a biologist whose research interests have centred on arms control and disarmament for 15 years, I had followed some of the more obvious issues in this area during the 1980s – Sverdlovsk, 'yellow rain', psychotropics, 'defensive research', and so on. My interest in pursuing further detailed research on biological weapons and arms control was stimulated by the growing realisation that these issues were causing increasing concern and activity amongst western governments, including that of the United Kingdom. This point was made very clearly at a seminar organised by the Foreign and Commonwealth Office in London in March 1993 on 'Export Controls to Prevent the Proliferation of Biological Weapons'.

If the UK government thought it necessary to follow up its previous warnings to the academic and research community by inviting over a hundred people to be briefed, by a Minister of State and the Vice-Chief of Defence Staff amongst others, about the threat of biological weapons proliferation and the co-ordinated export control system being put in place by the Australia Group of states, it seemed that an attempt to provide an up-to-date review of the problem could be useful. I therefore began to work more intensively on biological arms control, and devoted sabbatical work at the Indian Ocean Centre for Peace Studies (University of Western Australia, Perth) and the Peace Research Centre (Australian National University, Canberra) entirely to this topic. I was well aware of the deficiencies of the BWC from the outset, but soon became even more worried by the implications of the rate of change in the biotechnology revolution for the proliferation of biological weapons and consequently for the possibilities of biological warfare.

This book, then, is an attempt to clarify a complex military, diplomatic and scientific issue for a general audience. It draws on primary material in all these areas and attempts to present the important issues in a coherent and policy-orientated manner. I have tried to make the book more readable by avoiding some of the conventions that would be required in a more technical study, using 'party' rather than 'State Party', 'convention' rather than 'Biological Weapons Convention', and so on, but I have given a range of references in each chapter in order that an interested reader may follow the debate further. As the literature is diverse, I have also included a short guide which might be a useful starting point for anyone wishing to undertake more detailed study of the subject.

I would like to thank a number of friends and colleagues for their help. John Walker and Brendon Hammer supplied many of the VEREX papers, often at short notice; Alastair Hay kindly allowed me to use material he had obtained under the US Freedom of Information Act;

Sean Howard (of BASIC) obtained recent US studies for me; Owen Dando produced the figures for Chapters 6 and 7, and my wife kept an eye both on the biology and my use of English. I also benefited greatly from the formal presentations and informal discussions at the Wilton Park Conference on 'Controlling Biological Weapons' in September 1993. Erhard Geissler kindly pointed out the recent work on viruses to me, and Vivienne Mountner supplied the abstracts of the 1993 International Virology Congress. The translation of the Russian submission in the 1992 round of confidence-building measures used in Chapter 9 was made by Ed Jocelyn of the Department of Modern Languages at the University of Bradford.

I am particularly grateful to the New Zealand Public Advisory Committee for Disarmament and Arms Control for organising a speaking tour which allowed me to air my ideas on this subject before numerous members of the New Zealand Institute of International Affairs.[1] Finally, I would like to thank everyone at Perth, Canberra and Bradford who gave assistance with this book during my sabbatical term and to Bradford University, the Radley Trust and the Joseph Rowntree Charitable Trust for grants which helped to finance this study. I naturally accept responsibility for any errors that remain.

. 1 .

THE SPECTRE OF BIOLOGICAL
WARFARE RETURNS

Hopes that the ending of the Cold War would usher in a more benign new world order received a severe setback when large-scale warfare was undertaken by coalition forces to remove Iraq from Kuwait in 1991.[1] One unwelcome surprise for the general public was the realisation that the coalition forces were very concerned that they might have been attacked with biological weapons.

Even for most people involved with security and international affairs, biological weapons had been virtually a non-issue for two decades. Most members of the general public simply had not thought about the potential use of such weapons. Writing in the popular science journal *New Scientist* in early 1992, Graham Pearson, the Director General of the UK Chemical and Biological Defence Establishment (CBDE) at Porton Down, attempted to draw readers' attention to the importance of preventing biological warfare:[2]

> As to the suggestion . . . that the use of biological weapons is widely recognised by many military commanders as the least effective option, it is interesting to ask why some 10 nations have biological weapons programmes.

Turning specifically to the events of the previous year he added:

> . . . Why did the Iraqis have a military programme, uncovered by the UN Special Commission, focused on anthrax and botulinum toxin as agents? Why was there so much concern that such agents might be used by Saddam Hussein? Why is the UN instituting such a stringent future compliance regime? . . .

In short, Pearson argued that the potential for proliferation and use of biological weapons is something that we should take seriously and act to prevent now if we possibly can.

A similar position was taken in late 1992 by General Friel, Commander of the US Chemical and Biological Defense Agency. He was reported as saying that concerns over nuclear and chemical weapons during the Cold War had masked similar worries over biological weapons. Looking to the world after the Cold War he stated:[3]

> . . . the biological threat has been recently singled out as the one major threat that still poses the ability for catastrophic effects on a theater-deployed force . . .

More generally, President Clinton, in his autumn 1993 address to the United Nations, looked forward to a peaceful, prosperous world of market-based democracies, but also pointed out the problems that could prevent its achievement. In particular, he noted that if proliferation was not prevented no democracy could feel secure. In his view:[4]

> One of our most urgent priorities must be attacking the proliferation of weapons of mass destruction, whether they are nuclear, chemical or biological; and the ballistic missiles that can rain them down on populations hundreds of miles away.

The growing realisation amongst the general public that the Soviet Union had an offensive biological weapons programme for the last two decades of the Cold War has served strongly to reinforce that point in regard to biological weapons.[5]

It is true, of course, that concerns over the Soviet programme were voiced during the latter stages of the Cold War.[6] The accusations of the alleged use of 'yellow rain' in the Far East appear not to have stood up well to detailed analysis,[7] but the latest information strongly reinforces the view that the anthrax outbreak at Sverdlovsk in 1979 did result from an accident at a military research facility.[8] Moreover, the development in several countries of novel kinds of agents capable of affecting behaviour clearly requires careful analysis.[9]

Western governments have made their concerns over the proliferation of biological weapons very clear in recent years. There has also been a variety of estimates of the extent of proliferation presented in the open literature. The widely respected Office of Technology Assessment (OTA) in the United States attempted to summarise these sources in mid-1993. In its opinion 'countries generally reported as having undeclared offensive biological warfare programmes' were as follows:[10]

Middle East	Iran
	Iraq
	Israel
	Libya
	Syria
East Asia	China
	North Korea
	Taiwan

As the OTA noted, there is a considerable overlap between the nations in these two conflict-prone regions which are thought to have biological weapons programmes and those which are seeking other weapons of mass destruction and ballistic missiles.

The aim of this book is to provide the reader with the necessary information to make judgements about the dangers of the proliferation of biological weapons and how that process might be controlled. The conclusion is that we do have a chance to restrict the spread and use of these weapons, but success in that endeavour is far from assured. In particular, it will be argued that the rapid advances in commercial biotechnology will considerably complicate any efforts to achieve effective control. If we do not act effectively, it seems likely that we will see biological weapons used on a large scale sooner rather than later in the next century.

In the following part of this chapter an attempt is made to bring together some of the openly-available quantitative information on the effects of the use of biological weapons. It will be argued that the only possible conclusion from this evidence is that biological weapons are weapons of mass destruction, in many ways more equivalent to nuclear weapons than chemical weapons. A brief review will then be given of how biological weapons might be used.

Chapter 2 gives an account of potential agents that could be used in biological weapons programmes, and Chapter 3 deals with the offensive biological weapons programmes of the UK, Japan and the USA up to the unilateral renunciation of biological weapons by the United States in the late 1960s-early 1970s. Chapter 4 deals with efforts to control the production and use of biological weapons from the agreement of the 1925 Geneva Protocol through to the agreement of the Biological Weapons Convention (BWC) in the early 1970s and its five-yearly review conferences up to 1991.

In Chapter 5 we turn our attention to the relationship between science,

3

technology and warfare. The impact of the revolution in information technology on modern warfare is followed from the writings of Marshall Ogarkov in the Soviet Union and in the implementation of the new warfare in the coalition assault on Iraq in 1991. The related concerns over the basic industrial strength in crucial technical areas, which is required to underpin such an advanced military capability, are shown to include biotechnology.

Modern biotechnology and its impact are the subject of Chapter 6, and in Chapter 7 the implications of this new technology for the development and spread of biological weapons is analysed. Current developments following the Third Review Conference of the BWC in 1991 are the subject of Chapter 8. Particular emphasis will be placed on efforts to move towards the addition of verification conditions which are presently missing from the convention. Major attention is given to the VEREX meetings of government experts resulting from the third review and the possibility that these could lead to positive progress at the fourth review in 1996.

Chapter 9 is concerned with policy options available to western states, such as defensive research programmes, export controls and possible armed interventions against countries attempting to obtain or use biological weapons, which have to be integrated with efforts to improve arms control. The difficulties of combining assistance to Third World states with proliferation control in this area of overwhelmingly dual-use technology are stressed.

In Chapter 10 the proliferation and control of biological weapons are set within the wider arena of arms control and international politics after the Cold War. Discussion centres on two general theories about how the world might develop: one assuming that proliferation is inevitable but can be managed and the other that it must be prevented by all possible means. It is suggested that, as biotechnology is cheap and will become increasingly available, it is in this area of dual-use technology that we may well see which of these theories prevails.

Biological Weapons of Mass Destruction

In order to have a proper factual basis for the analysis presented in the rest of this book we now consider some open quantitative estimates of the potential effects of the use of biological weapons. These estimates are summarised in Table 1.1. The first column of the table gives the four major studies that we shall discuss. Within each study the cases investigated are then numbered and, where possible, briefly described. The

Table 1.1 Some publicly-available information concerning large-scale attacks using biological weapons

Study (Case)	Weapon System	Area Affected (km²)	Fatalities[1]
SIPRI			
(i) bomber	10 -kt nuclear	30	–
	biological agent	0–50	–
	VX nerve gas	0.75	–
	5–6-t high explosive	0.22	–
(ii) WEU	1.75–17.5 kg anthrax spores	1	–
(iii)	500–125,000 kg biological agent	500	50%
United Nations			
(i) line attack	10^{10} agent per gm along 100 km	5,000	50%
(ii)	1Mt nuclear	300	90%
	15t Sarin	60	50%
	10t biological	100,000	50% ill; 25% dead
International Security			
(i) missile on sparsely populated city	20-kt nuclear	–	40,000 dead ; 40,000 injured
	300 kg Sarin	–	200–3,000
	30 kg anthrax spores	–	20,000–80,000
(ii)	1 kg anthrax	0.2–2.6	50%
OTA			
(i) missile on sparse to moderately populated city	12.5-kt nuclear	7.8	23,000–80,000
	300 kg Sarin	0.22	60–-200
	30 kg anthrax spores	10	30,000—100,000
(ii) line attack	100 kg anthrax spores	46 (clear day)	130–460,000
		140 (overcast)	420,000–1.4m
		300 (clear night)	1–3m

[1]Numbers killed, unless otherwise indicated

second column specifies the weapon system or agent; the third and the fourth column give, respectively, the data available on the area affected and the consequences for people in the target area. It will, of course, come as no surprise that the publicly-available information on this topic is fragmentary, but enough is to be found for a reasonable picture of the deadly effects of biological weapons to emerge.

SIPRI

In the early 1970s the Stockholm International Peace Research Institute published a series of volumes under the general title *The Problem of Chemical and Biological Warfare*. In the second volume of the series, *CB Weapons Today*,[11] an attempt was made to compare the relative potencies of chemical, biological and other types of weapon both nuclear and conventional. It was suggested that a 10–15-kt nuclear weapon airburst over an urban target might cause 50 per cent casualties, half of which would be fatal, over an area of 3,000 hectares (30 km^2). The area over which a biological weapon would cause 50 per cent primary casualties was given as 0–5,000 hectares (0–50 km^2), a footnote pointing out that the result would be highly weather-dependent. The attack scenario was for a single aircraft with a bombload of 5–6 tons and, for comparison, the area for 50 per cent casualties from the use of VX nerve gas was given as 75 hectares and for high-explosive bombs as 22 hectares. Of course, the effect of the chemical weapon would be weather-dependent and that of the high-explosive bombs on the amount of shelter available. The general import of the figures, however, puts biological and nuclear weapons in a different class from other weapon systems.

Another indication of the potency of biological weapons was given in Volume V of the SIPRI study, *The Prevention of CBW*.[12] In this volume the authors were attempting to estimate the scale of a militarily-significant offensive biological weapons programme. We shall have cause to refer to their main argument in a later chapter. What is of interest here is that the authors referred back to the work on the usage of these weapons in volume II and suggested that, to achieve 50 per cent casualties with a non-communicable agent in a city of half a million inhabitants, some 10^{17}–10^{19} pathogens would be required. They then attempted to calculate the weight of agent necessary to provide that number of pathogens and suggested that a figure of 'something between hundreds of kilos and hundreds of tons of BW agent' would be required.

The SIPRI authors then went on to argue that their estimates were of a similar order of magnitude to those made by the Armaments Control

Agency of the Western European Union (WEU). This agency was concerned with verifying that WEU members were observing the armament limitations agreed in 1955. As the SIPRI authors noted, the official WEU figures available were somewhat deficient in that precise concentrations were not given, but biological and military experts had worked out what amounts of various agents would be required to obtain 'direct military effect' over an area of 1 km^2. In the accompanying table this weight of agent was, for example, given as 0.007 kg for botulinal toxins and 1.75–17.5 kg for anthrax spores. Scaling up from the least and the most effective agents given, the SIPRI authors stated that:

> . . . for an attack of a 500 km^2 town, the WEU would reckon that something between 500 kg and 125 tons of BW agent would be required.

An imperial ton is equivalent to 1,016 kg so the range of potency is wide, but the message remains clear: biological weapons could have devastating effects if used in amounts which are clearly capable of being delivered on to a target.

The United Nations

This point is amply supported by figures from a major United Nations study carried out at about the same time in the late 1960s.[13] It was suggested that pathogens can be produced at a concentration of 10^{10} per gm. The authors then outlined a scenario in which an aircraft sprayed such a mixture along a 100-km line when a 10-km per hour cross-wind was blowing. Assuming that a relatively fragile agent was used and therefore that only 10 per cent of the organisms survived aerosolisation in the spray, and that they then died off in the environment at a rate of five per cent per minute, it was concluded that 50 per cent of unprotected people over an area of about 5,000 km^2 would inhale a dose sufficient to cause infection (about 100 of the individual organisms).

The report continued:

> . . . This particular calculation is valid for agents such as those which cause tularaemia or plague, as well as for some viruses. The decay rate of the causative agents of Q-fever, anthrax and some other infections is much lower . . .

These organisms would therefore exert their effects over an even larger area.

Again a comparative table was presented in which it was suggested that a one-megaton nuclear weapon could kill 90 per cent of unprotected people in an area of 300 km², that 15 tons of nerve agent could cause 50 per cent deaths over 60 km², and that 10 tons of biological agent could cause illness in 50 per cent, and death in 25 per cent of people over an area of 100,000 km². The real equivalence of biological and nuclear weapons of mass destruction is again strongly demonstrated by this example.

International Security

A rather more precise comparison was provided by Steve Fetter in the journal *International Security* in 1991.[14] He estimated the number of people that could be killed if a missile with a throw-weight of one tonne were aimed at a large, sparsely-populated (30 people per hectare) city using different types of warhead.

He calculated that a 20-kt nuclear warhead could kill 40,000 people and injure another 40,000 in the absence of civil defence measures. A chemical warhead of 300 kg of Sarin (nerve agent) could, under the same conditions, kill 200 to 3,000 people, but 30 kg of anthrax spores could kill between 20,000 and 80,000 people.

As Fetter explained, anthrax readily forms spores which are resistant to environmental stress and therefore suitable for dispersal in weapon systems. As it is not infectious in the sense that a person who caught the disease as a direct result of an attack would pass it on to another person, Fetter argued that the organism could be used with some discrimination in an attack. Moreover, it is deadly at much lower concentrations than nerve gases. The estimated dose rate at which 50 per cent of an unprotected target population would catch the disease, assuming ideal infective-agent particle sizes of one to five micrometres (m^{-6}), is incredibly small. On Fetter's figures, just 1 kg of anthrax spores could produce such conditions, over 0.2 to 2.6 km², depending on the weather. If untreated, anthrax contracted from the air in such an attack, by inhalation through the lungs, would kill nearly everyone affected within a few days. Though vaccines are available they would have to be given *before* exposure and their effects following high infective doses of the organism are uncertain. Finally, whilst antibiotics can be used successfully, they have to be administered early before signs of the disease become apparent. Given the numbers of people who could be affected in the scenarios discussed here, it is doubtful whether any effective assistance could be organised in the time available.

Theoretically, civil defence measures could be more effective against attack with biological weapons than against nuclear weapons but, as Fetter himself concluded:

. . . even when used against a prepared population, anthrax warheads could rival small nuclear weapons in their ability to kill people . . .

This point was made very clearly in the detailed OTA study released in 1993,[10] which also clarified the reasons why different attack scenarios with biological weapons give such diverse effects.

Office of Technology Assessment

The OTA considered two hypothetical cases: first, an attack with a missile delivered on an overcast day or night, with a moderate wind, on to a city with 3,000 to 10,000 unprotected people per km^2. The authors stated that 300 kg of Sarin nerve gas could kill between 60 and 200 people in an area of 0.22 km^2. 30 kg of anthrax spores spread out in a cigar-shape across the city from the missile warhead could kill 30,000 to 100,000 in an area of 10 km^2. For a 12.5-kt nuclear weapon there would be a circular area of destruction of 7.8 km^2 in which 23,000 to 80,000 people could be killed.

In the second case, 100 kg of anthrax spores were released by an aircraft along a line to the windward side of the city (as in the case given in the 1969 United Nations report). The city chosen for illustrative purposes was Washington, DC. On a clear sunny day with a light breeze, 46 km^2 would be affected and 130-460,000 people could die. On an overcast day or night with a moderate wind, 140 km^2 would be affected and 420,000 to 1,400,000 people could die. On a clear, calm night an area of 300 km^2 would be affected and between 1 and 3 million people could die. Using the line source is a considerably more effective means of delivering a biological agent.

Whilst the central message of the potentially devastating consequences of the use of biological weapons is obvious from these examples, an understanding of the situation is sometimes complicated by the fact that the efficiency with which biological weapons could be produced and used undoubtedly increased from 1940 to 1969. It might also appear from the different scenarios and measures used (Table 1.1) that the results given in the examples were produced by *ad hoc* 'back-of-the-envelope' calculations. Nothing, of course, could be further from the truth. Much work has gone into the study of how micro-organisms react to environmental factors and how they infect individuals. The information gained has been used to develop complex mathematical models for predicting the consequences of employing biological weapons and assuming different conditions for attack.

US Army

Obviously it would not be sensible for all such official information and calculations to be placed in the public domain, but some of the relevant general data have been released. As an example, we may consider the study, *Biological Vulnerability Assessment: The US East Coast*, produced by the US Army at Dugway Proving Ground in 1983.[15] The document analysed potential clandestine biological attacks on the whole of the east coast, on Washington DC and on two large military facilities in the area. The report has two major sections, one on the topography and meteorology of the area and the other concerned with modes of attack, potential agents and examples of hypothetical attacks. Appendices cover the computerised methods used to analyse weather conditions and the attack scenarios.

For a region such as the east coast of the USA the meteorological conditions are very well known. The types of weather condition that occur at different times of year and how these can be predicted – at least over the short term – are well understood. Also, as previously pointed out, much is now known about how aerosols behave in different weather conditions, how different disease agents are affected by environmental stresses, and the mechanisms by which infection takes place through the lungs. As examples, the conferences organised in part by the US Army on aerobiology in the 1960s may be cited.[16,17]

Thus it is possible to know what particular set of weather conditions would be best to ensure dispersal of the aerosolised agent and its ideal spread over the envisaged target area on the wind. In this specific study one aim was to estimate the amount of anthrax necessary to attack various targets in the area. The types of favourable meteorological condition likely to occur in the area were examined and a mathematical cloud-diffusion model was used to determine the concentrations of the agent which would arrive downwind from the source in such conditions. The best kind of conditions would occur in what is called neutral air stability under cloudy or overcast skies. And because micro-organisms are damaged by UV light, night would be the best time for ensuring that high levels of most agents arrived at the target.

Calculations can be made of the probable dose rate required to infect 50 per cent of people in a particular target area if the following are known: the concentration of the organism in the source material spread along a line of attack; the efficiency of the munition in aerosolising the agent; the wind speed; the rate of decay of the agent in the air; and the number of organisms required to be inhaled, assuming normal rates of respiration in the target population. One such calculation indicated that a

900-km^2 area of Washington could be successfully attacked to produce 50 per cent deaths with 40 kg of anthrax, assuming ideal conditions of neutral stability and a 4m/sec wind speed. This is similar to the OTA figures, as the authors suggested that, because of uncertainties in the actual attack conditions, several times the calculated amount might be used.

The study contains a number of other relevant calculations for different scenarios, but the general point to be made is that there would be nothing necessarily *ad hoc* about biological warfare. Sophisticated calculations could be made in order to achieve different effects with various types of agent. For example, the required application rate for the fungal agent which causes black stem rust of cereals is 0.01 kg/km^2 to achieve an 85 per cent reduction in crop yield.[18]

In the light of the information that is publicly available, it is clearly necessary to investigate carefully why the United States renounced these weapons unilaterally.

The US Renunciation of Biological Weapons

Professor Matthew Meselson of Harvard University, who has long been involved in efforts to prevent the use or spread of biological weapons, gave testimony to the US Congress on this subject in 1989. He set out the reasons for the US renunciation as follows:[19]

> First, it was understood that biological weapons could be as great a threat to large populations as nuclear weapons and that no reliable defence is likely . . .

The USA already had nuclear weapons which could be seen as more versatile, for instance being also suitable for use against small hardened military installations such as missile silos. Meselson continued:

> Second, it was evident that biological weapons could be much simpler and less expensive than nuclear weapons to develop and produce . . .

and:

> Third, it was realised that our biological weapons program was pioneering an easily duplicated technology and that our program was likely to inspire others to follow suit.

Thus, according to Meselson, the biological weapons programme was 'a substantial threat' to the United States' own security. Better then to make a convincing show of giving up the weapons and attempt to erect some barriers to proliferation.

It will be seen that this explanation does not involve the widely-accepted and propagated argument[20] that 'biological weapons are not effective military weapons'. This argument was also rejected strongly in 1992 by a senior official from the British Chemical and Biological Defence Establishment at Porton Down. Writing in the *Journal of the Royal United Services Institute*, Gordon Carter stated that President Nixon's decision resulted from political considerations.[21] He specifically rejected the idea that it was caused by the stated rationale of the uncontrollability and unpredictability of these weapons. In his view:

> . . . The utility of BW had been demonstrated by all means, short of use in war, and the established feasibility could clearly not become disestablished with time . . .

He reinforced the point as follows:

> . . . The US had sustained its offensive BW capability for nearly a quarter of a century. During this period, the concept of uncontrollability and unpredictability (which would only be possible if certain agents of great epidemic potential were used) had not arisen . . .

Thus in Carter's view, there was no 'scientific, military or technical reason' why such an argument should have been put forward in 1969. By implication, the same holds true today and underlies the statement from the Director General of Porton Down which was quoted at the start of this chapter. We should therefore proceed on the assumption that biological weapons could be considered militarily useful in some circumstances. The proliferation of these weapons is therefore a real problem, not just an empty threat used in a propaganda war over the shape of the new world order.

We need to turn finally in this introduction to the question of the different ways in which biological weapons might be used, because it is certainly not just in relation to massive attacks on unprotected civilians that they have been considered.

Other Military Uses of Biological Weapons

We have been discussing in the main the use of biological weapons on a large scale against civilian populations. As the OTA report noted,[10] it is perfectly possible that a major state might choose to have biological weapons in order to deter any such attack or even for symbolic purposes just to demonstrate its capability. Furthermore, an attack with biological weapons need not necessarily be an overt act or be directed just against the human population. As Commander Rose pointed out in his prize-winning essay in the US *Naval War College Review*, Cuba charged the USA with a multifaceted, covert attack in the 1970s:[22]

> ... Allegedly, this campaign targeted vital crops such as tobacco (blue mold) and sugar cane (cane smut), livestock (African swine fever), and also the populace itself (hemorrhagic strain of dengue fever) ...

As Rose commented, whatever the source(s) of these diseases (natural or otherwise), they were certainly costly for Cuba.

Covert use of biological weapons against people, plants and animals could form a means of economic warfare to weaken an enemy indirectly before military action. Similarly, as the original SIPRI study noted[11], biological weapons could be used in a covert strategic attack against troops, either massively or against key facilities, for example, before a major invasion. Covert use would be suggested by the continuing difficulties of providing an effective detector system for biological weapons, and the possibility of protecting troops with masks, etc. if a biological attack were known to be under way.

Once hostilities had commenced between parties equipped with biological weapons, a variety of both covert and overt uses would obviously be possible. Raymond Zilinskas has suggested that if two Third World states became bogged down in attrition warfare there might well be a temptation to use biological weapons against the enemy's front-line forces, if only to cause logistic and morale problems.[23] Moreover, as attempts were made to circumvent the front-line stalemate, biological weapons could obviously offer means of attack at other points. As he suggested, terrorists might be employed to contaminate key transport nodes, such as airports and railway stations with persistent and deadly agents. Lest anyone should find such ideas far-fetched we can again refer to official US studies.

A 1975 paper entitled *Covert Biological Weapons Literature Review*[24] set out to give an overview of possible operations and the studies that had been made of them. After noting examples involving agents carried in aerosols, by insects or by other methods the paper stated that:

> In the past several years, all of these methods have been studied, prototype models have been produced, scenarios in their application have been written and tested, and hardware has been evaluated for covert use by unconventional forces ...

Such work ceased in the USA, the study stated, after the renunciation of biological weapons. Nevertheless, similar work could certainly have continued elsewhere, and the USA has continued to study vulnerabilities and the difficulties of taking effective defensive measures against terrorists.[25]

A final reason we might note for a major Third World state wishing to possess biological weapons could be to deter intervention in its region by forces from the rich industrial world, or even to use such weaponry if it was fighting forces from the West. That surely was the reason for concern about Iraq's biological weapons in 1991 and the thinking behind General Friel's worries over the 'biological threat' and 'catastrophic effects on a theater-deployed force' which were quoted at the beginning of this chapter.

Given that framework, which is intended to stress again the reality of the problem of the proliferation of biological weapons, we turn next to a more detailed study of biological agents.

. 2 .

POTENTIAL AGENTS
FOR BIOLOGICAL WEAPONS

During the course of evolution organisms have developed complex co-operative and competitive interactions. For example, ruminants such as cows depend on micro-organisms in their gut in order to digest the cellulose they eat. Without these micro-organisms cows would not be able to digest grass as efficiently as they do, and we would not have a dairy industry.[1]

We are more concerned here with the competitive interactions between organisms: specifically with the way in which bacteria, viruses and, to some extent, fungi, may be manipulated to cause harm to human beings and their economically important food-producing animals and plants. The definition and classification of bacteria, viruses and fungi are complex issues, the details of which need not overly concern us here.[2]

It is necessary, however, to recall that higher organisms like ourselves are made up of minute cells. Each cell consists of cytoplasm and a nucleus where the genetic material is held. Bacteria are simpler, single-celled organisms in which, for example, the genetic material is not separated off from the cytoplasm in the same way. Bacteria are visible with the light microscope, but are generally smaller than 10 micrometres (m^{-6}) in diameter. Viruses are much smaller again and consist predominantly of genetic material. They can only reproduce by invading a suitable cell and taking over its operations. Viruses can be seen through use of more powerful electron microscopes. Fungi are widespread and important organisms in nature; they include the common edible mushroom, toadstools, smuts, rusts and powdery mildew. They are very different from green plants in lacking chlorophyll and thus must obtain their nutrients from parasitism or the decomposition of dead matter.

15

We shall mainly be concerned here, however, with bacteria and viruses.

Given the constant threat of invasion from other organisms, animals have evolved complex mechanisms of protection. We human beings keep out as many invaders as possible by means of our tough waterproof skin. Where we are more exposed, for example in our eyes and mouth, tears and saliva contain enzymes to attack invaders. Additionally, other bacteria which normally live with us harmlessly, in our digestive systems, help in various ways to make it difficult for harmful invaders to become established.

If an invading organism breaches these outer defences it becomes much more difficult for the body to defend itself. However, a complex system based on the white blood cells (leucocytes) has necessarily evolved to protect us.[3] There is first a 'non-specific' internal defence system including cells which attack foreign invaders. To do this the cells have to recognise the foreign material, which they do with the assistance of various mediators. However, this non-specific system is supplemented by a highly sophisticated and very specific immune-response system.

The body's specific protective system depends on the class of white blood cells called lymphocytes. Two types of lymphocyte are of particular importance. These are the T-cells from the thymus gland and the B-cells from the bone marrow. The interactions between these two types of cell are complex, but it is clear that B-cells specialise in responding to foreign material in circulation whilst T-cells attack body cells showing evidence of having foreign material within their cytoplasm.

B-lymphocytes have very specific receptors (antibodies) for foreign molecules (antigens) on their surfaces. When an antigen molecule is encountered the B-cell is activated to divide and secrete its antibody protein. This then binds and neutralises the foreign material in a precise manner. T-lymphocytes are similarly highly specific, but they respond to pieces of foreign material brought to the surface from within cells.

This system can clearly be overwhelmed, for example by a massive injection of a toxic chemical in a snake bite which takes effect before a sufficient response can be produced. Similarly in an illness such as measles, there is a period of time required following initial infection for the body to produce enough antibody to kill off the invading organism. On the other hand, once a specific initial invasion has taken place, some cells which can respond specifically will persist in a dormant state in the body. If a subsequent attack by the same organism occurs, these cells and their reaction are more swiftly activated. We say that the person has become immune to the disease, and we make use of this mechanism when we vaccinate people against disease with harmless elements from threatening micro-organisms.

Agents of Human Disease

Until the public anxiety over HIV and AIDS arose in the last decade most people in the developed world had fewer concerns over infectious or contagious (communicable) diseases and agents of disease than for much of the past hundred years. Our medical concerns were related more to illnesses such as heart disease and cancer which are not often caused by infectious agents.

Indeed, as the science of biology and its application to medicine and agriculture developed, for those of us in the rich world an unstated assumption had arisen that infectious diseases were no longer a serious problem. Whilst AIDS and, to a lesser extent, Legionnaire's disease, Lassa fever, Marburg virus disease and Ebola virus disease have shaken that confident outlook, it is necessary to begin by reminding ourselves of just how dangerous infectious diseases can be.[4]

While the classification of bacteria is complex, they do have standard biological (generic/species) double names. For viruses the nomenclature remains less standardised. Thus, while bacteria are given standard names here, the scientific names of viruses are not always used, though family groups and genera within families will be mentioned where useful. One small complication that should be borne in mind is that some bacterial diseases, particularly rickettsial diseases such as typhus (agent *Rickettsia prowazekii*), Q-fever (*Coxiella burnetii*) and Rocky Mountain spotted fever (*Rickettsia rickettsii*), are caused by bacteria which are obligatory intracellular parasites. Like viruses, they can only metabolise and multiply within other living cells.

A full account of the infectious diseases would require a medical textbook but, bearing in mind our concern with the military use of infectious agents, we may simply concentrate here on the questions of which agents cause which diseases and how the agents are transmitted (this will help us to get to grips with later discussions about which agents have been used to produce weapon systems). Thus if we consider AIDS, we know that acquired immunodeficiency syndrome – the name from which the acronym is derived – is caused by the action of a human immunodeficiency virus (HIV) and that this is transmitted between people by sexual contact and the exchange of blood products (for example, in the re-use of needles for drug injections).

There has been little interest shown in weaponising living agents more complex than bacteria for direct use against man. Thus we are not concerned here with vitally important infectious diseases, such as malaria or African sleeping sickness, because these are caused by more complex (protozoan) organisms. Amongst the fungi, only coccidioidomycosis, a respiratory infection caused by airborne spores of *Coccidioides immitis*, is thought to have aroused much military interest. Thus other fungal infections will be discussed here only in relation to potential attacks on agriculture.

Although we have tended to forget about the extreme dangers of infectious disease, we still protect ourselves against their effects wherever possible. We carefully vaccinate our children against those childhood diseases – diphtheria (*Corynebacterium diphtheriae*), mumps (virus), poliomyelitis (viruses), rubella (virus), rubeola (measles virus), whooping cough (*Bordetella pertussis*) – from which previous generations suffered greatly. Sensible people keep their own, and their children's, tetanus jabs (against *Clostridium tetani* toxin) up to date; they ensure that they and their children obtain protection against typhoid fever (*Salmonella typhi*), yellow fever (virus), cholera etc. if they are travelling to areas where this is necessary. Similarly, anyone bitten by a rabid dog would avoid the fatal consequences by quickly obtaining the necessary injections to halt the growth of the viral rabies infection.

While we may not recognise the fact as directly, we are also the beneficiaries of the growing understanding of infectious diseases that forced new standards of public hygiene upon previous generations. Thus we know that cholera (*Vibrio cholerae*), viral hepatitis and typhoid fever can be greatly restricted if water and food supplies are clean. We know that brucellosis (*Brucella abortus*, *B. melitensis*, and *B. suis*) can be effectively controlled, particularly by the pasteurisation of milk. Bacillary dysentery, gastroenteritis (many possible causative organisms) and botulism (poisoning by *Clostridium botulinum* toxin) clearly also demand care in the preparation of food and drink if they are to be avoided.

Because of the protection available to us through modern medicine and improved public health and hygiene measures we have predominantly lost contact with the overwhelming impact of the great killer infectious diseases. We need to supplement the facts of everyday life in the West with a little history.

Major Infectious Diseases

To obtain a realistic picture of the issue we are discussing it is necessary to briefly review what is known of diseases such as those already mentioned and others such as bubonic plague (*Yersinia pestis*), influenza (viruses), leprosy (*Mycobacterium leprae*), smallpox (variola viruses), tuberculosis (*Mycobacterium tuberculosis*) and yellow fever (virus).

In his classic book, *Plagues and Peoples*,[5] William McNeill presented an overview of how the interaction of such diseases with the growing human population had often shaped historical events. His curiosity had been aroused by the ease with which 600 Spaniards under Cortez had conquered the Aztec Empire. He concluded that the major reason was the Aztec susceptibility to smallpox and other diseases carried by the Europeans. Moreover, he suggested that this was a specific example of a general feature of European expansion: that it was a disease-experienced society that, during the maritime voyages of recent centuries, frequently encountered native populations with no resistance to the diseases it carried.

The tragic consequences are illustrated by McNeill's account of the conquest of Mexico:

> . . . population decay was catastrophic. . . . less than fifty years from the time Cortez inaugurated epidemiological as well as other exchanges between Amerindian and European populations, the population of central Mexico had shrunk to about three million, i.e., to about one tenth of what had been there when Cortez landed . . .

The population decay continued, at a slower rate, for another 50 years. And, of course, such a devastating assault had profound psychological and social consequences on the native peoples.

McNeill attempted to explain how the gradual build-up of the human population and the increasing contacts between centres of population in Eurasia had produced the disease-experienced Europeans, and then to take the story forward to the present situation where the world's human population can be affected by a new influenza virus. As he pointed out, and as biologists stress today,[6] we are embarking on a radically new experiment with our massive population growth and the development of many megacities. Despite our medical technology, successful rapid conquest of opportunistic pathogens which might take advantage of these circumstances is not assured.

To understand the outcome of the impact any disease organism may have on a human population requires data on the characteristics of the organism and its mode of action, and on the population's environment and characteristics. With such data precise models of how diseases spread and are controlled may be obtained.[7] It is clear, for example, that the European population suffered similar devastation to the Aztecs when plague returned, after many centuries' absence, in the fourteenth century. McNeill suggested the best estimate is that one-third of Europe's population died between 1346 and 1350.

Such huge setbacks undoubtedly severely affected the build-up of the human population. Other diseases, such as smallpox, later became endemic amongst the European population. Those who survived childhood were likely to have a degree of immunity as adults. It took the development of vaccination at the turn of the eighteenth century to reduce the impact of this dreaded disease on children.

Other diseases, such as cholera, which began to affect the European populations more as contact with India increased and the rapid urbanisation of the last century provided conditions for its propagation, then triggered the changes in public health provisions required for effective control. Also, towards the latter half of the nineteenth century medical experimentation and theoretical advances allowed the development of specific control measures.[8] In recent decades, of course, the use of antibiotic drugs against bacteria has been of great importance.

Bubonic Plague

If most of us were asked to name an infectious disease which had profound effects in history we would most probably think of bubonic plague or the Black Death. Plague is caused by the bacterium *Yersinia pestis*, which is a natural infection of rodents. It is transmitted to human beings by the bite of fleas which have previously fed off infected rodents.

As we have a very poor natural immune response to this particular organism, death rates are high in untreated cases. In the bubonic form a lump – or bubo – arises in a lymph node near the site of infection within six days. This indicates the immune system's attempt to deal with the infection. After a week, typically about half of those infected in the great pandemics were dead. In the septicaemic form of the disease the bacteria rapidly enter the blood and spread widely throughout the body. Death rates then approach 100 per cent in untreated cases. Sometimes, after the bacteria reach the lungs of an infected person, there is a highly contagious spread of the deadly primary pneumonic form of the disease through the air from person to person. Death rates for pneumonic plague again approach 100 per cent for untreated cases.[2] Occasionally, after circulatory collapse, the surface of the victim's body blackens. 'Black Death' is the name given to the pandemic which ravaged Europe in the middle of the fourteenth century. This was the first devastating wave of the second great cycle of plague. The first occurred in late Greco-Roman times, but the second cycle persisted until about 1800. Since then a third cycle has spread through non-European parts of the world.

The Black Death had a profound effect on European society. It swept over vast areas and the *Cambridge History of Human Disease*[4] agrees with McNeill on its impact in numbers of deaths:

> . . . historians generally agree that death rates most commonly ranged between about 30 to 50 per cent in both Europe and the Middle East, with the best records indicating a mortality in the upper end of that range . . .

– and its unexpectedness:

> The Black Death was in many ways a completely unprecedented experience for those who suffered through it. Plague had virtually disappeared from the Middle East and Europe during the centuries between the end of the first pandemic in the eighth century and the beginning of the second pandemic . . .

Whilst vigorous efforts were made to combat the disease, given the suddenness of its onset, the intensity of its effects and the lack of medical understanding, the well-documented devastating impact of plague on the whole society is surely not surprising.

Cholera

Cholera is a diarrhoeal disease caused by the bacterium *Vibrio cholerae*. The bacterium is transmitted from one infected person's faeces through a contaminated water system to another person. The bacterium does not have other regular animal hosts.

Whilst some people appear to have a natural resistance to cholera, infection does not produce a strong lasting immunity. The bacteria adhere to the intestinal wall of human beings and secrete a toxin that causes an extremely severe diarrhoea. Patients may lose 10-12 litres of fluid a day and death results from the consequences of such a catastrophic loss. Modern treatment aims to safely replace the lost water and salts. Thus cholera is treatable today.

That was certainly not the case in the last century. Cholera appears to have long been endemic in the Ganges Delta of the Indian continent and since the early nineteenth century some seven pandemics are thought to have spread out from this source to many of the world's major cities. Mortality rates often reached 50 per cent during some of the epidemics, since medical knowledge was only gradually acquired and public health measures to prevent the spread of the disease were only gradually understood and implemented. Indeed, proper understanding of the cholera toxin and its role in the disease was only achieved in the 1950s.

Influenza

Influenza is a disease of humans and several mammal and bird species. It is a respiratory disease which may be complicated by other infections and which, though generally of low lethality, is always a threat to the young and old. Because of its highly infectious nature very large numbers of people are usually affected, and thus the total numbers of deaths caused by influenza are much greater than might generally be expected from its low lethality.

Influenza is caused by three viruses classified as A, B and C of the Orthomyxoviridae family. The most important influenza virus type is A and it exists in a number of sub-types which usually do not provoke cross-immunity to each other. Because of the normal airborne route of infection, influenza epidemics in temperate zones tend to occur in cold winter weather when people are crowded together in conditions of poor ventilation. Influenza A virus is genetically unstable. Between pandemics the proteins in the shell of the virus, which surrounds the genetic material, undergo continuous change which progressively invalidates acquired immunity and several times a century the virus seems to undergo radical change which invalidates most people's immunity.

There is no good evidence of influenza before its occurrence in Europe in the Middle Ages. Certainly there were pandemics in the sixteenth, the eighteenth and the nineteenth centuries. Yet, whilst the total numbers of deaths were probably higher than for the obvious killer diseases like cholera, it took the pandemic of 1918-19 to really bring concerted attention to the disease. The 'Spanish 'flu' pandemic began in the spring and proceeded with standard low lethality rates. In August a second wave of infection arose. This had different immunological characteristics and double or triple the death rates. The *Cambridge History* comments:

> ... It is possible that the 1918-19 pandemic was, in terms of absolute numbers, the greatest single demographic shock that the human species has ever received. ... The ... flu did most of its killing in a 6-month period and reached almost every human population on Earth ...

Over 21 million people died world-wide and, since many were young adults, the impact on affected societies was increased beyond that had only the very young and old died. Why the 1918-19 pandemic was so destructive remains unclear, but later pandemics have re-emphasised the threat. Not surprisingly, considerable research has been carried out on the disease and the World Health Organisation has a worldwide network of centres monitoring what is happening to the virus in order to detect new strains rapidly.

Leprosy

Leprosy occurs naturally only in human beings. The cause is an infection by the bacterium *Mycobacterium leprae*. This bacterium multiplies very slowly *within* human cells. Thus antibodies circulating in the blood are of little use against it. Immunity mediated directly against cells is therefore the body's main defence mechanism. Transmission is by sustained exposure to affected individuals, with nasal secretions thought to be the most likely source of infectious material.

The incubation period for the disease is usually three to five years. About three-quarters of those showing early signs of leprosy recover spontaneously. A milder form of leprosy develops in those with a hypersensitive reaction to the bacterial antigens. Severe progressive leprosy occurs in those who neither recover nor show a hypersensitive response. In untreated cases the bacteria kill skin tissue, leading to loss of facial features, fingers, toes etc.[9] There exists now, in fact, cheap and effective medication for leprosy, but it is estimated that there are still some 15 million lepers world-wide. These people are located predominantly in poor, rural parts of the world.

From the historical incidence of the disease, in which leprosy appears to be replaced by tuberculosis as urbanisation proceeds, it has been suggested that there is some limited cross-immunity with *Mycobacterium tuberculosis*, the causative agent of tuberculosis. As population density increases, it is argued that this favours the spread of tuberculosis and thus it could be that leprosy is replaced. Whether this explanation is correct, and, while accepting that true leprosy may have been difficult to diagnose in earlier centuries, there is no doubt that leprosy and the stigma it carries have been powerful factors within Judaeo-Christian history.

Measles

Measles is caused by a virus of the genus *Morbillivirus* of the family Paramyxoviridae. It infects only human beings. It is extremely contagious and spreads through the air or by direct contact. Infants have a passive immunity conferred by maternal antibodies for up to 6-9 months after birth, and infection bestows lifelong immunity thereafter in almost all cases. The same is true for vaccination.

Given these characteristics, in unvaccinated populations measles can be an endemic disease which causes epidemics every few years. Mortality is highest amongst the very young and very old and can reach 5 to 10 per cent in poor conditions. At present, it is estimated that there are 50 million cases and 1.5 million deaths annually world-wide as a result of measles. Vaccination programmes are thought to be preventing a similar number of cases and fatalities, but much work remains to be done on understanding the measles virus and providing an effective vaccine for the developing world.[10]

It has been argued that measles probably arose from a related animal virus as the human population reached levels which would sustain the virus. Some unidentified epidemics in Roman and Chinese history could have been due to measles. The disease was well characterised in the tenth century and was clearly present in Europe from the medieval period onwards. The most dramatic consequences of measles often occurred when a population without immunity was brought into contact with the disease. This frequently happened during the European expansion and led to high levels of death in many native populations.

Smallpox

Smallpox viruses (variola major and variola minor) of the Poxviridae family now only exist in laboratories. This viral disease was formerly transmitted primarily by airborne droplets being inhaled. It would infect almost all people at risk. The more dangerous variola major typically killed 25-30 per cent of people infected, and variola minor about 1 per cent.

After an incubation period of some 12 days there was an abrupt onset of high fever and related symptoms. Most people survived for a further 2-5 days when the characteristic rash began to appear. After a few days the small pimples of the rash turned to pustules. If the person survived, the pustules dried up and the remaining scabs fell off after a few weeks. The person could be left much disfigured, but with long-lasting immunity. Death rates could, however, be between a quarter and a half of children affected.

Although the disease may well have existed in antiquity it was only definitively described in the ninth century. It clearly became a predominant killer disease in the sixteenth and the seventeenth centuries. There are closely related diseases such as cowpox, but smallpox seems to have only affected human beings. Because it did not lie dormant within human beings and there was therefore no reservoir of symptomless carriers, it appears to have needed large populations – with numerous, new, non-immune, potential victims – to have persisted. This has led to speculation that the virus may have arisen from a related animal virus in Neolithic times as the human population began to increase. It has been estimated that in the eighteenth century smallpox accounted for 10-15 per cent of all deaths in some European countries, and that 80 per cent of victims were under 10 years of age. Even more terrifying, as we have seen, was the impact of smallpox on non-immune native peoples as they came into contact with the colonising Europeans.

Gradually techniques were developed to combat the disease. Variolation, the artificial infection of people with small amounts of smallpox material, was the first. This was a dangerous practice, but skilful practitioners did refine the technique to ensure only a very light pricking of the skin. The great breakthrough came when Edward Jenner noticed that those who had suffered cowpox did not catch smallpox. He then tested vaccination with cowpox as a defence against smallpox and wrote up his successful work in 1798.

The practice of vaccination spread extremely rapidly. The *Cambridge History* comments:

> . . . England led the way in the new practice – more than 100,000 were vaccinated there by 1801. . . . Within three years of the publication of Jenner's *Inquiry* it was translated into German, French, Spanish, Dutch, Italian and Latin. In France 1.7 million were vaccinated between 1808 and 1811 . . . and so on across the world.

By the end of the century some European countries had practically eliminated the disease, and by the middle of the twentieth century most wealthy countries were essentially free of it. The final action was then taken by the World Health Organisation which, in a vaccination campaign in the developing world, eradicated the disease in the 1970s.

Tuberculosis

Tuberculosis is an infectious disease caused by the bacterium *Mycobacterium tuberculosis*. It is usually a chronic disease which affects the lungs, but it may also affect almost any other part of the body. Given the right conditions tuberculosis may affect 100 per cent of the population and thus, despite its non-acute nature, it has killed many millions of people.

There are 30 species of *Mycobacterium* and many can cause disease in a wide variety of animals. Some cause serious diseases other than tuberculosis in human beings. Human tuberculosis is typically caused by *Mycobacterium tuberculosis*. There are three main types, I, A and B. These are distributed in different parts of the world and each seems to be strongly resistant to mutation. The bovine species (*Mycobacterium bovis*) can be transmitted through contaminated milk, and this may be prevented by pasteurisation. Usually, tuberculosis is transmitted by airborne droplets inhaled into the lungs after release from an infected individual coughing, sneezing or spitting. Very small numbers of bacteria are sufficient to infect an individual and these can lie dormant for long periods of time and then cause active disease.

Many environmental factors influence how the disease develops. In particular, the poor living conditions typical of early phases of industrialisation have repeatedly produced high rates of tuberculosis. Pulmonary tuberculosis begins when scavenging cells or macrophages engulf the bacteria in the lungs. The bacteria, however, are able to grow slowly within these cells. Thus only cell-mediated immunity is effective against the infection. T-cells and other activated scavenging cells or microphages move to the site and gradually form the characteristic tubercle. In most cases the bacteria become dormant within this structure. In some 10 per cent of untreated cases the disease is not halted and the bacteria spread throughout the body. Dormant bacteria can also be activated in times of stress and in old age. There is also little acquired immunity from an infection.

Tuberculosis appears to have been a human disease since the Neolithic period. Clear signs of the disease are evident in archaeological specimens. It appears to have been described in many early texts and was certainly present in the medieval period in Europe. As the population grew, and urbanisation proceeded, tuberculosis increased in severity. By the middle of the sixteenth century about 20 per cent of deaths in England are estimated to have been caused by various forms of tuberculosis. The great epidemics of tuberculosis developed with industrialisation and urbanisation. Whilst medical advances now make effective treatment possible, the improvement in living conditions in mature industrialised societies appears itself to have reduced the incidence of the disease dramatically.

On the other hand, the disease is still very significant in the developing world and could clearly return anywhere when social conditions deteriorate dramatically. There has also been increasing concern over the appearance of drug-resistant tuberculosis in some cities of the world in recent years, an example of the worrying growth of microbial drug resistance.[11]

Typhoid Fever

Typhoid fever is caused by infection with the bacterium *Salmonella typhi*. This organism attacks only human beings and should therefore be controllable by public health measures. However, there are a large number of related *Salmonella* bacteria which infect a very wide range of hosts and which can cause milder salmonellosis in humans. A variant illness called paratyphoid fever, which is also caused by *Salmonella* other than *S. typhi*, can exhibit similar symptoms to typhoid fever.

Typhoid fever is spread when *S. typhi* bacteria in faeces shed by an infected person are ingested by another person, either through drinking untreated water or eating contaminated food on which the bacteria can multiply well. Many bacteria are killed by acid in the stomach, but once in the small intestine the bacteria enter its cellular lining and are then ingested by white blood cells. Instead of being destroyed by these cells, *S. typhi* multiplies and then passes into the bloodstream. White blood cells in the liver and spleen then attack the bacteria, but, again, intracellular multiplication takes place and the organisms flood back into the bloodstream. Clinical symptoms of the disease – fever, weakness, etc. – may occur at this stage. The bacteria load the lymph nodes of the small intestine in particular and intestinal haemorrhage and perforation are major causes of death. Over a period of some weeks the immune system in survivors develops sufficient response to destroy the infection. In untreated cases the mortality rate is between 10 and 20 per cent. A particular feature of the disease is that some people who recover (about two per cent) maintain an infection in the biliary tract and continue to shed *S. typhi* in their faeces without showing signs of illness. Vaccination does produce immunity, but it is not 100 per cent effective.

Typhoid fever is thought to have long been a human disease. It was first effectively characterised in the early part of the last century and it was also the subject of some of the early analyses of how such diseases spread. *S. typhi* was one of the earliest of the bacterial agents to be identified. Despite all this, mortality rates caused by the organism amongst American soldiers in the Spanish-American War of 1898 and British soldiers in the Boer War were very high. Vaccination and improved military sanitation standards drastically reduced the incidence of the disease in the American and British armies during the First World War. Indeed, in the developed world the disease is now of limited concern. In poorer parts of the world though, typhoid fever still ravages many lives. Crude estimates suggest that there are 15 million cases of typhoid each year and that one million people, mainly children, still die of the disease.

Typhus

Typhus is a natural infection only in humans. It is caused by *Rickettsia prowazekii* and transmitted by the human body louse or sometimes the head louse. The rickettsial organisms are excreted in louse faeces and are transmitted to human beings mechanically through breaks in the skin. The louse is killed by the infection which is not passed on in its eggs. The disease spreads when infected lice move to new human bodies. Obviously, typhus flourishes where people are crowded together in unhygienic conditions. Mortality rates in untreated cases vary between five and 25 per cent, but can reach 40 per cent. Whilst people of all ages are susceptible to the disease, those under 15 years are less affected. An attack of typhus confers long immunity, although the organism persists in the tissues of victims and may reappear later in periods of stress.

Typhus is thought to have a long history. Accounts which appear credible date back to the wars of the fifteenth century. Napoleon's campaign in Russia in 1812, for example, was severely disrupted by typhus. Although modern armies can be protected by vaccination and the destruction of lice, it is clear that wherever the appropriate conditions arise in famine, war, or other forms of social breakdown typhus could quickly return. It may be noted that Howard Taylor Ricketts and Stanislaus von Prowazek, after whom the infectious agent of typhus is named, both died of the disease while investigating it.

Yellow Fever

Yellow fever is a natural disease of monkeys particularly and of non-human primates. It is transmitted between animals by blood-sucking mosquitoes. When such mosquitoes, especially *Aedes aegypti*, feed off human beings the yellow fever virus can be transmitted to the human population. In densely populated urban areas the disease can then be transmitted directly between humans by infected mosquitoes.

In humans symptoms arise three to six days after infection. After another two or three days, those who eventually survive begin to feel better. Others, however, experience a variety of symptoms as the remission is short-lived. Jaundice sets in if the liver is damaged and copious black vomit may be produced. Death follows between the seventh and tenth day of the illness for those who do not survive.

Reported mortality rates may be very high in urban-based epidemics, frequently between 20 and 70 per cent. However, as many mild cases are difficult to distinguish from other diseases the overall mortality rate is probably much lower. An attack of yellow fever which is survived gives a lifelong immunity to the disease. With these characteristics and the fact that the disease appears to affect children less severely, populations could, in the past, build up effective immunity to the disease. Epidemic outbreaks would then occur when large numbers of non-immune people arrived in an infected area or infected individuals encountered a non-immune community.

Examples of such events abound in the history of the New World. The *Cambridge History* gives many illustrations:

> During the first six decades of the nineteenth century, Savannah suffered from 15 epidemics, Charleston had 22, and New Orleans at least 33. The most notable of the New Orleans epidemics occurred in 1853 during which the city lost almost 8,000 individuals to the disease . . .

and, of course:

> . . . Chief among the victims of this and all other epidemics were Northerners and foreigners . . . along with white Southerners from the interior. Permanent white residents, however, seldom suffered from fatal yellow fever . . .

The discovery that mosquitoes transmitted the disease allowed it to be quickly controlled in North America during the first decade of this century, and effective vaccination is now possible.

The disease is still a threat. The virus remains within the monkey populations of Central and South America and there are cases of humans being infected each year. Severe outbreaks of yellow fever have been recorded in recent decades in Africa. Curiously, the disease is unknown in Asia. Some people have suggested that closely related natural diseases such as dengue and Japanese encephalitis in Asia have prevented the incursion of yellow fever there.

As may be seen from Table 2.1, the weapons designer would have a very wide range of choice even if consideration were limited to the foregoing ten diseases. Four are viral agents, six are bacterial agents. Transmission mechanisms range from air- and water-borne through to a variety of insect vectors. The diseases also attack human beings in a wide variety of different ways.

Table 2.1   Summary of major infectious diseases described

Disease	Agent	Transmission
Bubonic plague	*Yersinia pestis*	Flea bite
Cholera	*Vibrio cholerae*	Faecal-oral
Influenza	Virus (Orthomyxoviridae)	Airborne
Leprosy	*Mycobacterium leprae*	Sustained contact
Measles	Morbillivirus (Paramyxoviridae)	Airborne
Smallpox	Variola major (Poxviridae)	Airborne
Tuberculosis	*Mycobacterium tuberculosis*	Airborne
Typhoid fever	*Salmonella typhi*	Faecal-oral
Typhus	*Rickettsia prowazekii*	Contact with lice faeces
Yellow fever	Virus (Flaviviridae)	Mosquito bite

The choice for a weapons designer, however, is much wider than these major killer diseases. At a Royal United Services Institute lecture in 1981 Colonel Vicary and Wing-Commander Wilson of the Defence NBC Centre stated that there were at least 30 known micro-organisms and toxins suitable for use in weapons.[12] In its study, *Chemical and Bacteriological (Biological) Weapons and the Effects of Their Possible Use,* the United Nations in 1969 listed some 22 biological agents that might be used against human beings.[13] These are listed in Table 2.2. It will be noticed immediately from the table that the mortality rates (taken from epidemiological data and therefore not necessarily indicating the effects of deliberate use of high dosages delivered by the most dangerous route) do indicate a wide range of lethal and incapacitating agents. Moreover, the UN list does not include a number of the major infectious diseases that we have just discussed. Clearly, there are military considerations that have to be taken into account in selecting from the range of possible agents. It is to such considerations that we now turn.

Military Considerations

The UN study gives some general information on the characteristics of biological weapons that we need to take into account. First, of course, such weapons employ living organisms which multiply within the target organism, or extremely toxic chemicals which can be produced by living organisms. The high concentrations that can be easily achieved of these small living organisms or toxic chemicals imply that very large areas could be affected by the weapons, as was illustrated in the last

Table 2.2   Some possible biological agents for use against man[1]

Disease	Mortality
Viral	
Chikungunya fever	Very low
Dengue fever	Very low
Eastern equine encephalitis	High (>60%)
Tick-borne encephalitis	Variable (up to 30%)
Venezuelan equine encephalitis (VEE)	Low
Influenza	Usually low
Yellow fever	High (up to 40%)
Smallpox	Variable (but usually up to 30%)
Rickettsial	
Q-fever	Low
Psittacosis	Moderately high
Rocky Mountain spotted fever	Usually high (up to 80%)
Epidemic typhus	Variable (but usually up to 70%)
Bacterial	
Anthrax (pulmonary)	Almost invariably fatal
Brucellosis	Low
Cholera	Usually high (up to 80%)
Glanders	Almost invariably fatal
Melioidosis	Almost 100% fatal
Plague (pneumonic)	Almost 100% fatal
Tularemia	Usually low (can be up to 60%)
Typhoid fever	Moderately high
Dysentery	Low to moderately high
Fungal	
Coccidioidomycosis	Low

[1]Modified from reference 13.

chapter.

The SIPRI study, *CB Weapons Today*,[14] analysed a number of other considerations which allow a rough classification, from a military point of view, of the available biological agents. Some of these are illustrated in Table 2.3. Some agents are clearly much more infectious from the first to subsequent victims than others. The potentially infectious agents could therefore spread rapidly and uncontrollably. This makes such agents of limited attraction to military planners. Within the two categories, of potentially infectious and not, there is also a division

31

between highly lethal and merely incapacitating agents. From a military point of view one might not wish to use a lethal agent, for example against enemy troops in an area where there were also civilians.

Table 2.3   Military classification of biological agents[1]

Principal characteristics	Examples	Militarily significant features
Potentially infectious from first victim		
Incapacitating	Influenza virus	Military attraction limited by
Lethal	*Yersinia pestis* (plague)	potential uncontrollability
Not infectious from first victim		
Incapacitating	*Coxiella burnetii* (Q-fever)	Decay rate in air; incubation period;
Lethal	*Bacillus anthracis* (anthrax)	length of illness; etc.

[1]Modified from reference 14.

The SIPRI study analyses other military considerations, for example, the rate at which the agent's infectivity would decay when disseminated by a weapon system, the length of the incubation period for the illness caused, and the type and duration of the illness. Some of the complexities may be illustrated by considering the potential use of an agent which had an arthropod carrier (fly, mosquito, etc.) in an area where such a potential carrier was part of the local fauna. If such an agent were used it might be difficult to forecast the consequences even if the disease were not directly infectious from person to person.

The militarily-desirable characteristics of biological agents have been discussed in numerous open sources. Some of these are summarised in Table 2.4. Clearly, the weapons designer would require an agent which would produce a given effect at low dose in a predictable time and was easy to produce and use. Against this background we can now examine some of the weapon systems known to have been standardised prior to the agreement of the Biological Weapons Convention in the early 1970s.

Table 2.4   Some militarily-desirable characteristics of biological agents

---

1. An agent should produce a certain effect consistently.
2. The dose needed to produce the effect should be low.
3. There should be a short and predictable incubation period.
4. The target population should have little or no immunity.
5. Treatment for the disease should not be available to the target population.
6. The user should have the means to protect troops and civilians.
7. It should be possible to mass-produce the agent.
8. It should be possible to disseminate the agent efficiently.
9. The agent should be stable in storage and transportation in munitions.

The SIPRI study reviewed what was then known of the agents developed in the major post-war US biological weapons programme. The information on anti-personnel agents is summarised here in Table 2.5. We have already discussed yellow fever. We need now to briefly review the other agents and diseases mentioned in order to complete our overview of the biological possibilities that existed before the development of the new techniques of genetic engineering and other forms of modern biotechnology.

Table 2.5 Some anti-personnel biological agents standardised by the USA[1]

Species	Agent category	Incubation period in days	Duration of incapacity of survivors in weeks	Mortality rate %
Bacillus anthracis	Lethal	2–3	4–5	95–100
Yellow fever virus	Lethal	3–6	1–2	4–100
Francisella tularensis	Lethal	2–10	1–3	30–40
Brucella suis	Incapacitating	7–60	8–12	1–2
Coxiella burnetii	Incapacitating	15–18	1–2	0–1
VEE virus	Incapacitating	3–4	½–1	0–2

---

[1]Modified from reference 14.

Anthrax

Anthrax is a natural disease of herbivorous animals which can be transmitted to human beings. Although it has only been specifically characterised in recent centuries, there are many historical accounts which are almost certainly descriptions of outbreaks of this disease. The causative agent, *Bacillus anthracis,* can form spores which are extremely hardy and which can remain alive for very long periods after dissemination. The bacterium can enter the body through the skin and cause cutaneous anthrax or through ingestion of contaminated material. Infection through the lungs is particularly dangerous and untreated pulmonary anthrax has a mortality rate approaching 100 per cent. Fortunately, rather large numbers of bacteria are needed to cause the disease in human beings by this route.

After inhalation of a heavy dose of anthrax spores, however, the onset of the disease may occur within a day and death may follow rapidly after a couple more days. The pathological responses to the organism are caused by toxins that it produces. Vaccination is available but its effectiveness against massive doses is uncertain. Given these characteristics, it is not surprising that anthrax has been a choice agent for the designer of biological weapons. We shall return to its use in biological weapons programmes in more detail later.

Brucellosis

Three main infectious agents of domestic animals cause brucellosis in human beings. These are *Brucella melitensis* which attacks goats, *B. abortus* (cattle) and *B. suis* (pigs). Although the disease does not often cause death in human beings, it is very debilitating. The initial period of intermittent waves of fever (undulant fever) usually lasts up to a month, but it can last a year and relapses may continue over a period of several years. The usual means of transmission to human beings is from the ingestion of contaminated meat or milk products. Direct entry through skin wounds is also possible. The persistent nature of the disease results from the failure of the immune system to deal decisively with the bacterial invasion.

Descriptions of this kind of fever in the Mediterranean region date from classical times. Success in understanding the agent of the disease in goats and its transmission to human beings in milk dates from investigations in Malta at the turn of the last century. There are numerous other diseases which have similar symptoms to those of brucellosis and this obviously complicates diagnosis. Infection and recovery confer strong immunity, but no vaccine is presently available for human beings.

Q-Fever

Q-fever is caused when human beings become infected by *Coxiella burnetii*. This is a natural infection of many animal species, and, unlike other rickettsial infections, is not necessarily transmitted to man by an arthropod. Transmission can be by inhalation of the organism.

The illness begins two to four weeks after exposure and involves symptoms such as fever, pains, headache and so on. If untreated, these may last for one or two weeks and longer-lasting complications are possible. Infected animals produce large numbers of disease organisms, and these rickettsiae are extremely resistant to adverse environmental conditions. Furthermore, very low doses are sufficient to cause infection in human beings. With such characteristics, the organism can cause sudden, localised outbreaks of disease. There were a number of such cases, well-documented, amongst military personnel during the Second World War. Laboratory-acquired infections were also a serious problem in dealing with this organism and vaccines were first developed to protect laboratory workers.

Military interest would certainly have been aroused by the infectivity and environmental hardiness of this organism. Furthermore, it is easily grown in high concentrations. The effects of Q-fever in combination with those of other incapacitating agents such as tularemia or VEE virus have been studied.

Tularemia

This is a natural disease of rodents, rabbits and hares. The causative agent *Francisella tularensis*, however, has been found in a wide variety of other mammal, bird and insect species. It also can infect human beings. There are two variants (biovars) of the disease. The one found naturally in North America is *F. tularensis* biovar *tularensis* (type A) and is much the more virulent in human beings.

Infection can come about in a number of different ways: through an insect bite, through contaminated water or food, or through direct contact with infected material and passage through the skin or lungs. The incubation period is two to ten days and the debilitating disease lasts for about a month. Convalescence requires a further two to three months. Good immunity follows an attack and an effective vaccine is now available for laboratory workers.

There appears to be reasonable evidence of the presence of tularemia in the northern hemisphere in the eighteenth and the nineteenth centuries. Its wide distribution and adaptation to a range of hosts suggests that it is an ancient disease. It was the subject of detailed study in the

United States during the early years of this century. Given the complexity of the agent's natural ecology, eradication of the disease seems unlikely.

For the weapons designer the evidence that the bacterium can remain alive in the soil for weeks would indicate that it is a hardy agent. When given to human volunteers by aerosol (airborne into the lungs) in heavy doses the incubation period could be shortened to two to three days and the standard US BW agent was capable of causing 30-40 per cent mortality rates. It was also found that very small numbers of bacteria delivered by aerosol could cause infection with great reliability. Though, as noted previously, recovery from an attack confers long-lasting immunity and a vaccine is available, it has proved possible to produce strains of the organism resistant to specific drugs, such as the streptomycin-resistant strain used as the standard US agent.

Venezuelan Equine Encephalitis

VEE is one of a large group of arboviruses. These are arthropod-borne viruses which require multiplication in their vectors for transmission; other examples are yellow fever and dengue. VEE has a wide range of hosts. It causes a fatal disease of the central nervous system in horses and mules and an incapacitating influenza-like disease in humans. In natural occurrences in humans, VEE takes about two to five days to produce the symptoms of fever, nausea etc. The illness usually lasts between one and four days, and recovery takes a week or longer. An effective vaccine is available. Whilst the lethality of VEE for humans is very low, the virus is stable in aerosol dissemination and highly infective to human beings when administered by the respiratory route. This obviously would be useful in a weapons agent.

Even on the basis of such a brief review it is clear that some of the potential agents discussed satisfy well many of the requirements for biological weapons agents set out in Table 2.4. As an example, we might note that yellow fever is not known to have occurred in Asia. The weaponisation of this agent by the United States during the Cold War would therefore have produced a system which could potentially have been used against a target population with little or no natural immunity. We need now to turn to the question of attacks on plants and animals of economic importance.

Plant Diseases

We are dependent on plants for our staple crops (wheat, rice, corn, for example), for fibres (cotton, flax, for example), for wood and many other materials with industrial uses, and for vegetables, fruits and luxury items such as tea, coffee and tobacco. All these economically-important types of plants are subject to attack by plant diseases.[15] Well-known examples that can readily be called to mind are the Irish Famine of 1845–46 resulting from blight of the potato crop, and Dutch elm disease which has destroyed so many trees in Europe and America in recent decades.

Plants may be damaged by a variety of organisms but, as Table 2.6 shows, military interest, as with human pathogens, centres on viruses, bacteria and fungi. Fungi, the most important of the plant pathogens, are organisms which differ from plants particularly in lacking conductive elements, and chlorophyll in their cells. The vegetative body or mycelium of a typical fungus is made up of individual branches or hyphae which may or may not have septa or cross-walls. Some lower fungi (slime-moulds) do not have a true mycelium. Fungi reproduce by means of spores, specialised cells or small cell groups produced by asexual or sexual processes. In higher fungi asexual spores or conidia are produced from specialised hyphae.

Table 2.6 Illustrative examples of potential anti-plant biological agents[1]

Disease	Agent	Note
Viruses		
Tobacco mosaic	TMV	Natural airborne transmission
Sugar-beet curly top	CTV	Natural leafhopper transmission
Bacteria		
Rice blight	*Xanthomonas oryzae*	Many modes of transmission
Corn blight	*Pseudomonas alboprecipitans*	
Fungi		
Late blight of potato	*Phytophthora infestans*	Caused Irish potato famine
Black stem rust of cereals	*Puccinia graminis*	*P. graminis tritici* was a standardised agent
Rice blast	*Pyricularia oryzae*	Standardised agent

[1]Modified from reference 14.

37

Of the 100,000 species of fungi so far described 50 cause disease in human beings but some 8,000 are known to cause disease in plants.[15] About 200 of the 1,600 known species of bacteria are plant pathogens but a complication exists: a species may often have a number of pathovars, each of which is confined to one particular host. About 500 viruses are known to cause diseases in plants. These viruses come from a wide variety of different taxonomic groups.

We shall consider some illustrative examples of plant pathogens, again concentrating particularly on those known to have been standardised in the US offensive biological warfare programme.

Sugar Beet Curly Top

An example of a viral disease which has been studied as a potential agent is sugar beet curly top. Curly top occurs in the United States, Turkey and South America. The curly top virus (CTV) infects some 150 species of herbaceous plants, but is very destructive of sugar beet, bean and tomato.[16] The virus kills young plants and causes stunting and lower yields in older plants. Losses of sugar beet and tomatoes have been so severe as to cause cultivation of these plants to be abandoned over wide areas.

CTV is transmitted from plant to plant by the leafhopper *Circulifer tenellus*. The virus overwinters in infected weeds and other plants. The leafhopper feeds on these plants in the winter and spring and then carries the virus to cultivated crops in late spring and summer, transmitting the virus from crop plant to crop plant as it feeds. The insect feeds by inserting its stylet mouthpart into the phloem or sap vessels of the plant; the virus enters by this route and then quickly spreads throughout the plant and damages the phloem elements.

The disease can be controlled by the use of insecticides against the leafhopper, but resistant varieties of sugar beet, tomato, bean and other crops have been developed, producing a very effective means of control.

Bacterial Blight of Rice

Rice is probably the most important crop for human beings. The large and growing populations of Asia are extremely dependent on continued improvements in its productivity. Bacterial blight is widely distributed in Asia and can devastate crops. Yield losses in severely infected fields usually range from 20-30 per cent and may sometimes go even higher.[17]

Bacterial blight was first observed in Japan in the latter part of the last century and the bacterial nature of the disease was identified there in the early part of this one. The causative organism is *Xanthomonas oryzae*. This bacterium can enter the growing plant in many different ways, ranging from mechanical injury through to entry via natural stomata. It also overwinters in a variety of ways, either in a dry dormant form or in an active growing form in other plants. It is carried to the host plant by wind, rain, insects, etc. On infection, spots begin to appear on leaves, and infected leaves turn yellow, dry rapidly and then wither as the spots grow.

Enormous effort has been put into the development of resistant varieties of rice, work which began in Japan in the 1920s. At the International Rice Research Institute more than 100 cultivars have been developed as sources of resistance to bacterial blight. Mechanisms for forecasting blight attacks, for example by monitoring of the bacterio-phage population (which increases in advance of the disease), are also widely used.

Black Stem Rust of Cereals

Wheat withstands diverse environmental stresses – erratic rainfall and poor soil amongst others – and still produces stable, satisfactory yields. Epidemics of rust diseases can, however, cause severe crop losses. There are three types of wheat rust disease – black (stem) rust, brown (leaf) rust and yellow (stripe) rust. The fungus *Puccinia graminis tritici* is the causative agent of black stem rust in wheat and also causes black rust in barley. Other *Puccinia* species cause related diseases in cereals such as oats and rye.

The fungus has a complex life history which includes overwintering and alternation of hosts. The chief characteristic, however, is the massive production of uredospores on the wheat plant: one estimate for a moderate infection of black rust was 4×10^{12} uredospores/day/hectare. These can travel enormous distances on the wind and then be deposited, for example by rain, to infect distant areas.

It is known that there are occasional exchanges of spores between the very distant eastern and western wheat-growing areas of Australia, and there is regular infection of crops in New Zealand from Australia, 2,000 km away. In the United States there is regular movement of ure-dospores over 4,000 km northwards to infect the growing crop and then a movement back to the southern wintering areas. In order to minimise crop losses large numbers of different cultivars are used in the United States.

With the movement of spores over such vast distances, mathematical models, and even computer programs, have been developed in order to assist farmers in dealing with the arrival of clouds of potential infective agents. Much work has also been done on resistance and the genetics of resistance in wheat. Other measures such as the destruction of alternate hosts and chemical control regimes have also been employed.

Rice Blast

Rice blast disease has been documented for perhaps 200–300 years. It is known to occur in about 85 different countries. Yield losses during epidemics can be as high as 50–60 per cent. The causative agent of rice blast disease is the fungus *Pyricularia oryzae*. The typical symptoms of infection are small, bluish, water-soaked flecks on leaves which rapidly enlarge. The lesions may join up to kill entire leaves in susceptible varieties. The disease reduces the number of panicles and therefore grains that mature, and the total yield of the crop. Several toxins have been isolated from the pathogen and studies made of their role in the disease.

The fungus overwinters in a variety of different ways depending to an extent on climatic conditions. In the tropics conidia are present throughout the year, whereas in temperate regions the fungus can overwinter as a mycelium on straw. Mature conidia become airborne and lodge mainly on the leaves of plants where they germinate in the thin film of water provided by rain or dew. The fungus then goes through a cycle of further conidia production on the rice plant and the conidia are carried on the air to infect other plants.

Again, mathematical models have been developed to assist in the prediction and control of infections. Great efforts have also been made to understand the different races of the fungus, and resistant strains and resistance genetics of rice itself. Breeding of resistant strains of rice has been under way for some years in different countries. Chemical control methods are also available to combat the fungus.

As with the human diseases examined previously, it is clear that some features, particularly of the two plant diseases that were weaponised in the US, fitted well with military requirements. Both black stem rust and rice blast disease are caused by agents which are very well suited for widespread distribution and severely damage vital staple crops.

Animal Diseases

Whilst no animal diseases were weaponised in the US post-war offensive biological weapons programme, intensive studies were certainly made of a number of diseases. Some of the available information is summarised in Table 2.7. It should also be noted that, as we shall see in a later section, the British developed a crude capability to retaliate with an anti-cattle anthrax weapon during the Second World War. It is therefore necessary, as with the human and plant diseases, to provide a brief illustrative description of some of the more serious animal diseases in order to have a biological background for the discussion of the offensive weapons programmes carried out by major states.

Table 2.7   Illustrative examples of potential anti-animal agents[1]

Disease	Agent	Note
Viruses		
Foot-and-mouth disease of cattle	FMD virus	
Rinderpest or cattle plague		Intensively studied in World War II
Newcastle disease of poultry	NDV	Intensively studied in World War II
Rickettsiae (Bacteria)		
Heart-water of sheep and goats	*Cowdria ruminantium*	Tick carrier
Fungi		
Aspergillosis of poultry	*Aspergillus fumigatus*	

[1]Modified from reference 14.

Foot-and-Mouth Disease

Foot-and-mouth disease (FMD) is a highly contagious disease of cloven-hoofed animals (cattle, pigs, sheep, goats, etc.). It is caused by the FMD virus of the *Aphthovirus* genus of the Picomaviridae family. There are seven serotypes of the virus and no cross-immunity between the different types. Although the disease is of low lethality to adult animals, it does cause serious production losses and can have 50 per cent lethality rates in young calves.[18]

Major regions of the world, particularly North and Central America, and Australia, are free of the disease. Islands such as Japan and the UK are also free of the disease and it is on the decline in Europe. It is, however, enzootic in South America, the Middle East, Asia and Africa. Most wild cloven-hoofed animals, as well as some other animal species, are susceptible.

FMD is highly contagious. It is in fact one of the most contagious animal diseases known. Infected animals produce viruses from many sources, for example, exhaled air, saliva, milk, faeces and urine. Virus excretion starts one to five days before vesicles appear on the tongue, lips and feet. As antibodies build up the levels of virus excretion decline, but it can persist for weeks and some animals which recover may become long-term carriers.

Cattle appear to be most susceptible to airborne infection and pigs are thought to be major amplifiers of the disease because they produce high concentrations of the virus in exhaled air. There are, however, many other potential modes of transmission: from direct contact between animals, and, since the virus can survive for several weeks in the environment, indirectly from contact with contaminated straw and manure. The virus is also known to have survived airborne transmission of at least tens of kilometres and to have initiated infections thereafter. It is hardly surprising that countries free of the disease take tough precautions to keep it out and to deal with outbreaks vigorously if they do occur.

In natural infections the incubation period is two to eight days, but it can be induced experimentally in a shorter time. The first signs of the disease are fever, loss of appetite and cessation of milk production. Vesicles then develop, particularly around the mouth area and the feet. The vesicles quickly rupture to leave painful ulcers. In cases without complications the ulcers heal over about ten days and the animal begins to eat a few days after the vesicles rupture. The lesions on the feet make the animal reluctant to move and may result in long-term damage.

Foot-and-mouth disease may be difficult to distinguish from a number of other infections. Collection and analysis of samples has also to be carried out with great care because of the readily transmissible nature of the virus.

Newcastle Disease

This disease affects both domestic and wild birds and causes gastro-intestinal, respiratory and nervous problems. It is caused by a virus of the Paramyxoviridae family and genus *Paramyxovirus*. Paramyxoviruses affecting birds have nine serogroups, of which Newcastle disease virus is A/PMV 1. The different strains of the disease virus vary widely in virulence and affect domestic fowls, turkeys, pheasants, etc. Ducks and geese are susceptible, but the disease is rarely severe in these species. Newcastle disease is highly contagious with the virus being mainly spread by direct or indirect contact. It is excreted in faeces and in exhaled air. Windborne transmission of the virus is possible and in affected areas there are significant reservoirs of infection in wild birds.

The incubation period can vary between two and 15 days, but is generally five to six days. The effect of the disease is variable, depending for example on the virulence of the virus, the age of the bird and its immunological and health status. In its most virulent form, viscerotropic velogenic (VVND), there is a sudden arrival and spread of the disease. Birds lose appetite and egg production drops sharply. Profuse bright green diarrhoea is common and rapid dehydration occurs. Many birds die within a day or two and mortality rates can exceed 90 per cent. At death severe lesions are found in many internal organs.

Heartwater

This is a tick-borne rickettsial disease of ruminants. It is caused by *Cowdria ruminantium,* an obligate, intracellular, rickettsial parasite. Cattle, water buffalo, sheep, goats, and many species of wild ruminants are natural hosts. The disease occurs mainly in Africa, south of the Sahara. It is transmitted by ticks of the genus *Amblyomma* which prefer wooded or bushy country to the open plain. The ticks pick up the *Cowdria* when they are larvae or nymphs and then transmit them to other animals.

The incubation period for heartwater is between two weeks and a month. There is a sudden onset of high fever, and death within one to two days is possible. Mortality rates range from 10 to 100 per cent. Animals affected may circle and charge objects. In acute cases death occurs within a week. Dead animals show lung and other areas of oedema, and spleen and lymph nodes enlarged and congested.

Again, as with human and plant diseases, a minimal acquaintance with the wide range of possibilities[18] suggests that any weapons designer intent on attacking animal production would have a wide range of choice.

Toxins

Although toxins are chemicals and not living organisms, it is important to review the possible use of toxins derived from living organisms[19] as means of attack. Botulinal toxins, shellfish poison (saxitoxin) and staphylococcal enterotoxin are mentioned seriously in the literature.

Botulinal Toxins

The toxins produced by the bacterium *Clostridium botulinum* are much more poisonous than even nerve gases. They cause the food poisoning termed botulism and have been well-studied as potential warfare agents.

There are six types of toxin of which type A has been the most seriously investigated. It is quite simple to culture and harvest and can be stored as a dry white powder without great loss of activity. However, the toxin does decay in air and is therefore not much more lethal when released as an aerosol than nerve gas. Other possible uses are for sabotage or as a contaminant for small arms munitions.

Botulin poisoning results from interference with the normal transmission of impulses from nerves to muscles. Recovery from the poisoning does give some immunity and some protection by vaccination is possible, yet the lethal dose for the toxin is very low.

Shellfish Poison (Saxitoxin)

The planktonic dinoflagellate *Gonyaulax catanella* produces a toxin which can be accumulated by shellfish which feed on this source. If such shellfish are then eaten by human beings a severe form of poisoning results. During the 1950s procedures were developed for growing the toxin-producing organism and extracting the toxin at high yields. As a contaminant of small arms munitions, it was found to act much faster than botulin toxin.

Staphylococcal Enterotoxin

This is the causative toxin of the food poisoning which follows consumption of food contaminated with *Staphylococcus* bacteria. Again, simple methods have been developed to produce large amounts of toxin from strains of *Staphylococcus aureus*. This was designed to be used in a variety of incapacitating weapons systems.

Whilst toxins such as those described above are not biological warfare agents *per se*, there has been increasing interest in novel biological products in recent years. It is therefore necessary to include such products when considering future weapons systems and arms control measures. On the basis of this outline of possible biological and toxin agents, we may now consider the major offensive biological weapons programmes which were in place before the signing of the Biological Weapons Convention.

.3.

OFFENSIVE BIOLOGICAL WEAPONS
PROGRAMMES BEFORE 1969

In the first chapter an attempt was made to show that biological weapons have to be considered as serious possibilities for use in a variety of significant military situations. In the second chapter it was shown that a considerable range of potential agents are available to the military planner. In this chapter we are concerned with the offensive biological weapons programmes actually pursued by three major states – the UK, the USA and Japan – during and after the Second World War and, in the case of the United States, up to the late 1960s.

We shall begin by reviewing the official summaries of their offensive programmes from 1946 onwards provided by the UK and the USA as part of the enhanced confidence-building measures agreed at the third five-year Review Conference of the Biological Weapons Convention in 1991 (see Chapter 4). We shall then be able to fill in more of the detail of these programmes, within that official framework, from some of the investigations carried out during the Cold War period.

In a final section an attempt is made to stress the real meaning of this information. It is argued that in the early 1940s this was a very new area of military research. Great advances were believed to be possible in all aspects of the production and use of these weapon systems at this early stage of scientific and technological development. Many advances were indeed produced by rational application of vast amounts of money and the employment of many talented people in these research programmes so that, by the end of the 1960s, many effective weapons systems had been produced.

Information Provided in 1992 on Previous Programmes

The United Kingdom

The UK stated that it had a programme of offensive biological research and development from 1940 to the late 1950s.[1] Concerns over the possible advent of biological warfare had arisen before the Second World War and in 1940 a small unit had been set up at Porton Down to investigate biological warfare and possible defensive measures, and to develop the means to retaliate in kind if that became necessary. As is now well known, as part of the efforts to develop a retaliatory weapon, anthrax spores were released in tests carried out at Gruinard Island off the Scottish mainland, which led to its contamination for decades afterwards.

The UK report stated that the success of these trials led to a joint project with the USA and Canada aimed at the development of an anthrax cluster bomb. This was called the N-bomb project, but was not completed before the end of the war. Instead, the report indicated, the retaliatory capability during the war was met by an aircraft-delivered system consisting of cattle cakes filled with anthrax and directed against German livestock.

The stockpile of five million cattle cakes was almost totally destroyed after the war, and the remainder when the UK signed the Biological Weapons Convention in 1972. Whilst some research on offensive programmes continued after the war, the report concluded that by 1957 the UK had abandoned such work.

The United States

According to the US report, high-level official concern over biological weapons originated in the autumn of 1941.[2] During the war there were clearly links with the UK and Canada on offensive research. The report stated that, from 1946 to 1949:

> Most of the BW R&D programme concentrated on the antipersonnel aspects of BW such as highly infectious bacteria (*Brucella suis*, *Pasteurella [Francisella] tularensis*, Q-fever/rickettsia, Venezuelan Equine Encephalomyelitis (VEE), *Bacillus anthracis* and staphylococcus enterotoxin) . . .

There were also smaller programmes concerned with anti-plant and anti-animal agents. However, from the end of the Second World War until 1950 no production was carried out 'for the purpose of operational readiness' and no facilities were available for such work.

Field-testing sites had been closed or inactivated at the end of the war and testing was therefore carried out during this period in closed laboratory-sized chambers. Some small-scale outdoor testing was done with what were thought to be harmless organisms. In 1949 a one million-litre test sphere was built at Camp Detrick and explosive munition tests of some pathogens were undertaken there.

A change of policy occurred in mid-1950 when it was recommended that a biological weapons production facility should be established and that the testing of agents and munitions should be performed in the context of a general expansion of the whole programme. Open-air sea trials using *Bacillus globigii* (BG) and *Serratia marcescens* (SM), considered to be effective simulants, began with tests of the vulnerability and detection capabilities of US naval ships.

The Army was instructed to produce *Brucella suis* and *Pasteurella* [*Francisella*] *tularensis* agents at a facility in Pine Bluff Arsenal, Arkansas, and an anti-crop bomb was developed, tested and put into production in 1951. Moreover, large-scale tests of the vulnerability of the San Francisco Bay area were carried out with BG and SM in September 1950.

The biological weapons programme continued to grow from 1954 to 1958. Vaccine research on:

> . . . tularemia, Rift Valley Fever, and Q fever at Fort Detrick was supplemented by a major contractual effort at Ohio State University Research Foundation. The program included the use of human volunteers.

Partly in response to changing Soviet statements, official policy was substantially changed again towards biological warfare in 1956 from 'retaliation only' to a policy in which the USA 'would be prepared to use BW or CW in a general war to enhance military effectiveness'. Further enhancement of the offensive programme followed in the period from 1959 to 1962 and 'developmental work on Q fever and tularemia proceeded to their standardisation as BW agents'. A test centre at Fort Douglas, Salt Lake City, Utah, was also maintained at this time. During the period from 1963 to 1968, the report stated, the primary work was directed to producing the agents that had been found to be of military use. A number of munitions were filled and stored at the Pine Bluff Arsenal. This offensive programme was then curtailed by President Nixon.

One might conclude that these reports are less than comprehensive (see below) and it can be argued that there is a fine distinction between some aspects of the offensive programmes described and the defensive biological weapons programmes which have continued. It is clear, nevertheless, that these official reports confirm the existence of offensive programmes both during and after the Second World War.

More Detailed Information

The United Kingdom

An account of 'Biological warfare and biological defence in the United Kingdom 1940-79' was published in the *Royal United Services Institute Journal* in December 1992.[3] The author, Gordon Carter, was a senior staff member of the Chemical and Biological Defence Establishment at Porton Down.

Carter explained how British interest and concern about biological weapons predated the outbreak of the Second World War, suggesting that it was perhaps triggered by allegations of German biological weapons research.[4] This concern was heightened at the start of the war and was acted on at the highest level, Lord Hankey writing a key paper pointing out 'the need for studies of BW to leave the realm of hypothesis and enter that of practical experiment'. The group was established at Porton Down to carry out the necessary work.

From considerations of the knowledge of gas warfare it had been decided that the most effective means of using biological weapons would be:

> . . . to disseminate an aerosol of lung-retention size particles from a liquid suspension of bacteria in a bursting munition such as a bomb, delivered so that effective concentrations would be inhaled by anyone in the target area . . .

Work was concentrated on the anthrax bacterium and to a lesser extent on botulinum toxin. By 1942 laboratory work at Porton had determined what inhalation doses of anthrax were needed to infect and kill several animal species, and trials at the Porton ranges with *Bacillus subtilis* had determined how bombs might be used to spread spores effectively. It was then considered necessary to test the real agent at the secure site of Gruinard Island in Scotland.

The trials included use of a modified 30-lb high explosive/chemical bomb with some three litres of anthrax spores suspended near the ground and fired electrically. The trials in 1942 demonstrated just how deadly the weapon could be. It was realised that the weapon was more potent than any chemical weapons agent or munition of like size examined by the British, and in 1943 attention turned to the study of 4-lb bombs that might be more effectively used in clusters.

Work on the anthrax weapon (N-bomb) was transferred to the United States and Canada as the initial stage in a long association in regard to biological weapons.[5] Indeed, the leader of the British group had all the methodology data assembled and dispatched to the United States where it provided 'the foundations for the subsequent US BW programme'. This was the programme which was to grow to such massive proportions in the Cold War period, and, as we shall see later, utilised data from another national programme of offensive biological weapons research. The War Cabinet's requirement for a biological retaliation-in-kind weapon was met by the production of the five million anthrax cakes at Porton. Carter commented:[5] 'The likely impact of this weapon on the beef and dairy industry of Germany remains conjectural' but he pointed out its historical significance as 'possibly the first acknowledged biological weapon'.

Carter argued that, despite the post-war development of nuclear weapons and the discovery of the enhanced capability of the chemical nerve agents developed by Germany during the war, there was still a perceived need to develop a retaliatory biological weapons capability. A 'remarkable indicator' of the importance of biological weapons at this time, Carter suggested, was the construction of a new purpose-built laboratory at Porton:

> . . . The building, believed to have been one of the largest brick buildings of modern times had, eventually, 210,000 square feet of floor area, and for decades was regarded as the best designed and equipped microbiology institute in the world . . .

At a time of severe post-war austerity measures in the UK £2.25 m was spent on this single element of the biological weapons programme.

The armed services were particularly concerned to achieve a better understanding of the factors affecting the survival of pathogenic microorganisms in aerosols. It was considered that this could best be done safely at sea and in November 1948 tests were conducted off the Bahamas with munition effects being tested by sampling devices and animals in rubber dinghies upwind of the device. By this means the factors affecting the physical fallout, viability and virulence of the weapon pathogens in real conditions were correlated with laboratory findings.

Similar trials were held in 1952 and 1953 off Scotland and in 1954 and 1955 off the Bahamas. Carter concluded that the scale of resources devoted to biological weapons at the time emphasised official concern to have a proper assessment of this potential threat. Thus, whatever current views of the seriousness of biological weapons prevail amongst both specialists and the general public, the history of the British biological weapons programme confirms high-level interest, the allocation of large-scale resources, a perception of biological warfare as a real possibility, the perceived vulnerability of Britain to strategic attack and, finally, the production of offensive biological weapons.

The United States

The same themes are clearly evident in detailed documentation produced in Congressional enquiries and obtained under the US Freedom of Information Act. In its 'Summary of Major Events and Problems' for 1959, for example, the US Army Chemical Corps reported[6] that ten years previously, in its search for biological weapons agents, it had established a research project on tularemia. After describing the life-history of the disease organism and its effect on human beings, the report continued, in conformity with the information presented in the last chapter:

> . . . There are two forms of tularemia, the cutaneous and the typhoidal. The latter is much more dangerous, with the mortality rate in untreated cases about 30 percent. If pneumonia develops the mortality rate jumps to 40 percent. It is this typhoidal form which is of paramount importance as an agent . . .

The authors then went on to explain that antibiotics could be used to arrest the progress of the disease, but not its debilitating consequences. This was regarded as important because convalescence may take from six months to a year. Troops infected with the disease could therefore put a great strain on enemy hospital facilities. As was also mentioned in the last chapter, there are a number of strains of the organism and the one 'chosen by the Corps as an agent was a streptomycin-resistant strain'.

As for production of the agent, Fort Detrick developed and maintained the stock culture and large quantities were grown by the Directorate of Biological Operations at Pine Bluff Arsenal. The bacteria were maintained at a temperature of 4° C, at which half would remain alive after 40 days.

The weaponisation of the agent was also reported:

> The Corps CP-120 program, designed to evaluate the effectiveness of E120 bomblets loaded with *B.* [*Francisella*] *tularense*, had indicated that a single aircraft sortie would produce more than 50 percent casualties over an area of 16 square miles . . .

Moreover:

> . . . while the munitions are capable of causing widespread outbreaks of tularemia, they can be transported, stored, and handled logistically with no more hazard than with regular explosive munitions.

The report concluded that, as the development of this agent 'had reached the point of uniform mass production in a form specified to produce optimum military effects', it was accepted as a standard-type, biological anti-personnel agent in August 1958.

In a section devoted to yellow fever, the report noted that Fort Detrick had established a project to study the use of arthropods for spreading anti-personnel biological agents in 1953. One of the insects chosen for study was *Aedes aegypti*, the carrier of yellow fever virus. Some of its advantages as a vector were then set out, for example: since the mosquito injects the agent into the body, masks would provide little protection and since the insects survive for some time, a targeted area would remain dangerous for that period. The life-cycle of the mosquito and its mode of transmitting the virus were then briefly described.

The report stressed the dangerous nature of yellow fever, and its debilitating effects even amongst those who recover. The authors added that there was no known therapy other than treating the symptoms and that, 'Of the clinical cases since 1900, one-third of the patients have died'. The fact that the disease has never occurred in Asia was taken to indicate that 'the population of the USSR would be quite susceptible' to the disease. It was suggested both that an attack using mosquitoes would be quite difficult to detect and confirm and that, although a yellow fever vaccine exists, it would be impossible for the USSR to quickly mount a mass immunisation programme. Thus it was concluded that:

> . . . The difficulties that an enemy would face in detecting infected mosquitoes and protecting their population would make the *Aedes aegypti*-yellow fever combination an extremely effective BW agent.

As previous commentators have noted, the US Army did not appear to have considered that the yellow fever virus might have been transmitted to an animal reservoir population had it been used. Sources of reinfection could therefore always have been present as they are now in parts of Africa and Central and South America.[7]

The practicality of using the mosquito was tested by releasing uninfected females in a residential area of Savannah, Georgia, and checking how many had entered houses and bitten people. Also, in 1956, 600,000 uninfected mosquitoes were released from a plane on a bombing range and within a day the insects had travelled one or two miles and bitten many people. Further tests showed that the insects could be spread from helicopters, from devices dropped from planes, or from the ground.

The method of breeding mosquitoes was summarised and it was reported that Fort Detrick's laboratories could produce half a million mosquitoes per month. The yellow fever virus used was obtained from a person infected in Trinidad in 1954 and was propagated by infecting monkeys. The mosquitoes were in turn infected with the virus by immersing their larvae in infectious Rhesus monkey serum. The virulence of the infected mosquitoes was then tested by having them attack and infect mice. The Chemical Corps Technical Committee classified the yellow fever-*Aedes aegypti* mosquito as a standard-type biological weapon in June 1959. It was proposed to use an aircraft-delivered cluster bomb or missile warhead to disperse the mosquitoes over enemy territory.

Tests of different munitions continued. A contract was let in December 1957 'to determine feasibility of conducting large-area warfare attacks by means of spray tanks carried on low-flying aircraft'. The research was reported to have been very successful. The critical necessity was for the design of a nozzle that would spray out liquid particles of five micrometres in size or less in order that the drops would float in the air and spread over a wide area and, crucially, be very effective in penetrating the lungs of victims.

After the 275-gallon spray tank and nozzle had been tested in the laboratory, field tests were carried out at Dugway Proving Ground using an F-100A plane. This flew over a triangular area approximately 15 miles long and 12 miles wide. Sampling devices throughout the area allowed the behaviour of the aerosol cloud to be analysed. The results showed that spray attacks were feasible and that 'an area 10 miles or better downwind could be covered'.

Five of the trials were carried out using simulants, but on one flight the agent of Q-fever was used. The results indicated that 99 per cent of humans in the area would have been infected. Other 'important results' were said to demonstrate that the spray device was much more effective than bombs or shells for disseminating an aerosol of the biological agent and that the tank could hold a much larger amount of the agent relative to the weight of the spray system.

The report concluded that it had been proved that airborne attacks could be carried out at low level and that the system could contaminate

50,000 square miles in one sortie. The significance of this finding, according to the report, lay in the efficiency of this means of attack. It stated:

> . . . *on a night* when the wind was blowing ten miles per hour, *three large aircraft*, each carrying 4,000 gallons of liquid BW agent, and flying at a speed of 500 knots, *could spray an area of 150,000 square miles, causing more than half the people in the area to become ill.* [Author's emphases]

Presumably also, given the low altitude of attack, the aircraft would probably not be picked up on radar and the attack would therefore not be detected before people became ill.

The Release of Information to the Public

Information on the biological weapons research carried out in the United States during the Second World War became available through articles in scientific journals and in more popular books written by former scientists and soldiers who had been involved in the programme. The turmoil of the Vietnam War and the US use of herbicides on a large scale there provoked renewed concern about chemical and biological warfare. A number of books attempted to present the available information in the mid- to late 1960s before the publication of the major UN report in 1969 and the SIPRI studies of the early 1970s.

Seymour Hersh, writing in 1968, correctly identified the significant change of policy for use of biological weapons which had taken place in the 1950s:[8]

> In fact, by the mid-1950s official military policy toward the use of CBW agents had undergone a dramatic change, one that still remains secret. . . . The change in policy was simple enough . . . the military was free to wage chemical and biological warfare on a first-strike basis during conventional warfare . . .

He claimed support for his viewpoint in changes he recorded as occurring in Army field manuals in the 1950s.

Hersh's book attempted to summarise much of the information from other sources and was supplemented by his own extensive interviews and research. He was extremely critical of what had been done in the United States and emphasised that large increases in expenditure had occurred from the early 1960s to the time that he was writing. In his view, this allowed the Pentagon to make use of increasingly sophisticated scientific technology in its offensive biological weapons programme and the result was an inevitable series of spectacular advances across the entire spectrum of chemical and biological warfare. He argued indeed that behind a wall of secrecy a vast research programme had produced 'a massive array of killers'.

Hersh attempted to analyse both the results of the research and the organisations involved. He discussed evidence given to Congress by military officers and what he had gleaned from papers published in the open literature by scientists working for the military, and from diseases contracted by them during the course of the work. Regarding the research results, he noted, for example, the potential advantages of using dry powders rather than liquid sprays of biological organisms and of protecting the agents in better sub-packages.

As for anti-crop research, Hersh noted that:

> . . . the program has been emphasised in recent years. Research is now under way into various forms of bacteriological, viral, and fungal crop diseases, with two of the latter – rice blast and *Puccinia graminis* (stem rust) – receiving special study.

Considering the time at which he was writing, Hersh was naturally mostly concerned with the use of herbicides in Vietnam.

His description of the bases at which biological research, development, testing and production were being carried out is useful in giving a snapshot of the final stages of the offensive biological weapons programme in the USA. Noting that Fort Detrick was located near the small town of Frederick and had been in operation 'since 1943 when the base – then a top secret operation comparable only to the Manhattan Project – was opened', he stated that it controlled the procurement, testing, research and development of biological munitions and vaccines and defence measures. But he argued that the emphasis was on 'the offense'. The base had a budget of $38 million in 1966 and covered 1,300 acres. It employed '2,500 civilians and 500 military personnel . . . including 320 B.S., 110 M.S., 120 Ph.D., 14 M.D. degree holders and 34 veterinarians'.

Hersh estimated the number of animals used for experiments at various times in Fort Detrick's history. He suggested that usage per month in the early 1960s could have been as high as 60,000 assorted mice, rats, guinea pigs, monkeys, etc. He also reviewed work on human volunteers, particularly 'Seventh Day Adventists serving noncombat Army duties as conscientious objectors [who] were exposed to airborne tularemia'.

The organisation of the base, with its greenhouses for work on anti-crop agents and simulated rice paddy for work on rice blasts, was described in some detail from Hersh's own visit there. He also argued that the heavy investment in Fort Detrick from the late 1950s had produced an organisation very expensively equipped for its intended research programme and particularly for aerobiological experimentation. Cloud chambers, which were used to study the dispersal of micro-organisms, were described as available 'in volumes of 6,200 litres, 50,000 litres, 100,000 litres, 850,000 litres, and a new 1 million litre sphere constructed of steel 1¼ inches thick'.

Pine Bluff Arsenal, in Arkansas, was described by Hersh as the centre for the production of biological agents and their processing into munitions. Again on the basis of research and a personal visit in 1967, a description of the site was given. Hersh noted that:

> . . . The base's 1966 budget was $18.8 million; more than $5 million of this went directly for biological operations.
>
> Initially, the Chemical Corps considered building the whole laboratory underground, but it finally settled for a 10-storey building with only three floors below ground level . . .

Hersh's efforts to see the highly secret X201 production laboratory were unsuccessful.

Dugway Proving Grounds with its one million acres in distant Utah was also described. Hersh recorded that Dugway had six major divisions, with the meteorological division being added in 1953 just before the first testing of biological agents and that 'the station was redesigned and vastly overhauled in 1962'. The biological test compound was kept under tight security and Hersh could get little information on its operations. Finally he described the associated airforce and naval bases where biological warfare research was being carried out alongside the main army programme.

In the United Kingdom, at the same time, Robin Clarke published his analysis of the prospects for chemical and biological warfare.[9] He described in detail the problems of the aerosol dispersal of agents. He pointed out that the US Army had even sponsored two conferences on this subject (referred to in Chapter 1) and that research had shown the optimal size of aerosol particles to be between one and five micrometres. The reason for this was explained. Such minute particles – a micrometre is one ten-thousandth of a centimetre – are small enough to pass down into the lung and penetrate its wall. Clarke gave examples of the effect size has on infectivity:

... The infective dose of Venezuelan equine encephalomyelitis virus increases by a factor of 14,000 if the particle's diameter is increased by a factor of ten.

Of course, even if the particle diameter is of the right order the weapon system designed to carry it must achieve an even spread of the organism over the target area and protect it from the environment. Clarke reviewed some of the problems in handling micro-organisms, including their sensitivity to the ultraviolet (UV) rays in sunlight. He also discussed how temperature and humidity can be important in determining the survival time of the organism. Hence, as Clarke pointed out, Fort Detrick's interest in ways of protecting the organisms during dispersal.

It is clear that there was sufficient information available even to the general public for the importance attached to biological weapons by the USA to be understood. Yet it is unlikely that the full scale and significance of the programme was widely appreciated. More recently, Bernstein[10] has provided a detailed account of the origins of the US programme during the Second World War, and Susan Wright[11] has reviewed the offensive programme from the end of the war until the late 1960s as part of her account of the entire post-war programme. According to Wright the whole of the offensive programme period was punctuated by reviews of the problem which continually led to increased funding. She argued that the reviews were influential:

... The role and status of CBW programs rose. Total support for the CBW programs increased from approximately $10 million in the early 1950s to $352 million in 1969 – an increase of over 2,000 percent, allowing for inflation ...

Support for CBW (chemical and biological weapons) research and development also trebled in real terms between the late 1950s and the mid-1960s. In summary, the results, according to Wright, were that eight anti-personnel and five anti-crop agents were adopted by the US military. There was one other significant input to the US programme that we must now discuss – the work done by Japanese scientists and military before and during the Second World War.

The Japanese Offensive Biological Weapons Programme

As Hersh stressed,[8] the Russians indicted members of the Japanese army for crimes involving biological weapons in 1949 and found them guilty. The transcripts from the trial were published in English. The same information was reviewed by other authors (for example, see[7 and 9]) but until recently was not given much general credence in the West. That position has changed as the full story has been more widely reported.

The detailed study by William and Wallace[12] shows how the Japanese attempted to research, develop and deploy biological weapons before and during the Second World War. The main group involved was called Unit 731 and was based in Manchuria under the direction particularly of General Ishii. According to Williams and Wallace, Unit 731 had eight divisions. The first of these was concerned with bacteriological research, the second with warfare research and field experiments, and the fourth with bacterial mass production and storage. They stated that:

> Unit 731's bacteriological research division was divided into more than a dozen squads, each investigating the warfare possibility of a wide variety of diseases.

The studies carried out were extensive. The authors continued:

> Plague, anthrax, dysentery, typhoid, paratyphoid, cholera and many other exotic and unknown diseases were studied. So too were vaccines and blood sera for the prevention and treatment of diseases. Various disease vectors, mainly insect, were investigated, as were new drugs, chemical toxins and frostbite.

They suggested that Ishii was centrally interested in developing weapons for sabotage and clandestine use and for causing mass outbreaks of disease through the aerial delivery of pathogens by plane. They thought that he had managed to 'solve' the latter problem.

Extensive work was carried out on the use of infected fleas to carry plague. A porcelain bomb was designed so that the fleas would more easily survive. Named the *Uji*, the 25-kg bomb exploded in the air, cracking the porcelain like eggshell and spreading the fleas over the target area. Porcelain bombs were also thought useful for deploying tetanus, anthrax, typhoid and dysentery. Another type of bomb, the *Ha*, was a steel bomb containing 1,500 cylindrical shots immersed in anthrax or tetanus emulsion. It was designed for battlefield use against troops whereas the *Uji* bomb was thought more suitable for use against civilians. Clearly, what is being described here is an intensive, expensive programme which must have had serious, high-level support. Besides anti-personnel weapons, research was also carried out on anti-animal and anti-plant diseases.

The uniquely terrible aspect of the work was that 'Ishii based his unit in remote northern Manchuria so he could experiment on human beings'. Williams and Wallace record that the human beings, called 'marutas' or 'logs':

> ... were 'used up' at the rate of two or three per day. Every now and then the number would be topped up from the holding posts in Harbin. Researchers would submit a requisition to the Unit's commander to gain charge over a new maruta . . .

There was no escape for anyone who entered the clutches of the unit. It was estimated that some 3,000 people were killed in all manner of horrifying ways in order to improve the knowledge that was thought necessary for the success of the programme.

The Unit appears also to have *used* biological weapons. For example:

> During the operation that followed, the germs of cholera, dysentery, typhoid, plague, anthrax and paratyphoid were all used. Flasks containing pure germs were poured by BW cadres into reservoirs, wells and rivers. Containers were also tossed into houses. Three planes from Nanking Unit under fighter escort dropped germs from the air . . .

The Chinese losses resulting from this 1942 Chekiang Campaign were said to be 'inestimable'. There were also high Japanese casualties when a unit overran a contaminated area inadvertently.

All the results from this Japanese programme fell into US hands after the war when a deal was done granting immunity from prosecution in exchange for the information available from members of Unit 731.

Research Aims and Results

Even on the scale of these research programmes, not all avenues of work would have led to successful outcomes, but it is clear that the programme directors believed significant advances would accrue if enough were pursued. This point was made very strongly in a report by the US Secretary of Defense's *Ad Hoc* Committee on Biological Warfare in 1949.[13] It stated:

> Biological warfare is in its infancy. . . . Foreseeable improvements in the production and distribution of existing biological weapons would increase their effectiveness by a very large factor.

Even at the end of the 1940s, therefore, the United States felt that work in the area had only just begun, but that enough was known to be sure that great improvements in these weapons systems were assured.

It is not difficult to envisage what the aims of the post-war US offensive research programme might have been. Work would surely have been directed, for example, to studying whether other agent types were available, whether the efficiency of the production and storage of agents could be improved, and whether the release of agents from weapon systems could be achieved more effectively and the agent dispersed with better yield on to the target. There would surely also have been aims related to an understanding of how agents were taken up by victims and caused infection, and of how agents could be made more virulent and drug-resistant, and work would have been directed towards improving the available vaccines against potential agents.

The important point is that the US offensive biological weapons programme did deliver many of the expected advances by 1969. As Perry Robinson has noted[14] the data:

> . . . suggest an increase in BW efficiency of four orders of magnitude over the period 1940 to 1965.
>
> In other words: if, for regular military purposes, an agent-production capacity of 5 tons per day was judged necessary in 1945 . . . improvements in technology could have reduced the requirement to 0.5 kg per day 20 years later.

An imperial ton is equal to 1,016 kg, so the necessary capacity had been reduced from 5,000 kg to 0.5 kg per day over just two decades. To move through four orders of magnitude – 5,000-500-50-5-0.5 – in just 20 years implies a rapid rate of technological change in biological weapons systems.

Some sense of perspective on the whole US programme, which has to be seen as the major driving force in the immediate post-war period of offensive research, can be gained from the information available now – although it is undoubtedly true that much is still withheld from the general public. For example, we referred earlier to arthropod vectors of diseases and studies made of mosquito carriers for yellow fever. A publication of the early 1980s, *An Evaluation of Entomological Warfare as a Potential Danger to the United States and European Nato Nations*,[15] has a section on the history of entomological (insect) field testing in the post-war US programme. A summary of this information is set out in Table 3.1. The first column of the table gives the name of the particular field test, the second column the year of the test and the final column a brief summary of what was done. It is obvious that the field trials discussed earlier were part of an extended series which, at the least, carried on for almost a decade. Furthermore, the later trials appear to have been building on and refining the information gained earlier. A similar general sequence of activity would surely have occurred in regard to other potential weapons systems.

Table 3.1 Some entomological warfare field tests in the USA[1]

Name of Test	Date	Description
Big Itch	1954	Tests of E-14 munition for distribution of fleas.
Big Buzz	1955	To demonstrate mass production and dissemination of mosquitoes from aircraft and determine if they survived and took blood meals from humans.
May Day	1956	Tests of dispersal of mosquitoes from a ground source carried out in an urban area of Savannah, Georgia.
Munition Dissemination Tests	1957	Report states: 'A minimum of five infected mosquitoes, five houseflies, and 30 fleas or ticks per person . . . required for effective coverage of a target area.'
Bellwether I	1959	To determine the effects of environmental factors 'on the biting rate of starved, virgin female *A. aegypti* mosquitoes on troops in the open'.
Bellwether II	1960	Series of trials with up to 100 military personnel in each to determine effects of victim distance, movement etc. on mosquito biting.
Bellwether IV	1962	To compare strains of *A. aegypti* for biting propensity, dispersal and building penetration.

[1]Modified from reference 15.

Whilst the SIPRI study, *CB Weapons Today*[16] was careful to point out that many of the biological munitions it provided data on in the early 1970s were experimental, the data show that a wide range of systems had been developed in the United States. Table 3.2 summarises some of the SIPRI information on biological munitions. These ranged from 'depositors' for small scale use by troops through free-fall cluster bombs in the 1950s, to missile warheads and spray tanks in the mid- to late 1960s.

Table 3.2 Some munitions developed by the USA for biological warfare[1]

Type	Mechanism	Note
Generator E44R2	Depositor	Under development in 1965.
Warhead for guided missile M210	Bomblets in warhead [M143]	Under development in 1967.
Spray tank for liquid agent A/B45Y-1	Spray	Expendable for high-speed tactical aircraft. Under development in 1965.
Spray tank for dry agent A/B45Y-4	Dispenser	Tested with PG toxin agent. Under development in 1966.
Cluster bomb E133	Bomblets [E61R4]	Under development in 1958.
Submunition E61R4	For E133	Under development in 1958.
Submunition M143	For M210	Entered inventory in mid-1960s.

[1]Modified from reference 16.

The SIPRI data also included information on the agents for these munitions. It was suggested, for example, that if sufficient agent reached the target for each person to receive 20,000 anthrax spores, or 3,000 plague bacteria, or 25 organisms of VEE or tularemia, or 10 of Q-fever, about 50 per cent of those people would become ill. Much more detail was given, however, on production concentrations, half-life in storage and aerobiological decay rate after dispersal. These data are set out, in part, in Table 3.3.

As a further example of the improvement in capabilities derived from the research programme we may consider the dissemination of the agent from the munition. The *Joint CB Technical Data Source Book*, Volume VIII of 1973, was concerned with anthrax.[17] It was noted that:

> The dissemination component of the . . . model describes the transformation of the biological agent (aqueous slurry or presized dry

Table 3.3 Characteristics of agents used in US munitions[1]

Species	Symbol	Production concentration (organisms/gm)	Half-life in store (weeks)	Aerobiological decay rate[2] (min^{-1})
Bacillus anthracis	N (wet)	3.10^{10}	80 at 15°C	Insignificant
Coxiella burnetii	OU2 (wet)	1–5.10^{10}	>170 at –50°C	0.001 at any RH
VEE virus	NU (wet)	2–4.10^{10}	>40 at –40°C	0.02 at 85% RH
Puccinia graminis tritici	TX (dry)	2–4.10^{8}	100 at 4°C	Insignificant

[1]From reference 16.
[2]Probably in aerosol chambers in the dark and at room temperature. RH=relative humidity.

particles) into a viable, infective, inhalable aerosol cloud of specified strength, size, and location . . .

The source strength of the initial cloud of spores released by the munition is a function of the concentration of the agent in the munition and the dissemination efficiency of the weapon. The dissemination efficiency of the munition is defined as 'the ratio of the number of viable spores aerosolized in particles with ≤ 5 microns [micrometres] diameter to the number of viable spores in the agent fill'. As we have seen, the size of the particles had been found to be of critical importance, particularly in relation to penetration of the lungs.

It is known that the efficiency of the early munitions, even with anthrax as an agent, was very limited. In regard to an anthrax agent (TR) the source book noted:

> . . . Efficiencies of aerosolization of TR from the . . . A/B45Y-1 and A/B45Y-4 spray tanks are based on data obtained with a biological simulant and are . . . 17.2 per cent, and 49.1 per cent respectively.

Similarly, the source book for agent PG (staphylococcal enterotoxin) stated that the dissemination efficiency for the A/B45Y-4 munition was:[18]

> . . . 63 per cent if all aerosolized particle sizes are considered; 26 per cent if less than 5 micron particles only are considered.

Thus, although more fragile agents could not be used with such efficiency, the extent of the technical change in the period from the end of the Second World War is apparent in the increasing capability to release agents effectively from munitions.

Returning to the kinds of question that might have been asked at the start of this period, it is obvious that the range of agent types had been substantially expanded. In the case of tularemia a virulent strain had been selected and some drug resistance developed in it. As we have just seen, the engineering problems of releasing agents from munitions had been tackled with some success and, probably most critically of all, great strides had been made in understanding the behaviour of agents in the air, during dispersal to the target and inhalation. Much of this knowledge had been subject to specific, systematic refinement that allowed the development of relatively precise mathematical models on which weapons usage could be based.

There can be little doubt that, since the termination of the US programme, another country undertaking an offensive biological weapons programme would be able to benefit from the US experience and expect to move along the same trajectory with greater ease. It has often been said that the fact that something has been done once is the crucial information a technologist or engineer requires. With that knowledge, a way to proceed is likely to be found. Additionally, of course, much of the information necessary to help a country achieve success has become publicly available over time.

The whole idea of using biological weapons is so repellent that it is difficult for most people to imagine anyone wishing to set up an offensive biological weapons programme even if it were feasible. It is perhaps as well to remember that the conditions in which it might once have seemed reasonable and sensible were very different from those prevailing in relatively peaceful parts of the world today. It should be recalled that in the depths of the Second World War the British decided that it was necessary to carry out field trials with anthrax on the Scottish island of Gruinard, and only after 45 years[19] was it:

> . . . possible for the island to resume its rightful place as just one of the many islands which so enhance the beauty of the rugged coastal scenery of NW Scotland.

We may all agree with that view of the island's rightful place, but the pressures to procure and perhaps consider using such dread weapons will doubtless recur in the future.

An illustration of what could possibly happen was put forward in a recent paper about the war in Rhodesia.[20] It was argued that an unusual outbreak of anthrax, involving many cases above the normally low level, occurred between 1979 and 1980. The unusual geographical distribution of the disease at the height of a bitter war indicated to the author that it had resulted from deliberate use by the losing side in a futile attempt to stave off defeat.

All such suggestions naturally require the most careful analysis, but the point that the pressure of warfare or the threat of warfare may be used to justify behaviour of a desperate inhumanity has to be accepted. In the light of evidence presented in this chapter, it is hardly necessary to raise questions over the possible consequences of the misapplication of modern biotechnology to see the value of arms control and disarmament measures in this area of potential proliferation. It is to the halting quest for such international agreement that we now turn.

.4.

EFFORTS AT CONTROL TO 1991

In analysing past efforts to control the proliferation of biological weapons it is necessary to begin with a brief consideration of the 1925 Geneva Protocol. This consists of what is, in effect, a short preamble, a declaration of the central purpose of the protocol and then five subsidiary paragraphs dealing with accession, treaty language and so on.[1] The protocol is best viewed as a continuation of efforts to ameliorate the calamities of war, which had begun in earnest in the last century, for example with the St. Petersburg Declaration of 1868, and which was then carried forward at the Hague conferences of 1899 and 1907.[2]

The initial part of the protocol provides a link with those earlier developments of international humanitarian law in stating that:

> Whereas the use in war of asphyxiating, poisonous or other gases, and of all analogous liquids, materials or devices, has been justly condemned by the general opinion of the civilized world; and
>
> Whereas the prohibition of such use has been declared in Treaties to which the majority of Powers of the World are Parties; and
>
> To the end that this prohibition shall be universally accepted as part of International Law, binding alike the conscience and the practice of nations.

The question of controlling biological (bacteriological) weapons then arises in the following 'Declaration':

> That the High Contracting Parties, so far as they are not already Parties to Treaties prohibiting such use, accept this prohibition, agree to extend this prohibition to the use of bacteriological methods of warfare and agree to be bound as between themselves according to the terms of this declaration.

65

It is important to be clear about exactly what this declaration implies.

It will be seen first that the prohibition concerns *use*, not development nor production, of biological weapons. Secondly, it will be noted that the text refers to 'use in war' at the beginning but does not define war. Thirdly, it will be seen that the text of the declaration ends by making it clear that the prohibitions apply to fellow parties to the agreement.

It must be remembered that the states which negotiated this protocol had recently experienced the widespread use of chemical weapons in the First World War. Thus the undertakings in the text were diminished by reservations, made by many states, which restricted the states to which it should apply to fellow parties only. Crucially also, this reservation restricting application to fellow parties only was supplemented by a further reservation that the prohibition should only apply to an enemy whose armed forces or allies observed the provisions. Thus many commentators have suggested that the protocol is best seen as a 'no-first-use' agreement amongst the parties.

As far as proliferation is concerned, the Geneva Protocol is best not regarded as an arms control or disarmament agreement. There are no restrictions, as we have seen, on the development or production of biological (or other) weapons and there are certainly no provisions in the text for any kind of verification. It was not a legal barrier, for example, to the UK developing biological weapons in the 1940s. Furthermore, the United States only became a party to the agreement much later, in 1975. Yet it is on that fragile base that the control of biological weapons is founded.

The Concept of an International Control Regime

Winfried Lang, the Austrian diplomat who chaired the second Review Conference of the Biological Weapons Convention (BWC) in 1986, has provided a useful framework within which the convention may be discussed. As a lawyer, he pointed to the fundamental problem of a mismatch between the instrument of control and that which is to be controlled:[3]

> . . . negotiators are required to invent devices that match the static nature of law with the dynamics of security perceptions . . . and scientific/technological progress.

Using also his experience in international environmental law negotiations, Lang suggested that this mismatch could be dealt with successfully by the agreement of a series of legal elements over time. These elements, in effect, would eventually add up to a regime, which he agreed could be seen as a 'network of rules, norms, and procedures that regularise behaviour and control its effects' in a particular sphere of activity.

From his experience in negotiations on environmental issues, which have been rather successful and innovative in recent years, Lang drew a number of lessons in regard to the BWC. He argued that first agreements in a new area of environmental concern are frameworks only; they are followed by more detailed protocols at a later stage. He argued further that such later protocols are best made as specific as possible, but with built-in periodic review and revision to keep up with new scientific findings. He believed issues of verification to be just as important in environmental agreements as in disarmament and arms control negotiations, but argued that the major lesson concerned the need for institutional arrangements. In his view:

> . . . Treaties become operational only to the extent that they are administered and serviced by institutions. Institutions have to look into the issue of definition: is the list of substances or activities prohibited or controlled still commensurate with scientific and technical progress? . . .

He went on to suggest that institutions are needed, for example, to ask similar questions in regard to arrangements for verification and co-operation between rich and poor states.

Thus in the view of a very experienced diplomat, the crucial problem relating to the regime for controlling biological weapons is that:

> . . . the biological weapons regime may be qualified as an 'imperfect' regime because it lacks an international organisation for monitoring compliance and adapting legal rules to scientific and technological progress.

If we take this problem seriously, he seemed to suggest, we shall understand the need to set up an international institution (however modest) in order to help match the static law with the dynamics of security and scientific and technological change.

At present the regime in place, in addition to the 1925 Geneva Protocol, consists of the Convention on the Prohibition of the Development, Production and Stockpiling of Bacteriological (Biological) and Toxin Weapons and on Their Destruction of 1972 – the BWC. The text of the convention is set out in Appendix 1 and we shall analyse its contents in more detail shortly.

As we shall see, the convention resulted from intense diplomatic activity in the late 1960s and early 1970s. There are three depository states: the USA, the UK and Russia (succeeding the former Soviet Union). Gradually the number of parties to the convention has grown until now there are over 130 states involved and it is these which meet for three weeks every five years at a review conference. Lang argued that the next element in the biological weapons regime has to be seen to be the results of these reviews, as set out in the final documents of 1980, 1986 and 1991. A further element is the set of confidence-building measures established at the second review in 1986 and amended and enhanced at the third in 1991. It is also possible that another element may be developed as a result of the VEREX meetings resulting from the 1991 review. It is possible, as will be described in Chapter 8, that these meetings of experts could lead to the provision of greatly enhanced verification requirements for the BWC through the mechanism of a Special Conference and further meetings leading up to the fourth review in 1996.

With that framework set out we can now discuss the BWC systematically: analysing how it came about; what it consists of; what its major deficiencies are; how attempts have been made to put these deficiencies right; and finally assessing the present state of the treaty.

The Biological Weapons Control Regime

It has been argued that the BWC was a trail-blazing agreement, the first global-level disarmament agreement designed to rid the world of a class of weaponry. More often, the convention, rather than being hailed as a great achievement, is roundly criticised for its inadequacies and seen as an almost inevitable result of the suspicions of the Cold War period. As is often the case, the truth may lie between these two extreme positions. The BWC may have been all that could have been achieved at that time of partial *détente* midway through the Cold War. Whilst the regime-building to date has been largely concerned with trying to remedy its inadequacies, that does not preclude the development of a really effective agreement on the basis of the BWC. To get to grips properly with these issues we need to understand how the BWC came about in the early 1970s.

Origins

The problem of biological weapons of mass destruction had appeared on the agenda of UN bodies at intervals almost from the very establishment of the organisation after the Second World War. Usually, however, chemical and biological weapons were considered together and in the context of discussions of General and Complete Disarmament. The Secretary General's report of 1967-68 indicated the start of a period of intense activity. After observing that chemical and biological weapons were usually overshadowed by the question of nuclear weapons, as we have argued in previous chapters, he continued:[4]

> . . . Nevertheless, these too are weapons of mass destruction. . . . In some respects they may be even more dangerous than nuclear weapons because they do not require the enormous expenditure of financial and scientific resources that are required for nuclear weapons . . .

As the report went on to note, even small and poor countries could manufacture such weapons cheaply. By using small facilities, such production could also be done quickly and secretly.

The special UN report on chemical and biological weapons referred to in previous chapters[5] was prepared by a group of experts, and forwarded by the Secretary General to member states, the General Assembly, the Security Council and the then-18-nation Committee on Disarmament. Its foreword included a strong call for the conclusion of an agreement to eliminate these weapons.

The United Kingdom, which had taken a leading role in the discussions on biological weapons control, then submitted a draft convention to deal with these systems separately from chemical weapons. The draft was tough in a number of respects. Given the many reservations lodged by parties to the Geneva Protocol, it proposed to supplement the ban on use with a first article which read:

> Each of the parties to the Convention undertakes, insofar as it may not already be committed in that respect under Treaties or other instruments in force prohibiting the use of chemical and biological methods of warfare, never in any circumstances . . . to engage in biological methods of warfare.

In Article II(b) parties would also have undertaken:

> . . . not to conduct, assist or permit research aimed at production [of agents, equipment or vectors] . . .

This contrasts with the elimination of references to research in the BWC.

Although a process of removing state reservations to the Geneva Protocol has recently begun to reduce the saliency of the British point on use, as we shall see in later chapters, the issue of permitted research is still important. Yet as one distinguished commentator has noted, the great difficulty of verifying a ban on research was a likely reason for its eventual removal from the draft.[6]

There was initially strong opposition to the idea of considering biological weapons separately from chemical weapons, particularly from the Soviet Union and its allies. However, this position changed and the two superpowers undertook a period of intense negotiations which resulted in a draft convention being presented in December 1971.[7] Many interested parties had reservations about the BWC which resulted from these bilateral negotiations. Opinions vary as to whether the superpowers were just wanting to clear the decks for more important nuclear questions to be discussed, or whether a very cynical exercise had taken place. For whatever reason the resulting convention had many deficiencies.

The BWC

When compared with modern treaties such as those covering strategic nuclear or chemical weapons, the BWC is an extraordinarily slight document. It consists of a short preamble and just 15 articles. It was opened for signature in 1972 and came into force in 1975. The full text is set out in Appendix 1 and the provisions are summarised in Table 4.1.

Table 4.1 Summary of the biological weapons convention[1]

1. Not to develop, produce, stockpile or acquire agents, weapons etc.
2. To destroy stocks.
3. Not to transfer to or assist others.
4. To take national measures.
5. To consult and co-operate in solving problems.
6. May lodge complaint with the Security Council.
7. To provide assistance in the event of a violation.
8. No detraction from Geneva Protocol.
9. Obliged to continue negotiations on chemical weapons.
10. Co-operation for peaceful purposes.
11. Amendment.
12. Review.
13. Duration.
14. Signature, ratification, deposition.
15. Languages.

[1]Data from Appendix 1.

For comparison, we may consider the recently agreed Chemical Weapons Convention (CWC) which has the primary objectives of destroying all chemical weapons and of preventing the proliferation and production of new ones. The long and detailed text was negotiated over a period of nine years.[8] The organisation to take charge of the treaty will consist of a Conference of the States Parties, an Executive Council and a Technical Secretariat and it will have its headquarters at The Hague. A feature of the convention is the very careful delineation of the lists of chemicals that are to be controlled and the different means of verification that will be used. Such means include on-site challenge inspections.

The heart of the BWC lies in Article 1 in which each party:

> . . . undertakes never in any circumstances to develop, produce, stock-pile or otherwise acquire or retain:
> 1. Microbial or other biological agents, or toxins whatever their origin or method of production, of types and in quantities that have no justification for prophylactic, protective or other peaceful purposes;
> 2. Weapons, equipment or means of delivery designed to use such agents or toxins for hostile purposes or in armed conflict.

This all sounds splendid, but, as many people have pointed out, it gives little guidance on what is legal or illegal. How can a judgement be made about whether some activity has no justification for peaceful purposes if no list of agents or substances which might cause concern is given and there is also no indication of what quantity of an agent or substance might be acceptable? Considerable attention has been paid to this article at the review conferences, but the basic difficulty remains today.

In Article 2 the parties undertake, within nine months of the convention entering into force, to safely destroy or divert for peaceful purposes the elements banned in Article 1. In order to emphasise the lack of effective verification for the BWC, it only needs to be remarked that the Soviet Union apparently decided to enhance its offensive biological weapons programme just at the time the convention came into force and continued this programme for more than a decade and a half. Under Article 3 parties undertake not to transfer to other states, nor assist them in any other way to manufacture or acquire, agents, toxins or weapons. As we shall see in Chapter 9, the Australia Group of countries has extended the informal co-operation that it developed in regard to export controls related to chemical weapons to the field of biological weapons. This arrangement, however, is not formally related to the BWC.

Article 4 requires parties to enact national legislation to prevent the banned activities from taking place in their territories. Like much else related to the BWC, the implementation of this article by states has taken place only slowly. In Article 5 parties undertake to 'consult one another and co-operate in solving any problems which may arise in relation to the objective of, or in the application of the Convention'. Consultation and co-operation, it is noted, 'may also be undertaken through appropriate international procedures within the framework of the United Nations.' Furthermore, in Article 6, parties which believe another party 'is acting in breach of obligations' are given the right to 'lodge a complaint with the Security Council.' Other states party to the convention undertake to co-operate with any subsequent investigation. Not surprisingly, these two articles, embodying what passes for verification provisions in the BWC, though never used have been the subject of much discussion, and some development, at review conferences.

In Article 7 parties agree to provide assistance to other parties which are believed by the Security Council to have 'been exposed to danger as a result of violation of the Convention'. Article 8 makes clear that the BWC in no way limits or detracts from obligations undertaken under the Geneva Protocol. In Article 9 parties then undertake to continue negotiations towards a Chemical Weapons Convention. Those negotiations eventually led to a major treaty being agreed and implemented in the 1990s, two decades later!

Article 10 has caused considerable friction between developed and developing countries. In potential contradiction to the objective of Article 3, parties undertake:

> . . . to facilitate, and have the right to participate in, the fullest possible exchange of equipment, materials and scientific and technological information . . .

on the use of agents and toxins for peaceful purposes. It is also agreed that the convention should be implemented:

> . . . in a manner designed to avoid hampering the economic or technological development of State Parties . . .

or international co-operation in peaceful purposes related to the convention. This seeming clash between Articles 3 and 10 highlights the question of how to prevent dual-use technology from being misused, as it implies some restriction of the developing countries by the developed countries while at the same time helping them in their industrial development.

It is perhaps not as well understood as it should be in the West that the possibility of restriction works both ways in these issues. As Lang emphasised:[3]

> ... the North-South dimension cannot be easily dismissed. ... Developing countries know very well that such international regimes are unlikely to work without their full participation ... they demand special treatment concerning access to research and development ...

As the concerns of the poorer countries have not, in their view, been adequately addressed, it is hardly surprising that they have sometimes been less than enthusiastic supporters of some Western ideas. This important theme runs through the remaining chapters of this book.

The subject of Article 11 is amendment of the convention. Any state party to the convention may propose amendments, but the text states:

> ... Amendments shall enter into force for each State Party accepting the amendments upon their acceptance by a majority of the State Parties ...

There is always a reluctance to amend arms control agreements for fear of unpicking the whole of what is usually a complex set of balances but, for the BWC, an amendment risks producing a situation in which two different treaties are in operation: one for states that accept and another for those that do not accept the amendment! Not surprisingly, there has been a reluctance to go down this road.

The first review of the convention was mandated in Article 12. The conference was to:

> ... review the operation of the Convention, with a view to assuring that the purposes of the preamble and the provisions ... are being realised ...

It was also required that:

> ... Such review shall take into account any new scientific and technological developments relevant to the Convention.

The second Review Conference was agreed by parties to the first, and so on to date. Noting only that the convention is of unlimited duration but allows for withdrawal (Article 13), that the mechanisms of signature, ratification, etc. are covered in Article 14 and treaty languages in Article 15, we turn next to the results of the reviews.

The Review Conferences

The final declarations of the Review Conferences are ordered in terms of the articles of the convention.[9,10] It is convenient therefore to discuss the evolution of the convention in terms of the crucial individual articles.

Article 1: At the first Review Conference the parties reaffirmed their support for the provisions of this article and expressed the belief that it:

> ... has proved sufficiently comprehensive to have covered recent scientific and technological developments relevant to the convention.

This reflected the reviews of these developments presented by the three depository states and the discussions at the conference.[11]

At the second review more concern was evident regarding new scientific and technological developments (see Chapter 7) and it was thought necessary to state that the conference:

> ... reaffirms that the undertakings given by the State Parties in Article 1 apply to all such developments.

In a second point the conference sought to deal with the possible production of toxins by new methods, stating that the convention applied to all natural or artificial agents or toxins and:

> ... Consequently, toxins (both proteinaceous and non-proteinaceous) of a microbial, animal or vegetable nature and their synthetically produced analogues are covered.

These points were reaffirmed at the third Review Conference. Additionally, at the third review the parties attempted to tighten up the requirements by stating that:

> ... experimentation involving open-air release of pathogens or toxins harmful to man, animals or plants that has no justification for prophylactic, protective or other peaceful purposes is inconsistent with the undertakings contained in Article 1.

Open-air testing of pathogens is, of course, an important element in an offensive research programme. It should be understood also that in reference to this article the final declarations of the second and the third reviews contained expressions of grave concern over possible non-compliance with the convention by some states and over the inability of the parties to resolve these doubts.

Article 4: The first and the second Review Conference called upon parties which had not already done so to take the necessary measures to prohibit and prevent acts in contravention of the convention in their national legislation. Parties were also exhorted to supply the necessary information on what had been done to the UN Department of Disarmament Affairs. The second review gave more explicit instructions on what was required and this all became incorporated into the enhanced confidence-building measures (Declaration of legislation and regulations, and other measures) agreed at the third Review Conference.

Article 5: The doubts about the adequacy of the verification provisions of the BWC resurfaced at the first Review Conference, particularly from Sweden.[11] In the end, however, only a modest advance could be agreed. This allowed that the consultation procedures:

> . . . include, *inter alia*, the right of any State Party subsequently to request that a consultative meeting open to all State Parties be convened at expert level.

By the time of the second review, concerns over scientific and technological developments and over possible illegal activities had considerably increased. Sweden had also, in 1982, unsuccessfully attempted to have a special conference called with a view to establishing 'a flexible, objective and non-discriminatory procedure' to deal with compliance issues related to the BWC.

Considerable progress therefore became possible at the second review because of these pressures. It was agreed, for example, that the consultative meeting should be promptly convened, that it could consider any problem, suggest ways in which clarification might be achieved, use technical experts and initiate international procedures through the United Nations. Lang commented that the consultative meeting was thus more clearly defined and the former bilateral procedures more firmly transformed into a multilateral system. However, he was also critical of the fact that:

> . . . All efforts . . . failed to make the Secretary-General of the United Nations the key to this machinery, the depositories (Soviet Union, UK, US) refused to relinquish their dominating position.

Still, at the third Review Conference in 1991 the procedures were again substantially elaborated. A request for a formal consultative meeting could be preceded by bilateral or other consultations, it had to be addressed to the depositories, and they were required to convene the meeting within 60 days. The rules and costs of the meeting were defined and it was agreed that 'the Secretary-General may be kept informed' under certain conditions.

Under Article 5 the second and the third Review Conferences also elaborated a series of confidence-building measures which we shall discuss in the next section, and the third review put in place the VEREX experts' meetings that are the subject of Chapter 8.

Article 8: The first and the second reviews strongly reaffirmed the importance of the 1925 Geneva Protocol and that the BWC in no way limited or detracted from it. Both final documents urged states not yet party to the protocol to adhere to it at the earliest possible date. The final document of the third review went much further and stressed:

> . . . the importance of the withdrawal of all reservations to the 1925 Geneva Protocol related to the biological and toxin weapons Convention.

This reflected the process whereby an increasing number of states had removed such reservations over the period since the BWC was agreed.[9]

Article 9: The final documents of the BWC Review Conferences undoubtedly demonstrated that a link was still felt to exist between the issues of chemical and biological weapons. The first review document stated that:

> . . . The Conference deeply regrets that such agreement [on chemical weapons] has not yet become a reality despite the fact that eight years have already elapsed since the [BW] Convention was opened for signature.

The second and the third reviews, on the other hand, noted with satisfaction the progress being made in negotiations on the CWC. The general easing of East-West relations was clearly the cause of the progress made in the CWC and the BWC during this period. However, the divide between the North and the South – developed and developing – states surfaced very strongly in regard to Article 10.

Article 10: Noting the importance increasingly attached to the view that disarmament should assist economic and social development, the first Review Conference concluded that developed countries should increase their co-operation with developing countries in the peaceful uses of biological agents and toxins. The final document specified that:

. . . Such co-operation should include, *inter alia*, the transfer and exchange of information, training of personnel and transfer of materials and equipment on a more systematic and long-term basis.

The same subject was given much more extensive treatment in the second review final document.

Pointing to the 'increasing gap' between the developed and the developing countries in the fields of biotechnology and genetic engineering the conference called for the wider sharing of knowledge. Parties to the convention were urged to take a wide range of specific measures in order to bring this about. The link between disarmament and economic development was again referred to and it was noted in conclusion that the fulfilment of the measures suggested would 'positively strengthen' the convention.

Unfortunately, even as sympathetic a commentator as Winfried Lang was forced to conclude that:[3]

. . . In interpreting such understandings one should take into account that, under real life conditions, the transfer of technology takes place on the basis of commercial contracts; it cannot be organised by decrees issued by national governments . . .

Thus, he argued, they do not carry much weight, but they do serve to remind parties that developing countries cannot be taken for granted.

At the third review this point was emphasised once again. The final document referred to the increasing importance of Article 10 and the gap between developed and developing countries. It again set out a wide range of measures that could help the developing countries, including new elements such as co-operation in epidemiological surveillance to improve identification of major outbreaks of disease. The document also welcomed efforts to elaborate an international programme of vaccine development.

Yet even as committed a supporter of the convention as Nicholas Sims was moved to comment that all of these proposals presented:[9]

. . . problems for the North, where the benefits expected from the Convention are primarily security benefits: the reduced risk of being attacked with BTW [biological and toxin weapons]. From the point of view of the North, Article X is being misread. . . . there is not true consensus.

Sims suggested that the way forward was to concentrate on the prevention of disease as a co-operative activity, as it is clearly in the treaty itself (Article 10), whereas economic development is not. To a Western reader that may seem a reasonable and realistic approach. However, it sits uneasily with Lang's idea of a developing treaty regime in which the final documents of the five-yearly Review Conferences are central elements, for there is no doubt that Third World states have put their concerns over Article 10 very clearly into these documents.

While there may have been additional reasons for their actions, the Third World states showed clearly at the third review that their co-operation *is* needed for progress to be made. As Sims has stressed, the third review failed to set up any supportive institutions because some parties refused to allow a fund, which would have cost very little, to be set up. The fund would have financed a small unit in the UN Secretariat to handle the convention's confidence-building measures. He continued:[9]

> ... These State Parties, overwhelmingly from the Third World, had already blocked all proposals for even the most minimal form of inter-sessional committee; now they sought, and again with regrettable success, to prevent the creation of just two Secretariat posts, within the Geneva Branch of the Department of Disarmament Affairs ...

This was no trivial matter for supporters of the convention because the implementation of the confidence-building measures agreed in the second and the third reviews could undoubtedly have been assisted by such a small organisational initiative.

Confidence-Building Measures

The second Review Conference of the BWC was held as the first signs of the thaw in the Cold War were appearing. The successful conclusion of the Stockholm Conference, with its recognition of the role of confidence-building measures (CBMs), occurred in the same month as the review.[11] Thus there was a positive atmosphere for the introduction of such new measures into the convention.

The final document, in its section on Article 5, stated that 'mindful of the provisions of Article V and Article X' and in order to strengthen confidence in the convention and its implementation, parties had agreed to implement measures:

> ... in order to prevent or reduce the occurrence of ambiguities, doubts and suspicions, and in order to improve international co-operation in the field of peaceful bacteriological (biological) activities.

The agreed measures are summarised in Table 4.2. It is obvious that, while the security implications are usually stressed in the West, the measures clearly also refer to issues of international co-operation covered by Article 10. The Review Conference decided that a special group of scientific and technical experts should meet in the following year (1987) to work out the details of how data would be exchanged and the system was then put into operation.

Table 4.2   Summary of the confidence-building measures agreed in 1986[1]

Measure	Description
1	Exchange of data on research centres and laboratories that have very high safety standards in handling biological materials that pose a high risk.
2	Exchange of information on outbreaks of disease and similar occurrences caused by toxins that appear to be different from normal.
3	Encouragement of publication of results of research directly related to the convention and promotion of the use of such knowledge for permitted purposes.
4	Active promotion of contacts between scientists engaged in research directly related to the convention, including exchanges for joint research.

[1]Data from reference 9.

Unfortunately, the results of this data exchange CBM exercise were extremely disappointing. Reporting on the results of the first three rounds of data exchange in 1987, 1988 and 1989, Geissler noted that 18 parties took part in the first, 23 in the second and 14 in the third. The total number of different states taking part in the first three rounds was only 27, with the majority of parties to the convention declining to do so.[12] Geissler reported a slight improvement in the fourth round of 1990. By that time 36 states had participated, but the majority of parties to the convention had still taken no part.[13] In both reports Geissler pointed to the disturbingly low level of participation by developing countries from the Third World.

Regarding the information provided, there were also concerns because it was less than complete in some cases and there were ambiguities, for example, about what was intended by the words 'directly related to the Convention' in the questions provided as the basis for the exchange. As an example, Geissler noted that although something like 70 unusual outbreaks of disease or similar outbreaks caused by toxins had occurred and should therefore have been reported by parties during the period of the information exchange, only one such outbreak was reported under the confidence-building measures. This was an occurrence of Q-fever in the West Midlands in 1989 affecting more than 100 people and reported by the UK in 1990.

Although Geissler's second report was somewhat more enthusiastic about the promotion of contacts through symposia, its general conclusion was quite negative about the level and the quality of the responses. Nevertheless, the value of CBMs in increasing confidence is well understood by many government specialists. The greater the transparency about activities in this area of biological research, at least in the short term, the fewer suspicions there are likely to be. The third Review Conference attempted both to improve the previously agreed confidence-building measures and to add a further series. The CBMs agreed in 1991 are summarised in Table 4.3. A detailed set of forms relevant to all the measures was attached as an annex to the final document of the Review Conference.[10] Because the poor response to the first attempt at CBMs in the period 1987–91 may have been partly due to states with nothing to declare failing to return the documents, a new additional initial declaration form listed each of the new measures in turn and asked, for each of them, whether there was nothing to declare or nothing *new* to declare.

Table 4.3 Summary of the confidence-building measures agreed in 1991[1]

Measure	Description
Declaration Form A	Nothing to declare or Nothing new to declare
(1)	Exchange of data on research centres and laboratories.
(2)	Exchange of information on national biological defence research and development programmes.
B	Exchange of information on outbreaks of infectious diseases and similar occurrences caused by toxins.
C	Encouragement of publication of results and promotion of use of knowledge.
D	Active promotion of contacts.
E	Declaration of legislation, regulations and other measures.
F	Declaration of past activities in offensive and/or defensive biological research and development programmes.
G	Declaration of vaccine production facilities.

[1]Data from reference 10.

As we shall see in Chapter 8, one important aspect of building confidence and eventually having an effective verification system for the BWC is to develop understanding of the different national patterns of activity in relevant areas of biological research. A brief review of the submission by the UK in 1992 shows how such a picture could be built up from these enhanced CBMs.[14]

We have already referred in Chapter 3 to the summary provided of the UK's past offensive biological research and development programme. This was set out in response to measure F, with a further summary of the UK's past *defensive* biological research and development programme. The initial declaration form (nothing to declare or nothing new to declare for each of the measures) was left blank, indicating that a full response would be required for each of the CBM measures.

Nine facilities were listed in form A(1). These included the Coppetts Wood Unit of the Royal Free Hospital and Medical School in Muswell Hill, London. This was stated to be financed by the Department of Health, to have a laboratory isolator of $1.5m^2$ and to be 'the only comprehensive, high-containment patient management laboratory in the UK' dealing with patients having, or suspected of having, diseases such as Lassa, Ebola and Marburg fevers. Also listed was the Chemical and Biological Defence Establishment at Porton Down in Wiltshire, recorded as wholly financed by the Ministry of Defence and having a BL3 (lesser) containment unit of $300 m^2$. It was stated that there was no BL4 facility. The work of the establishment was summarised as:

Research and development into protective measures as defence against the hostile use of toxins and micro-organisms such as anthrax, tularemia, flaviviruses and arenaviruses.

This information on the current National Biological Defence Research and Development Programme in the UK was considerably amplified over the next 14 pages of the report.

An organisational structure was described for CBDE at Porton Down. The annual budget was reportedly in the region £30m, of which the biological defence element accounted for about £10m. Extra-mural contracts to universities and industry totalled about £4m, approximately one-third of which was concerned with biological defence. The total numbers of personnel involved in biological defence work at Porton Down are set out in Table 4.4.

Table 4.4 Numbers of people involved in the biological defence research and development programme at CBDE Porton Down[1]

Description	Numbers
I. Total number	215
II. Division of personnel	
Civilian	210
Military	5
III. Division of civilians	
Scientists	105
Engineers	5
Technicians	70
Administration/support	30

[1]Data from reference 14.

The programme was categorised under four headings: hazard assessment; detection; protection; and medical countermeasures. There is obviously not space here to detail the whole programme but some examples may help to illustrate its nature. Under hazard assessment, recent publications had included:

> . . . a comprehensive and authoritative review of the survival of micro-organisms, particularly bacteria, in the atmosphere and methods for their assaying and monitoring . . .

and:

> . . . a paper on the molecular biology of a model toxin, the alpha toxin of *Clostridium perfringens*, to facilitate the understanding of the potential hazard together with underpinning gene probe technology for detection.

Under detection, an example of a recent publication was given which:

> . . . outlines the ability specifically to identify a strain of a model DNA virus (Herpes B virus) using genetic fingerprinting.

Under medical countermeasures, a recent paper described:

> . . . the use of an anti-viral drug to counter a model DNA virus (Herpes B virus).

Under current projects there, work on vaccines included:

. . . the development of improved vaccines for anthrax and tularemia, including the use of recombinant vaccines and the use of vaccinia virus as a multi-agent vaccine carrier.

We shall return to these fascinating applications of modern biotechnology in greater detail in later chapters.

In regard to confidence-building measure B, specified at the third Review Conference, the recording of outbreaks of reportable infectious diseases was dominated numerically by BSE in animals, 22,607 cases of which were registered for 1991. Particular attention was given to an outbreak of blue-eared pig disease which began in Humberside and spread throughout the country, deviating from the normal expected pattern of disease. The disease was first recognised in North America in 1987 and arrived in continental Europe late in 1990. The agent of the disease can be spread by the airborne route and causes economic losses, through reproductive disorders in particular. Suggestions of economic sabotage were dismissed as very unlikely in causing the outbreak.

Under measure C it was stressed that it was UK policy for basic research, particularly that related to the convention, to be generally unclassified. To the extent possible without infringing national or commercial interests, applied research was also to be unclassified. Information on the journals in which unclassified research is published is discussed in more detail in the literature appendix at the end of this book.

The UK had a stated nil return for measure D on promotion of contacts. Under measure E legislation was reported in regard to matters specified in Article 1 of the convention and regulations regarding the export and import of micro-organisms and toxins relevant to the convention. Finally under measure G, eight vaccine production facilities were listed. One of these was the Public Health Laboratory Service Vaccine Production Unit, at the Centre for Applied Microbiology and Research (CAMR), Porton Down. It was reported to be concerned with anthrax and Kveim skin test antigen.

Whilst all such information might previously have been obtainable by a foreign intelligence service, such a level of disclosure by parties could not help but clarify national patterns of activity for all concerned. It remains to be seen whether the data exchange lives up to expectations when it is evaluated at the fourth Review Conference in 1996. The lack of organisational back-up for the BWC leads many observers to doubt that it will be successful.

The Present State of the BWC

In the period before the third Review Conference the United Nations Institute for Disarmament Research in Geneva produced a research report on the issues that needed to be addressed and proposals for solutions.[15] Its two experienced authors also issued a summary of the paper[16] and reflected on the outcome of the review shortly afterwards.[17] Together with the latest annual review by SIPRI,[18] these publications provide a good basis for a current general assessment of the health of the BWC and the biological weapons control regime.

In their post-conference review, Goldblat and Bernauer pointed first to the continuing need to recruit new parties to the convention. Despite the welcome increase in the number of states joining, they emphasised the large number of states still remaining outside this agreement. Particularly worrying are the states in conflict-prone regions of the world, such as the Middle East and North Africa, which have not joined the convention (they mentioned Algeria, Egypt, Israel, Morocco and Syria as examples).

Goldblat and Bernauer considered that the scope of the convention would remain imprecise until what was actually prohibited was spelt out clearly and it is to be hoped that the VEREX process (Chapter 8) will encourage this clarification. They remained dissatisfied with the relationship between the BWC and the 1925 Geneva Protocol, noting that in 1992 over 20 states retained reservations to the protocol. In their view, the Review Conference should have stated bluntly that such reservations contradict the undertakings given in the BWC never in any circumstance to acquire biological or toxin weapons. They also pointed out that few states have enacted the legislative or administrative procedures required by Article 4.

Following a careful review of the development of the new consultative mechanisms in Article 5, Goldblat and Bernauer suggested that 'the competence of the consultative meeting is still not quite clear', and they were fairly pessimistic about the possibility of international economic and technological co-operation under Article 10 of the convention, viewing it 'primarily as a disarmament measure'.

The basic weakness of the BWC remains its lack of any organisational underpinning between the brief five-yearly reviews. The real scale of the deficiency may be gauged from Sims' analysis of what might best serve the purposes of the convention.[19] He suggested a Committee of Oversight composed of some 20 representatives of parties to the convention, chosen with due regard to geographical and political factors and charged with promoting the effectiveness of the convention in all its aspects, including its constructive evolution. This committee would be supported by a scientific advisory panel and a legal advisory panel. The state which held the presidency of the Review Conference would also provide a small secretariat for the Committee of Oversight and its advisory panels until the next review, when it would hand over to the next president.

Unfortunately no such organisational system exists, and, given the expenditure necessary to implement the Chemical Weapons Convention, it must be doubtful whether extra expenditure for the BWC will be easily obtained. Perhaps the best that can be hoped for is that a small sub-section of the CWC organisation will eventually be mandated to handle verification issues associated with the BWC.

Meanwhile the 1993 *Yearbook* of the Stockholm International Peace Research Institute saw fit to add an appendix on 'Benefits and threats of developments in biotechnology and genetic engineering' to its chapter on chemical and biological weapons.[18] Jointly written by a former Senior Director of Research at Sweden's National Defence Research Establishment (FOA), the current head of Stockholm University's Department of Neurochemistry and Neurotoxicology, and the Director-General of FOA, this appendix is a sobering reminder of the pace of technical change in biotechnology relevant to the development and production of biological weapons. It is to such issues that we now turn.

.5.

SCIENCE, TECHNOLOGY AND
WARFARE

In his classic work, *The Pursuit of Power: Technology, Armed Force and Society since A.D.1000*,[1] William McNeill attributed the rise of the West partly to the relationship between technology, public finance, war and political power. Because there was no central power established in Europe, different political groups were able to use superior military technology to secure and extend their own power.

McNeill's book is part of recent rich and diverse developments in the historical study of technology and war,[2] but what is of particular interest here is that there are clearly historical periods when the technology of warfare develops very rapidly. We are in such a period of rapid change now: the technology of war is changing and with it the nature of modern warfare. To illustrate the point we may refer to work by Captain J. W. Bodnar who has a doctorate in biochemistry and is a member of the Chemistry Department at the US Naval Academy. He suggested in a paper titled, 'The military technical revolution: from hardware to information', that there has been a three-phased change in military technology since the Second World War.[3]

First there was an engineering revolution which steadily transformed weapons and platforms. This began during the last war and had practically ended by the 1980s. Then there was a revolutionary change in the capabilities of military sensors which began in the early 1970s and greatly increased the ability of individual platforms (e.g., ships) to analyse data and use weapon systems effectively. Bodnar believed this second phase of the military technical revolution would end in the 1990s. The third phase, in his opinion, began in the late 1970s and is concerned with the enhancement of command, control, communications and intelligence as applied to military forces. This phase was evident in the DESERT STORM operation against Iraq in 1991 but is far from complete. Ten years from now the effectiveness of military forces will therefore be very different again from what it was there.

A similar but more general argument was put forward by two analysts from the US RAND organisation in a paper entitled 'Cyberwar is coming'. They argued that industrialisation led to the development of mass armies and attrition warfare, as in the First World War; mechanisation then allowed manoeuvre warfare with tanks, as in the Second World War, but now:[4]

> ... The information revolution implies the rise of cyberwar, in which neither mass nor mobility will decide outcomes; instead, the side that knows more, that can disperse the fog of war yet enshroud an adversary in it, will enjoy decisive advantages.

Whilst the information technology revolution, which has affected so many spheres of civilian life, lies at the heart of this analysis, the authors were quite clear that enormous consequential changes would occur in military organisations and forces.

The argument was taken a stage further by an engineer, Flt. Lt. P. C. Emmett, of the Royal Air Force, in a paper entitled 'Software warfare: the emerging future'. He pointed out that the software used in the new information technology is of crucial importance: any effective modern force must understand its characteristics and production and integrate them, not just into weapon systems, but into the very preparations for war.[5] He envisaged a two-way influence whereby the process of software production would alter the character of war which would then feed back to accelerate the process of software production.

Such interest in new military technology and its consequences obviously stems in part from the dramatic events of Operation DESERT STORM. A few brief illustrations of the practical application of the new technology in the 1991 war against Iraq are given below. Marshall Ogarkov of the Soviet Union, whose writings were closely followed by some observers in the West, had anticipated much of what happened. We shall therefore also briefly consider Ogarkov's views.

Technology and Warfare

Operation DESERT STORM

Bodnar listed some of the instances where the communications capabilities of the coalition forces permitted operations of a new character against Iraq. He referred, for example, to the way in which individual buildings or bridges were bombed by laser-guided weapons: the weapons were fired from planes which were co-ordinated by airborne AWACS and which had reached the target area through the use of precision navigation. But most importantly, he pointed out that the information necessary to guide the planes was derived from satellite reconnaissance systems: the data passed first to rear-area analysts before being used to guide the attack squadrons. Bodnar also instanced the remarkable long-range bombing operation whereby B-52s flew from bases in the United States to bomb Kuwait and were then able to fly on to land in Diego Garcia.

Bodnar also remarked on the ground attack which concluded the war so rapidly through a co-ordinated, multinational operation in the desert. Much has been written about that operation and one of the most interesting comments was made by Rear Admiral Sir Peter Anson, chairman of Matra Marconi Space Limited, and his co-author, in a paper entitled 'The first space war'. According to them, the coalition serviceman:[6]

> . . . was able to move with confidence over difficult desert terrain, avoiding enemy defences, assured of resupply and able to pinpoint and target enemy arms and installations with remarkable precision, thanks to the technological 'discovery' of the war – Global Positioning System (GPS).

Whilst the military receivers for GPS were being provided as quickly as possible, $3,000 hand-held models were on the commercial market and some US troops asked their relatives to buy units for them. Although it is necessary to exercise a certain caution over some of the claims made about the nature of the Gulf War, this image of the coalition soldier being able to pinpoint his exact position with a hand-held instrument surely shows the superior information-processing capability of the coalition to that of Iraq.

Marshall Ogarkov's Views

Like their Western counterparts, Soviet military analysts studied the 1991 war in the Gulf with great care. Also, as might be expected, Western analysts of Soviet military affairs were scrutinising Soviet conclusions about the war. One such analyst, Mary FitzGerald, of the Hudson Institute, contributed a long article to the US *Naval War College Review* in the autumn of 1991.[7] What is striking in FitzGerald's analysis is her argument that the Gulf War essentially confirmed what the Soviet military had already concluded about the form that warfare would

increasingly take. She argued that, while the Soviet military had under-
gone profound change during the Gorbachev period, the mainstream
military view still reflected the focus that Marshal Ogarkov had put on
'emerging technologies' from the early 1980s onwards. She suggested
that the civilian leadership had not sought to block the development of
technologies perceived to be at the heart of future military capabilities,
such as advanced conventional munitions and space-based systems.
Moreover, they regarded the developments as inevitable; as she put it,
'the Soviet military had developed a comprehensive and revolutionary
vision of future war long before the Persian Gulf conflict'. In another
paper[8] she made the point even more strongly, suggesting that for Soviet
military analysts 'the Gulf War is said to have confirmed Marshall
Ogarkov's forecasts on the nature of future war'. If that was so, then
Ogarkov's views are important for anyone trying to grasp the current
relationship between science, technology and warfare.

Marshall Ogarkov's ideas had, in fact, been the subject of Western
analysis for most of the 1980s. Dale Herspring, a Foreign Service officer in the US Department of State, had written on the state of the Soviet
military in the aftermath of the 27th Party Congress. His paper of 1986
gave a good insight into Ogarkov's importance.[9] He argued that current
events then had to be seen against the backdrop of the period from 1977
to 1984 during which Ogarkov had dominated military politics from his
position as Deputy Defence Minister and Chief of the General Staff.
Ogarkov had not been reticent in openly expressing his disagreement
with politicians. Herspring argued that though this led to his dismissal
in the uncertain times of 1984 Ogarkov was not disgraced: he had a
major book published in 1985 and was, in fact, transferred to head the
critical Western Theatre of Military Operations.

In another article, Herspring attempted further to explain Ogarkov's
importance.[10] In his view, the impact of the scientific-technical revolution in military affairs was a matter of concern to all Soviet military
officers, but Ogarkov devoted more time and passion than anyone else
to the subject. He argued throughout his period as Chief of the General
Staff that it was crucial for the Soviet military to understand and adapt
to the major scientific-technical advances being made. Herspring
thought that Ogarkov was awarded the top post precisely to drag a force
dominated by the large-scale manoeuvre warfare of the previous war
into the modern age of computers and information technology.

As a Foreign Service officer, Herspring's analysis was naturally
largely concerned with the political aspects of Ogarkov's work. More
detail on the technical issues is available from a study published by

FitzGerald in 1987.[11] She argued that Ogarkov's views fitted into the evolution of Soviet views on nuclear warfare. From 1966 to 1976, she suggested, a segment of the Soviet military held the view that a defence against nuclear weapons would be found. This idea was firmly countered by Brezhnev's address in Tula in 1977. Thus after 1977 it was accepted that offence would always predominate in the balance between nuclear offence and defence and that there was essentially a stalemate between East and West at the nuclear level. There was little sense in developing further offensive systems since both sides would retain the capability for retaliation whatever the other did. However, the implication then was that beneath this nuclear 'umbrella' conventional systems would become more important .

Ogarkov's views were well known to the military in the West. For example, two officers serving in the Intelligence Division at Headquarters Allied Forces Central Europe (AFCENT), one British, one American, contributed an article entitled 'Ogarkov's revolution' to the journal *International Defense Review* in 1987.[12] They stressed the revolutionary nature of his thinking, its technological basis and its link to the nuclear stalemate. As they saw it, Ogarkov's view was that nuclear war becomes unnecessary if conventional technology is exploited:

> . . . Wars can remain conventional, according to Ogarkov, because new technologies, guided by new highly accurate delivery systems, will 'make it possible to conduct military operations with the use of conventional means of qualitatively new and incomparably more destructive forms than before . . .

It is hardly surprising, given the changes under way in Western military technology at the time, that Soviet writings were replete with accusations that the West might attack the Soviet Union in precisely this manner.

FitzGerald's 1987 article set out Soviet views on some of the main characteristics envisaged in the new form of warfare. First she noted the extended range of operations and Soviet fears that the West's AirLand Battle operation could involve conventional strikes against the entire strategic depth of the Warsaw Pact. She then stressed that the targets of the conventional attack were seen to be equivalent to the standard targets for nuclear weapons, for example, command-and-control points, communication networks and nuclear missiles. On top of that there was the possibility of surprise:

> . . . Soviet military figures have repeatedly stressed that the new conventional means will be used to deliver 'surprise' or 'preemptive'

strikes against the opponents' most important . . . targets. . . . Ogarkov wrote that Air-Land Battle envisions simultaneous, surprise strikes with the latest conventional means by air, naval and ground forces . . .

Against that background one can see the force of the later argument that the form of the DESERT STORM assault on Iraq came as no great surprise.

Writing in 1991, FitzGerald added more technical detail on what the new form of warfare was expected to be.[7,8] She noted that since the early 1980s military theorists in the Soviet Union had focused their attention on technologies related to automated decision-support systems, microelectronics, and so on. She stressed that the potential for continued evolution of technology and warfare was recognised and that two periods of change were suggested by the Soviet theorists. In the first, up to the turn of the century, there would be a continued development of enhanced types of current systems, for instance, for surveillance and target acquisition; in the first two decades of the *next* century it was expected that very different systems, such as directed-energy weapons and advanced robotics would come into use. Future war was seen as potentially global, with the control of space systems being of particular importance. The integration of means of reconnaissance, decision-making and action through new technology was to be at the core of the new warfare.

The importance accorded to high-technology capabilities in Soviet military writing during the 1980s is beyond doubt, but the Soviet Union lacked the industrial strength to put the ideas fully into effect. Although the USA was able to *implement* similar ideas, they were likewise concerned about their industrial capabilities and the long-term health of their defence industrial base. In order to pursue the issue further we need to consider the debate in the USA.

Industry and Warfare

The United States emerged from the Second World War as the dominant world industrial power. Following the war it is undoubtedly true that investment in military systems led to spin-on advances of use to the civil sector. Areas which benefited from military-related investment in the USA included aviation and computing. Yet it is now widely acknowledged that, as the information technology revolution has progressed, the speed of technological change in the civil sector has overtaken that in the military.[13] More fundamentally, new developments are occurring less often in the United States and more often elsewhere.

It is now well understood that the modern world economy is essentially a single market.[14] This has well-defined characteristics, such as its division into three tiers of states: core, periphery and semi-periphery. However, the position of states in these tiers can change over time, and the whole system has followed a cyclic pattern of growth and recession. Periods of growth over the last two hundred years correlate well with major periods of innovation in core technologies: smelting iron with coal, and the mechanisation of textile manufacture in the original 'industrial revolution'; steam engines and railways in the mid- to late nineteenth century; electrical and heavy engineering in the late nineteenth and the early twentieth centuries; Fordist mass production of cars, trucks, etc. from the 1930s to the 1980s; and electronics and information technology in our own times. What is more, the innovatory changes occur not just in technology, but in what has been termed the whole techno-economic paradigm:[15]

> The new key factor does not appear as an isolated input, but rather at the core of a rapidly growing system of technical, social and managerial innovations, some related to the production of the key factor itself and others to its utilisation . . .

The centre of the current pattern of growth is Japanese commercial industry and the rate of change is very fast, with flexibly-organised firms able to rapidly alter their mix of goods in the core electronics and information technology sector. Moreover, this commercial capability is increasingly allowing Japan to enhance its military potential.[16]

As the revolution in technology has progressed, a wide-ranging debate has developed in the USA on the implications for its continued military dominance. The debate has covered such aspects as strategy, foreign dependence and the technological base, and industrial policy. From our present perspective, the aspect of the debate concerned with 'critical technologies' is of particular interest. The attempt within the US Department of Defense to define what technologies are crucial for future military requirements, and to put plans in place to ensure their development, has been subject to extensive Congressional scrutiny.

One point came out very clearly in the first report of the National Critical Technologies Panel to Congress in April 1991. As may be seen from Table 5.1, the panel found that there was considerable overlap between its own identifications and previous Department of Defense analyses of critical technologies, and those considered to be important commercially.[17] The table illustrates the overlap of interest in new materials, advanced manufacturing and computer software. It is somewhat difficult to grasp what is really involved in these newly-developed technologies. Two examples may demonstrate the level of sophistication involved.

Table 5.1 Some critical technologies identified in the USA[1]

National critical technology panel	Commerce emerging technologies	Defence critical technologies
Materials e.g., Electronic and photonic materials	Advanced semiconductor devices	Semiconductor materials and microelectronic circuits
Manufacturing e.g., Intelligent processing equipment	Artificial intelligence	Machine intelligence and robotics
Information and communications e.g., Software	High-performance computing	Software producibility
Biotechnology and life sciences e.g., Applied molecular biology	Biotechnology	Biotechnology materials and processes

[1]Modified from reference 17.

Gallium Arsenide Technology

The core technology driving both economic growth and the revolution in military operations of the late twentieth century is information technology (IT) based on electronics. This technology is founded on scientific discoveries in physics which began at least a century ago. An example was the discovery by Thomas Alva Edison that electricity flows through space from a heated metal. By the early years of this century it had been shown that the electrons (negatively-charged particles which are constituents of all atoms) released from such a heated metal flow only to a positively-charged anode. Thus an alternating current which switches from positive to negative could be changed or rectified to direct current through the Edison effect. Later developments showed that the Edison effect was much stronger in a vacuum (tube or valve), and that other processes such as amplification could be achieved. The practical applications developed clearly depended not just on the flow of electricity (as in motors) but also on the control of the behaviour of electrons: hence electronics.

It was known that similar effects could be produced in crystals of some materials but, while valve technology predominated, little interest was shown in such solid-state devices. This changed when Shockley, Bardeen and Brattain, working at the Bell Laboratories in the 1940s, discovered how to make crystals which could rectify as well as valves, and which could amplify. The new crystals were called 'semiconductors' and for a long time the preferred material was silicon.

A semiconductor is a crystalline material whose electrical conductivity is between that of a conductor and that of an insulator. Addition of small amounts of different impurities allows an increase in the number of negative-charge carriers (electrons) in n-type semiconductors, and the number of positive-charge carriers (holes) in p-type semiconductors. The introduction of such impurities is called 'doping'. The creation of solid-state devices such as transistors (the basic elements of modern amplifiers and logic circuits) and thus integrated circuits (many connected elements) depend on the properties of junctions between p-type and n-type regions in the same piece of semiconductor crystal.

There are two main types of transistor. Bipolar transistors are the basic elements in a computer's central processing unit, and field-effect transistors (FETs) are generally used in a computer's memory and increasingly in the logic operations of smaller computers. Both types, in effect, are switches which may be either turned 'on' or 'off' by the application of an electric charge to particular regions of the transistor. The performance of both types of transistor depends crucially on the quality of the silicon crystal. Relatively uniform and defect-free crystals are grown to a size of about six inches in diameter in a complex process involving dipping and then slowly removing a small seed crystal from molten silicon. The large crystal produced is then sliced and polished to produce thin wafers of material. Integrated circuits are etched on to the surface of the wafers in another complex process, and doping is carried out to generate regions which have different electronic properties. Finally, the wafer is cut into a number of chips, each of which may have as many as a million transistors.

The possibility of using gallium arsenide (GaAs) instead of silicon has been known about for at least 30 years.[18] Gallium arsenide has distinct advantages: because of the speed with which electrons move through it; in weak-signal operations; and in the generation and detection of light. Thus GaAs chips are well suited for use in computing, television reception and the opto-electronic transmission of data (photonics). Gallium arsenide light-emitting diodes and lasers, used in visual displays and audio-disc players, are widely employed; domestic satellite-receiver dishes use gallium arsenide detectors. Gallium arsenide is also superior to silicon because of the ease with which its electronic characteristics may be manipulated, for example in alloys of aluminium gallium arsenide. Very thin layers of two or more alloys may also be alternated on a chip to create so-called heterojunctions in which the precise electrical properties vary from layer to layer.

Given these advantages, why has gallium arsenide not superseded silicon as the preferred semiconductor medium? The answer to that question lies in the difficulties of producing high-quality, low-cost gallium arsenide chips. One of the most serious problems in manufacturing is the lack of a native oxide. Silicon oxide readily forms on heating silicon in air. It constitutes an electronic and mechanical seal and can thus be used as the insulator between adjacent transistors on a chip or as a protective mask through which 'windows' can be cut and chemicals allowed to react in etching and doping processes. Much more difficult approaches are needed in gallium arsenide chip manufacture. A further disadvantage is that gallium arsenide is a compound. Defects in the element silicon may be annealed by heating the crystal, but heating gallium arsenide leads to selective loss of arsenic. Again this greatly complicates manufacture since defects caused at various stages of the production process are difficult to correct.

Applications of gallium arsenide technology, not surprisingly therefore, have been limited to devices where specific, desirable features compensate for the relatively high cost of production. The most familiar example in everyday use is at the focus of satellite receiver-dish antennae, since communications satellites use microwaves for which gallium arsenide's speed characteristics are eminently suitable. Additionally, it can amplify the weak signals practically without distortion ('noise'). Gallium arsenide is therefore also particularly important in many current defence systems which rely on microwave technology.

Almost certainly, gallium arsenide's most important future applications will be found in the photonic transmission of information. Light propagation in fibres (fibre optics) allows transmission of more information further and faster than the transmission of electrical signals in conventional metal wires is capable of. As optical fibres are increasingly used, gallium arsenide usage is also likely to increase because of its advantageous optical properties. Furthermore, the advantage that gallium arsenide has in speed of operation could eventually lead to its increasing incorporation into the central functions of computers by the displacement of slower-acting, silicon-based systems.

Micromachining Technology

Micromachining is the process of fabricating miniature objects and structures, often on the surface of a silicon chip. It is similar to the technology for etching electronic circuits on to silicon chips, but differs in that mechanical structures, not electrical circuits, are created.

Micromachining technology is important because it provides a direct means of linking information on other aspects of the physical world, such as pressure or acceleration, with modern electronic systems. This combination allows the development of extremely powerful and economically important new devices. Such devices already have important commercial applications, but technical developments in the 1980s have opened up a huge range of potential new applications.[19] Some of these are already coming on stream, but many more possibilities look likely to emerge.

The oldest micromachining technology is called bulk micromachining because the entire mass of the chip is used: areas of silicon are marked (burned) by light shining through a patterned template (photolithographic mask). The marked areas are then etched away by alkaline chemicals. Micromachining work in the 1960s produced the silicon-diaphragm pressure sensor. In such a device a silicon chip is modified so that it has a very thin layer in one part its surface. This layer or diaphragm distorts slightly under pressure, the distortion creating stress in the crystal which, in turn, generates electrical signals (a piezoelectric effect). By this means, changes in pressure may be detected through the electrical signals generated, and this information may then be processed in an electronic system. However, this technology is very different from that used to make standard chips and thus, although successful and subject to refinements which allow greater control, is not easily integrated into standard chip manufacture.

A second process called surface micromachining is much closer to the standard chip technology. For example, a small structural projection or 'beam' can be constructed on a silicon chip in four stages. First, ultraviolet light passed through a photolithographic mask is used to define an area on the surface which is susceptible to etching in the next stage. The defined area is then partially etched out by hydrofluoric acid to form a depression. A layer of new silicon can then be deposited on the whole surface from silicon vapour. A supporting base in the depression and a projecting 'beam' lying on top of the *original* silicon outside the depression can be patterned out of the newly-deposited silicon. Finally, the 'beam' is released by etching away some of the original silicon beneath it.

However, even this newer technique has limitations because the struc-

structures so built are extremely thin. Another technique, LIGA (*Lithographie, Galvanoformung, Abformung*), solves this problem to some extent. Again, lithographic patterning is used, but instead of ultraviolet light patterning and chemicals etching into silicon, high-energy X-rays are used to cut directly into X-ray-sensitive polymers laid over the surface of the chip. The shorter wavelengths of X-rays allow more detailed features to be constructed, and deeper cutting into the polymers allows wider and thicker structures. Unwanted surface polymer is removed by chemicals, leaving a mould which can be filled to create the microstructure, or used as the template for a further moulding process.

The United States probably remains the leading actor, at least in academic research on micromachining, and its Defense Advanced Research Projects Agency (DARPA) is funding a programme at the level of $20 million over three years. In Japan, the Ministry of International Trade and Industry (MITI) has started to support an integrated research programme to run over 10 years.

Reports suggest that future developments will require a much greater understanding of the materials used in micromachining technology. One particular problem with silicon-based devices is that they tend to have high levels of residual stress which cause difficulties if parts are moving. Some researchers are investigating non-semiconductor materials with magnetic properties; others are investigating combinations of silicon chips and biological enzymes or antibodies. Formidable technical problems will obviously be encountered in such new applications, but the commercial rewards for success could be considerable.

The general debate on critical technologies in the United States which was referred to earlier in this chapter naturally also encompassed assessments of the relative capabilities of other countries in all of these technologies. Table 5.2 shows comparisons made in the USA in 1991 for defence technologies. It is clear that the main competitors in these advanced industrial systems are the USA, Europe and Japan and that most Third World countries have very little chance of competing at such levels of sophistication even though the capabilities are spreading around the world.

Biotechnology

Biotechnology was considered important in the US assessments of critical technologies (Table 5.1). This is reflected in Europe where the life sciences have a prominent place in the Fourth Framework Programme.[20] In the UK a new Biotechnology and Biological Sciences Research

Table 5.2   Illustrative comparative technological capabilities[1]

Critical technology	Dual-use	USSR	NATO allies	Japan	Others
Semiconductor materials and microelectronic circuits	√	*	***	****	**Israel
Machine intelligence and robotics	√	*	***	****	**Finland, Israel, Sweden
Software engineering	√	*	**	**	**Various countries
Biotechnology materials and processes	√	**	***	****	**Various countries

Others relative to USA
****	Broad technical achievement, capable of major contributions.
***	Moderate technical achievement, capable of important contributions.
**	Generally lagging.
*	Lagging in all important aspects.

[1]Modified from reference 17.

Council has been established recently,[21] which again serves to emphasise the growing importance of this aspect of technological development.

The stark fact is that biotechnology is cheaper and simpler to master than the advanced information technologies we have just discussed, but the biological weapon systems that could result would nevertheless be extremely powerful. Not surprisingly, therefore, the American literature contains frequent references to the possible development of biological weapons by other states as a relatively inexpensive means of countering sophisticated Western conventional military technology.[22,23] The nature of this new biotechnology requires careful study, for it would be almost inconceivable were such a new and powerful technological capability not at least *considered* for application in the military sphere.

.6.

THE NEW BIOLOGY

For our present purposes it is necessary to get a sense of the huge scale of investment in modern biotechnology brought about by clear commercial possibilities, and then to review briefly the basic biology and techniques on which current advances are founded. With that information it will be possible to focus on what new knowledge has become available which might be relevant to the production of biological weapons.

Biotechnology

Biological organisms have long been used by human societies, for example in the brewing of beer, the baking of bread and in cheese-making.[1]

Bread is made from wheat flour, salt, sugar and yeast. Water is added and the thick sticky dough is repeatedly folded. The mixture is then left to rest for some time. Enzymes from the yeast cells then act on sugars in the mixture to produce carbon dioxide through fermentation. As this gas cannot escape from the mixture it causes the dough to rise. At the same time, other enzymes from the yeast act on proteins in the flour to make them less tough. Baking then inactivates the yeast, stops the enzymatic reactions and drives off by-products such as alcohol produced by the fermentation of sugars. Though this system of making bread is very old, genetic engineers are currently trying to improve yeasts, for example by making them more active and able to operate more quickly at lower temperatures.

Beer is produced from the starch and proteins of barley through a series of stages. In the first, called malting, the seeds are allowed to

99

germinate. Enzymes in the seeds break down the stored material there to simpler compounds that yeast is able to ferment. The germination is halted by slowly heating the barley. The malted barley is then milled and mashed. Hot water is percolated through the mash to obtain a rich solution of nutrients called wort. The wort is then mixed with hops to give the required flavour and heated to obtain a sterile solution. Fermentation of this sterile liquid is carried out by adding yeast. This stage takes between a week and ten days. As a thick crust builds up on the surface, carbon dioxide produced during fermentation dissolves in the liquid and makes it effervesce. Final processing consists of filtering off the solid material from the beer and finishing its presentation in bottles, cans and barrels. Beer is usually about four to six per cent alcohol. Low-alcohol beers can be made by removing alcohol from ordinary beers or directly, by use of an engineered yeast strain that produces beer of only low-alcohol concentration.

Vinegar is produced by a second fermentation of beer, cider or wine. A mixture of *Acetobacter* species is used to convert alcohol to acetic acid. Traditionally, this was done in large pine vats and the bacteria were obtained by passing the liquid repeatedly over bundles of birch twigs coated with the bacteria. Nowadays the process is carried out in aerated fermenters.

In cheese-making the milk is first pretreated by pasteurisation in order to kill off any contaminating micro-organisms. The milk is then coagulated by means of lactose-fermenting bacteria and rennet. The liquid whey is separated from the solid curd which is processed further to produce cheese. Gas-producing bacteria are used to give the cheese its particular texture and acid-producing bacteria give it flavour. The ripening of cheeses requires storage under conditions that allow micro-organisms to improve the flavour. Fungi are used at this stage to give some cheeses their individual characteristics of flavour, colour, texture and appearance.

Official reports in many countries have emphasised the increasing importance of biotechnology. For example, the UK Advisory Council on Science and Technology (ACOST), in a 1990 report, *Developments in Biotechnology*,[2] suggested that:

> Biotechnology is a broad term used to describe the production of innovative products, devices and organisms by exploitation of biological processes . . .

The report explained the crucial features of the new developments as follows:

... Traditional biotechnology was based on enrichment and purification, modern biotechnology on the *manipulation of genes* and on the *alterations of the genetic structure of cells*. Much of its importance stems from recent advances in genetics and biochemistry and from the emergence of molecular biology. [Author's emphases]

The central importance of the new understanding of genetics at a molecular level was clearly emphasised. In the view of the report's authors:

Underpinning the future progress on genetic manipulation will be advances in molecular genetics and the knowledge of genomes of organisms . . .

Major new commercial opportunities are confidently expected to arise from the acquisition of this deeper understanding.

Five distinct new technologies were identified in the report (Table 6.1) and it was suggested that these have led to advances in the production of: high-value chemicals (mainly for medical use); intermediate-value chemicals or enzymes; monoclonal antibodies for diagnostic purposes; novel plant species or increased yields; transgenic animals; and detection of particular genetic factors in human beings. A paper produced for the European Community's Forecasting and Assessment in Science and Technology (FAST) Programme in 1992 also summarised some of the progress and prospects in these different areas of application.[3]

Table 6.1 Novel technologies[1]

---

1. *Sequencing of genes and proteins*: elucidating the order of the constituent chemicals.

2. *Genetic engineering*: cutting and splicing of DNA, moving genes between organisms and getting these genes to work.

3. *Fused cell techniques*: fusing two cells to produce a new cell with all or parts of the genetic material of the two parent cells, for example to produce monoclonal antibodies or new plants.

4 *Protein engineering*: altering the structure and thus the properties of proteins by manipulation of the DNA which controls their production.

5. *Fermentation and cell culture*: growing large amounts of microbial or animal or plant cells.

---

[1]Data from reference 2.

Fifteen first-generation protein drugs and vaccines were reported in the FAST paper to have been approved for use in the USA and a hundred others created by recombinant DNA techniques (rDNA, see below) were said to be awaiting approval. Great advances in understanding are expected to lead to much more sophisticated and specific products being available in the future. A number of genetically-engineered Hepatitis B vaccines are already on the market and human growth hormone has been used for the treatment of dwarfism in children.

In regard to intermediate-value chemicals, it is expected that over 50 per cent of the industrial enzyme market will be taken over by biotechnology products within a decade. Numerous medical diagnostic kits depending on monoclonal antibodies are already in clinical use. Examples are an AIDS diagnosis kit and a *Legionella* rapid assay.

Plant biopesticides based on toxins produced by the bacterium *Bacillus thuringiensis* (Bt) have been commercially produced for three decades. Two rDNA Bt products have now been approved in the USA. Toxic genes have been cloned, sequenced and introduced into different organisms and further applications are likely despite concerns such as those over the development of resistant strains of insects. Plants, of course, have been subjected to mutagens and selected for altered genes for many years. Now new plant transgenic techniques are available and over 50 species of crop plant have been transformed by these methods. Progress has been rapid in the development of plants with resistance to herbicides, insects and viruses. Genes which encode for an enzyme that inactivates a herbicide have, for example, been transferred into cotton and oilseed rape.

In regard to animal husbandry, bovine growth hormone (bovine somatotrophin, BST) can now be produced by microbial organisms and fed to cattle. Some 15-30 per cent increases in milk production have been reported. Monoclonal antibody technology is also being used in the diagnosis of animal diseases. There is, for example, a system that screens for a wide range of poultry diseases.

The general conclusion is that during the next few decades we may expect major impacts from applications of the new biotechnology to the food and drinks industry, health, pharmaceuticals, chemicals, agriculture, and the environment (Table 6.2). What then is this new technology, and on what scientific knowledge is it based?

Table 6.2 Commercial areas affected by biotechnology[1]

1. Foods and drinks.
2. Pharmaceuticals and health care:
   – Human medicine;
   – Veterinary medicine.
3. Chemicals and fuels.
4. Agriculture and horticulture.
5. Environment clean-up.

[1]Data from reference 1.

Some Basic Biology

The basic facts that we need to understand are straightforward, even though the detail of how living cells operate may be extremely complex. There are differences in the details of how simple bacterial (prokaryotic) and more advanced (eukaryotic) cells operate. Bacterial cells do not have their genetic material or DNA (deoxyribonucleic acid) enclosed in a distinct nucleus as, for example, do the cells in our bodies, and this has profound implications. Nevertheless, for both prokaryotic and eukaryotic cells, we know that the enzymes that effect their operations, and many other biological compounds of importance, are proteins. These are made up of one or more chains of amino acids called peptides. The sequence of amino acids determines the three-dimensional structure of the chains and this is crucial to the function of the protein.

The sequence of amino acids in the peptide chain is determined by the information coded in the DNA gene for that particular chain. In a eukaryotic cell the information in the DNA is transferred out from the nucleus to the cytoplasm surrounding it by a particular kind of RNA or ribonucleic acid called messenger RNA (mRNA). The mRNA has a structure which is complementary to the DNA from which it has been transcribed. The peptide chain is then synthesised on the mRNA by a process called translation. In bacteria, which do not have their DNA separated off in a nucleus, mRNA operates in a similar way but tends to be much shorter-lived.

The sequence of events is summarised thus: transcription of the coded information from DNA to mRNA and then translation from mRNA to form the peptide chain of amino acids. The particular sequence of amino acids of the peptide chain then dictates the three-dimensional structure and therefore the properties of the protein coded for by the original

DNA gene. Although the existence of nucleic acids has been known for over a century, the hereditary function of the material was only clearly demonstrated in the early 1950s. The detailed investigation of the structure and function of DNA and RNA effectively dates from that time. Hence our understanding is very recent and has developed extremely rapidly.

The structure of DNA was suggested by Watson and Crick in 1953. The structure of the DNA double helix is now well known. The DNA molecule is composed of two linked strands of nucleotides. Each nucleotide consists of a base, a sugar called deoxyribose, and a phosphate. The backbone of each DNA strand consists of linked and linearly alternating deoxyriboses and phosphates. The base can be one of adenine (A), guanine (G), cytosine (C) or thymine (T). Because of their particular characteristics A on one strand always links with T on the other, and similarly G always links with C. The important point is that the genetic information is encoded in the order of the bases. In the code a particular non-overlapping triplet of bases determines a particular amino acid of a peptide chain.

Certain other characteristics of DNA should be noted. First, the two strands are coiled around each other in a helical manner. The sugar and phosphate backbones of the strands are on the outside whereas the linked base pairs are on the inside (forming the 'rungs' of the helical 'ladder'). It is also known that the phosphate may be attached at either of two positions of the deoxyribose, conventionally numbered 5' and 3'. The two DNA strands have opposite polarity in the sense that in one the attachments run from 5' to 3' and in the other from 3' to 5'. When DNA replicates itself the two strands split apart and a new strand is built up on each in what is a semi-conservative process – each new length of DNA being made up of one old or conserved strand and one new 'daughter' strand. The structure of genes is, of course, by no means as simple as this description might suggest. There are, for example, specific sets of triplets which determine where protein synthesis will start and finish on mRNAs, and segments which regulate the transcription of mRNA from the DNA.

RNA or ribonucleic acid differs from DNA in that the sugar present is ribose and the base uracil occurs instead of thymine; RNA is also single-stranded but the same principle of a non-overlapping triplet code determining amino acids applies. Messenger RNA is produced on the DNA template, in the 5' to 3' direction, by the action of enzymes called RNA polymerases. The DNA strands separate locally, but only one is used for copying into mRNA. The mRNA then undergoes a variety of further processing stages before it is ready to act as a template for protein synthesis. In the simpler bacteria groups of genes are often transcribed together as they are located close together along the bacterial DNA. Such a group of genes is called an operon; the individual genes are called cistrons. The mRNA remains in one piece as the different cistrons are translated into proteins. In more advanced eukaryotic cells each mRNA codes for only one amino acid chain or peptide. Moreover, when the mRNA is first transcribed there are many apparently non-functional pieces (introns) between the pieces (exons) which code for peptide. The introns are sliced away within the nucleus before the passage of the mRNA into the cytoplasm and the subsequent production of the peptide.

Protein synthesis takes place in the cytoplasm on ribosomes. These are proteins where mRNA can be brought together with the appropriate amino acids. The genetic code includes the signals of initiation (AUG) and termination (UAA, UAG and UGA) of protein synthesis and 61 other possible base combinations which code for the 20 different, naturally-occurring amino acids. The code is therefore degenerate because some amino acids are specified by more than one type of triplet.

This simplified description of the basics of molecular biology will raise as many questions as it answers. For example, if the same DNA is present in each of the cells of our bodies why are liver cells different from skin cells? Clearly, there have to be very complex means by which the operation of genes is controlled and means by which these central processes within cells can be integrated with regulatory elements outside the cell. In short, while it is not necessary for us to follow all the details here, an enormous amount of work has gone into elucidating how the basic mechanisms of heredity actually function within the intact cell and the whole organism.

It can be logically argued that, amongst other things, a gene would need:[4]

- the code for the protein product;
- a switch to turn it on and off;
- a regulator to make sure it produced the correct amount of protein.

As we shall see, some of these elements have certainly been identified, and the fact that they seem to operate in the same way in a wide variety of organisms suggests that certain very important aspects of the operation of the genetic machinery have been conserved essentially intact through long periods of evolution. This allows the elements to be manipulated between different organisms by man.

The New Technology

We shall not attempt to provide here a comprehensive listing of the major technologies now available in this rapidly-advancing field, nor to detail the technical aspects of those we do describe. The aim rather is to give sufficient information on some of the crucial technologies for the reader to be easily able to follow what is being done in regard to the organisms of interest. It is important to stress that the techniques to be described did not arise *de novo* but from an extended background of scientific research. For example, much of the work which will be of interest to us later has concerned micro-organisms: bacteria and viruses in particular. There has been a long period of intensive study of such organisms including the initial 'Golden Age' of work from the last quarter of the last century through to the start of the First World War.[5] Nevertheless, advances are now being made very rapidly and the pace of developments over the last two decades has accelerated.

DNA Sequencing

One standard method of analysing the sequence of bases in DNA is named the Maxam-Gilbert method after its originators.[6] Identical pieces of DNA are cut into fragments (by methods detailed later) and the fragments are then sorted according to size by subjecting the whole set to gel electrophoresis. In this technique the DNA fragments are acted upon by an electric current and migrate along the gel to a distance dependent on their size, the smallest migrating furthest. Batches of similar-sized fragments can then be obtained directly by washing them off different sections or bands of the gel.

Batches of DNA pieces of identical length are then radioactively labelled at one end and split into four separate lots (Figure 6.1). Each lot of DNA fragments is then treated with a different reagent. The reagent attacks the DNA at one (or two) specific bases. Conditions are set so that only a small number of sites will be attacked by each reagent, but every potential site should be cut in each lot of DNA.

The result is a series of differently-sized fragments in each of the four lots. These fragments have different sizes depending on how far away from the radioactive end they were attacked. The four lots of fragments can therefore be subjected to gel electrophoresis again to separate out the different lengths of fragments. The bands obtained can then be detected in each case by autoradiographs revealing the labelled fragments, and the sequence of the DNA can be deduced by comparing across the four sets. For example, in the third lot of DNA shown in

Figure 6.1 The Maxam-Gilbert method of sequencing DNA*.

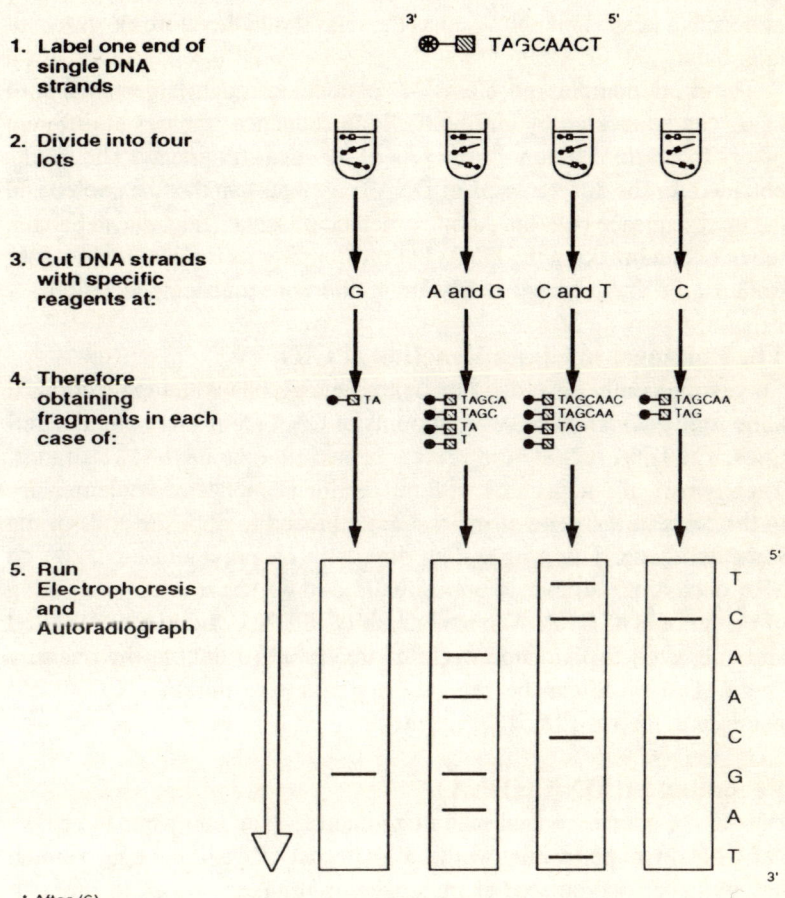

1. Label one end of single DNA strands

2. Divide into four lots

3. Cut DNA strands with specific reagents at:

   G   A and G   C and T   C

4. Therefore obtaining fragments in each case of:

5. Run Electrophoresis and Autoradiograph

* After (6)

Figure 6.1, the strand can be cut at T immediately after the radioactive label. Thus a band will be obtained at the far end of the electrophoresis gel, since small fragments migrate furthest. On the other hand, the strand can also be cut at the T at the far end of the strand away from the radioactive label. This shows up as the largest and therefore slowest-running band.

The more complex problems of sequencing much larger strands of DNA can be tackled by cutting the long sequence of bases at different places to obtain different initial sets of identical fragments. The results obtained for the different sets of DNA fragments can then be pooled and the total sequence built up. Another method of sequencing, due to Sanger, relies not on breaking the DNA, but on stopping its replication in a controlled way. There is also steady automation of sequencing techniques.

The Polymerase Chain Reaction (PCR)

This is a recently developed technique which has wide application. It allows the generation of large amounts of DNA from small initial quantities. The DNA region of interest is heated to separate the two strands. Then two synthetic primers with nucleotide sequences complementary to the parts of the gene of interest are attached to opposite ends of the separated gene. The primer then directs DNA polymerase enzyme to copy each of the strands in opposite directions. The result is a doubling of the amount of DNA. The new quantity of DNA can then be reheated and subjected to the same cycle of treatment to double the quantity again. The cycle can be repeated ten times to obtain a 1,000-fold increase in the specific DNA of interest.

Recombinant DNA (rDNA)

DNA is, of course, recombined in animal reproduction when the paternal DNA in a sperm joins with the maternal DNA in the egg. Human beings have manipulated such processes for many years in order to breed animals for particular purposes, and similarly with plants. There were severe limits though to what was achievable. As Gerald J. Stine commented:[7]

> . . . for millions of years of biological evolution recombination of DNA, as it generally occurs in nature, stays within species lines and within their mechanism of reproduction. . . . the investigator only brought together packages of evolutionarily-prepared DNA and asked whether or not the DNA within these packages (gametes) would recombine.

The discovery of site-specific restriction enzymes in 1970 dramatically changed that situation and led to the rapid developments in genetic engineering that we see today.

Restriction enzymes occur in bacteria where they function to protect the bacteria against invading foreign DNA. Entry of such DNA into the cell stimulates production of these enzymes which specifically attack and therefore degrade the function of the foreign DNA. Type II restriction enzymes have been mainly used in rDNA techniques because they cut DNA at absolutely specific sites no matter where that DNA originates. Thus it is possible to cut two different types of DNA at the same site and then to join the two different types together.

As is shown in Figure 6.2, two species of DNA can be cut by the EcoR1 restriction enzyme which makes a staggered symmetrical cut leaving bases exposed on both. These bases can then join up and be sealed together to form a new mixture of DNAs. By the late 1980s over a thousand such enzymes had been isolated, mostly of type II. Many of these enzymes were isolated from different bacterial species cut at the same site, but, even so, one hundred specific cleavage sites were known and about 150 restriction enzymes were commercially available.[7]

In order to use such a restriction enzyme, for example to produce large amounts of the product of an animal gene, it is necessary not only to find a way of inserting the gene into another piece of DNA but to get it to function in another cell such as a bacterium which can be easily cultured. This may be done, for example by inserting the DNA from the higher organism into a plasmid vector. Plasmids are autonomously replicating DNA molecules able to function in bacterial cells.

The example shown in Figure 6.3 outlines the steps that are taken. The plasmid DNA is in the form of a circle which is cut or opened up by a specific restriction enzyme. The DNA to be inserted is cut by the same enzyme and the fragments of the two types of DNA (gene and plasmid) are mixed. The 'sticky ends' join up and are sealed with DNA ligase. As the joining-up is not a controlled process, some plasmids simply close up again, but some will incorporate the foreign DNA. These are called recombinants. In the next stage the plasmids are mixed with bacteria and some enter the bacterial cells. This process is termed transformation, and some of the bacterial cells so transformed will have incorporated the recombinant DNA plasmids. The bacteria containing recombinant DNA may be selected in various ways, for example by having recombinant plasmids confer antibiotic resistance on the bacteria which then allows the ones containing such plasmids to be selected out by subjecting the whole batch to the action of an antibiotic. Once the

Figure 6.2 Joining up DNA from different species using a restriction enzyme*.

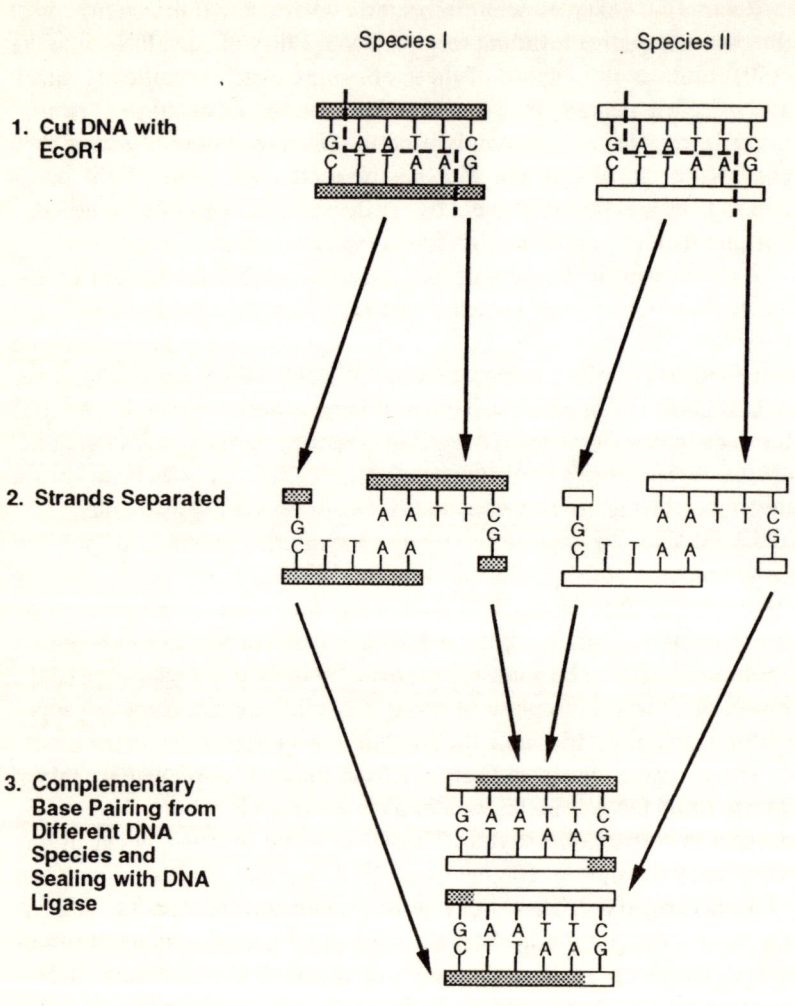

* After (7)

selected bacteria containing the foreign DNA are identified, they can be grown on (cloned) to yield large quantities of this DNA and its products.

Just how large are the quantities that can be produced is illustrated by the fact that a concentration of *Escherichia coli* bacterial cells of one per millilitre may be transformed into a concentration of one billion cells per millilitre in 24 hours. If each cell has a copy of the plasmid there will be billions of copies available. Additionally, a plasmid of *E. coli* can be enabled to multiply in the bacterial cell without the bacterium reproducing and thereby splitting itself. In this way 1,000-3,000 plasmids can be obtained within each bacterial cell and each of these plasmids will also reproduce when the bacterium itself does.

Although the use of plasmids is a very successful means of producing functioning rDNA in bacteria it suffers from the disadvantage that only relatively short pieces of DNA can be carried. One way of carrying larger sections of DNA is to use bacteriophages (or phages). These are viruses which attack bacteria. They naturally insert their own DNA into bacteria where it can replicate and produce large numbers of new phage particles (lytic phase) or become integrated within the bacterial chromosome and replicate at the same time as the bacterial cell (lysogenic phase).

The phage lambda (λ) has been intensively studied. It has 60 genes which have all been mapped and the complete sequence of its 48,000 base pairs is known. The genes which govern the integration of the phage into the bacterial chromosome and replication alongside the bacterium can be removed from the phage DNA. Then foreign DNA inserted into the phage DNA will be injected into other bacteria when new phages are produced in the lytic phase. Over 100 vectors have been derived from the λ phage, as there are many sites where restriction enzymes may be used and which do not interfere with the independent phage replication.

There are further ways of cloning still larger pieces of DNA. Advances in the understanding of yeast genetics, for example, have made it possible to develop cloning vectors called yeast artificial chromosomes (YACs) which can be transferred into yeast cells and will function there.

Gene Probes

With the techniques just described, it is possible to take the fragments of DNA produced by a variety of different restriction enzymes and to prepare a 'library' of clones of these fragments for the whole DNA of a particular organism of interest.

Figure 6.3 Genetic engineering of a bacterial plasmid and cloning of foreign DNA*.

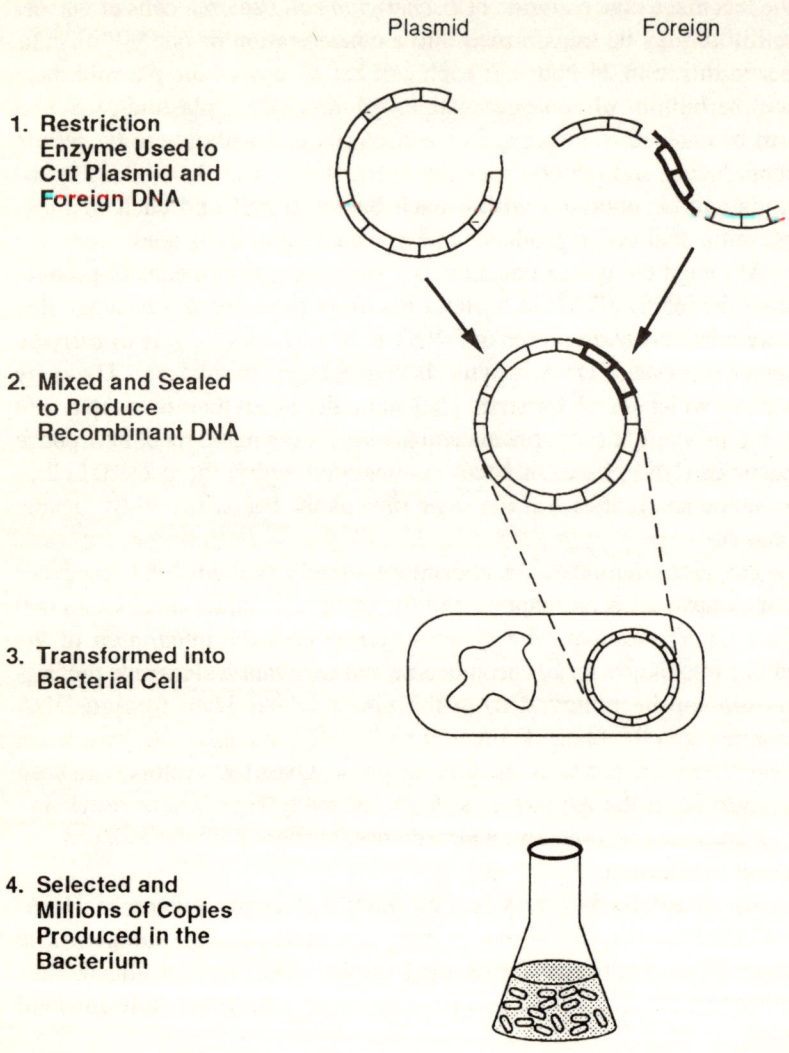

Plasmid   Foreign

1. Restriction
   Enzyme Used to
   Cut Plasmid and
   Foreign DNA

2. Mixed and Sealed
   to Produce
   Recombinant DNA

3. Transformed into
   Bacterial Cell

4. Selected and
   Millions of Copies
   Produced in the
   Bacterium

*After (7)

The question eventually arises as to how the investigator can recognise what gene has been cloned. What does a particular piece of DNA that is now functioning within the bacterial cell do within the whole living organism? The enzyme reverse transcriptase was discovered in 1970 in certain viruses which cause cancer and which have RNA as their genetic material. In a viral infection the enzyme produces a DNA strand complementary to the virus RNA. In the laboratory, therefore, the same enzyme may be used to produce a DNA copy (complementary DNA or cDNA) from any piece of messenger RNA.

Take the simple case of human reticulocytes (red blood cells). The mRNA in these cells is almost entirely made up of material used to produce the globin chains that compose the oxygen-carrying haemoglobin molecule. So it is not too difficult to purify the mRNAs for single globin chains and to make radioactively-labelled cDNA from this mRNA. Given that DNA bases always pair A to T and C to G, such DNA molecules can be used to 'recognise' chemically exactly similar sequences to their own. Thus it would be possible to use a cDNA made from the globin mRNA to find the 'gene' amongst a set of fragments of DNA that have previously been cloned.

A standard procedure for screening cloned DNA sequences was developed by Grünstein and Hogness. This is illustrated in Figure 6.4. The transformed bacterial cells are grown to visible size in a solid medium. The colonies are then transferred on to a replica plate (basically by stamping the replica plate into the original and thereby picking up some of the material from each colony). Chemical treatment of the replica colonies then kills the cells and denatures the DNA. The denatured DNA sticks to the replica plate and protein material etc. may be washed away.

Radioactive cDNA can then be flooded on to the replica plate where it will hybridise or join up with any DNA which it specifically complements. Unhybridised DNA is then washed away and the replica plate subjected to autoradiography. If there is a match with the cDNA it will show on the radiograph of the replica plate and this will indicate the colony on the original plate which has the DNA of interest in its plasmids.

Monoclonal Antibodies

When foreign proteins (antigens) enter an animal its immune system responds by producing clones of different individual plasma cells, each clone of which produces a different single antibody. A disease called multiple myeloma arises when an individual clone of plasma cells

Figure 6.4 Screening for cloned DNA sequences using the Grünstein-Hogness method*.

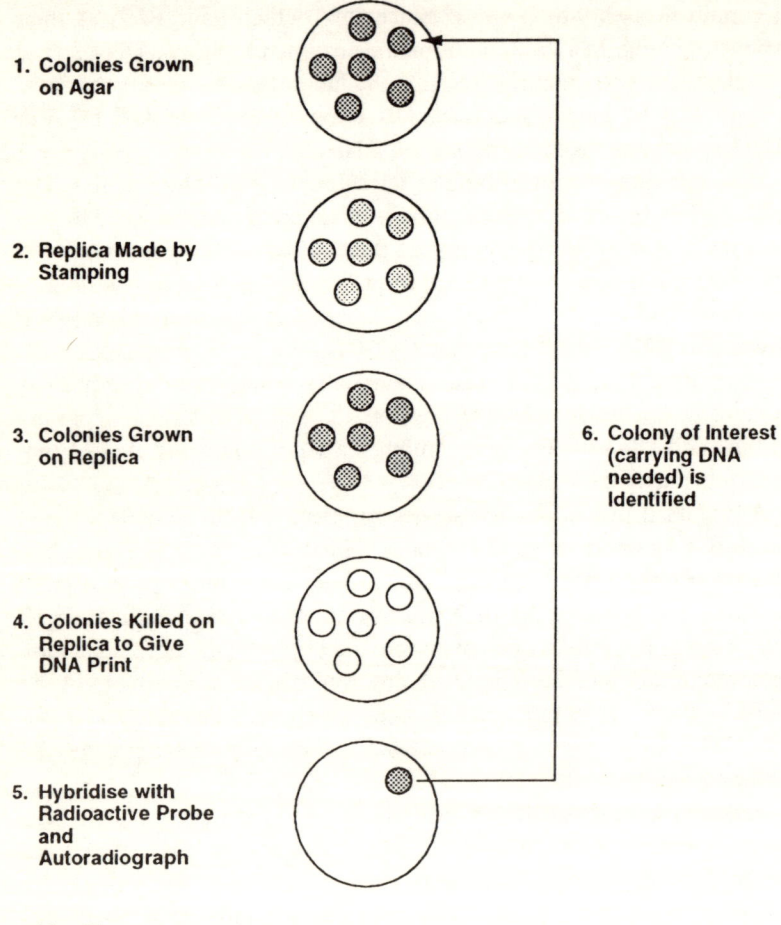

1. Colonies Grown
   on Agar

2. Replica Made by
   Stamping

3. Colonies Grown
   on Replica

6. Colony of Interest
   (carrying DNA
   needed) is
   Identified

4. Colonies Killed on
   Replica to Give
   DNA Print

5. Hybridise with
   Radioactive Probe
   and
   Autoradiograph

* After (7)

becomes malignant and proliferates uncontrollably. The antibody it produces, however, is against an unknown antigen. A revolutionary
technique was developed in 1975 by Kohler and Milstein to take advantage of such cells.[8]

The technique consists of fusing the malignant cells with antibody-
producing cells (from an animal spleen) which are operating in their
normal manner and producing a specific antibody to a known specific
antigen (Figure 6.5). In practice, mouse myeloma cells are used and the
programmed spleen cells also come from the mouse. There is actually
a very, very low rate of fusion of the two cell types and as myeloma
cells grow very rapidly in culture they would soon swamp any hybrids
were special measures not taken. Since the myeloma cells lack an
enzyme that spleen cells possess it is possible, by selecting the correct
growing medium, to block the growth of myeloma cells but allow the
growth of the hybrids (spleen cells themselves do not grow and divide
in this situation). The result is a hybrid cell which proliferates as the
myeloma cell did but also produces a specific antibody as the spleen
cell did.

Clearly the capability for producing large amounts of specific antibodies has opened up a wide range of new applications, for example in
diagnosis, because the antibodies produced have affinity of a precise
character for specific antigens.

Bioprocessing

While it is perhaps less fascinating than the key recombinant DNA
(rDNA) and monoclonal antibody techniques, equally critical for the
advance of biotechnology has been the steady improvement in understanding of how to use cells and molecules in industrial processes.

Progress may be categorised in four areas.[9] Firstly, means have been
found of carrying out large-scale culture of plant and animal cells which
permits products to be obtained in commercially-significant quantities.
Secondly, improved methods of fermentation of microbial cells have
been introduced which again allow larger yields to be obtained, and
from a wider range of organisms. Following on from such production
processes, new and very specific means have been discovered to separate and purify the products required at a reasonable cost. Lastly,
techniques have been developed which allow cells and enzymes to be
immobilised, thus creating a means by which the bioprocessing can be
carried out through a stationary bioprocessing matrix.

Taken together, such developments are transforming what can be
done and the yields, purity levels and rest-levels of production that can

Figure 6.5 Production of monoclonal antibodies*.

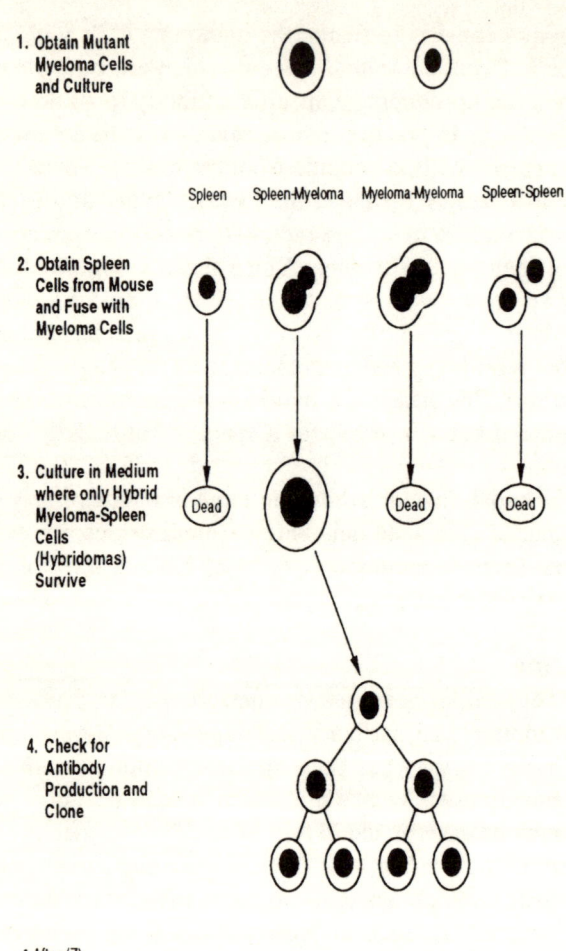

1. Obtain Mutant
   Myeloma Cells
   and Culture

   Spleen   Spleen-Myeloma   Myeloma-Myeloma   Spleen-Spleen

2. Obtain Spleen
   Cells from Mouse
   and Fuse with
   Myeloma Cells

3. Culture in Medium
   where only Hybrid
   Myeloma-Spleen
   Cells
   (Hybridomas)
   Survive

   Dead   Dead   Dead

4. Check for
   Antibody
   Production and
   Clone

* After (7)

116

be achieved in a manner which can only expand the applications of biotechnology in the future.

The New Biotechnology in Operation

It is necessary to grasp the nature of the commercial driving forces behind the growth of biotechnology. This is not an industry of giant, mature companies like the chemical industry. Particularly in the United States there are many small companies competing for vast commercial profits. An example is Amgen, which was a struggling start-up company in 1980. In 1983 a molecular biologist with the company succeeded in cloning erythropoietin (EPO), a substance which induces red blood cell production.[10]

After linking up with the giant Japanese company Kirin (a brewing company seeking to diversify) and jointly developing a second drug (granulocyte colony-stimulating factor, which increases white blood cell production) Amgen made more than $1bn profit in 1992. Given such opportunities, it seems likely that many small companies will be the driving force for change in biotechnology for some time to come.

What we are dealing with then is first a drive for commercial profit through practical implementation of new product discoveries. This is linked to two other factors: methodological breakthroughs (such as recombinant DNA technology) and developments in theoretical understanding (such as the intron/exon structure of the genome of higher organisms). Together these factors interact in a mechanism that produces extremely rapid scientific and technological change. Moreover, it is not at all easy to predict what changes will occur and what the shape of science, technology and commercial industry will be a decade from now.

The intention here is not to attempt an overview of current developments, but rather to illustrate what is happening in the areas vital for our consideration of possible new biological weapons. We shall therefore deal mainly with certain recent developments in medicine and agriculture. We shall also limit our discussion to developments closely related to our interest in micro-organisms. Thus most of what we read in newspapers on new gene therapies and the sequencing of the human genome will not be covered. Nevertheless, it is necessary to briefly illustrate the capabilities for intervention that are now possible, even for human beings. One example is the cure that now seems possible for adenosine deaminase deficiency (ADA).

In this disease the victim lacks an enzyme that breaks down deoxyadenosine; the chemical builds up in the body and unfortunately kills the T-lymphocytes of the immune system. The victim is therefore unable to fight off infections.[11] The cure consists of extracting some of the victim's bone-marrow cells and introducing the missing gene into these cells by means of a harmless virus. The properly functioning cells may then be returned to the victim's body where they continue to produce blood cells capable of manufacturing the missing enzyme. The person is then able to lead a normal life.

We concentrate here on biotechnology developments, particularly relating to infectious diseases: both new threats from old diseases, like the resurgence of tuberculosis in the developed world resulting from changes in our life-styles, and the potential evolution of new threats from previously unknown diseases.[12] We shall also cover some aspects of biotechnology in relation to agriculture where, for example, it seems there is an increasing threat from a new form of the late blight fungus of potatoes which caused the Irish potato famine in the last century.[13]

Somatostatin

This a peptide which controls the release of insulin and human growth hormones from the pituitary gland. Somatostatin is known to be an amino acid chain of 14 components (Figure 6.6). From this sequence it has been possible to produce a synthetic human gene with the correct sequence of nucleotides by chemical methods. This gene was then inserted into the plasmid pBR322. The plasmid contains a control region for the *lac* operon of *E. coli*.

It will be recalled that genes in bacteria are found in groups called operons. The *lac* operon of *E. coli* is concerned with the production of lactase which splits the lactose of milk into monosaccharides. However, it would be wasteful for a small bacterium to have this system in its functioning state, directing the production of lactase, if no milk were available in the gut of its human host. The bacterium therefore has a group of regulatory genes to switch production on and off.

The *lac* operon has three structural genes and two other signalling sequences called the promoter and the operator. Nearby there is an associated regulator gene. If there is no lactose in the environment the regulator gene produces a protein that binds to the operator site and overlaps the promoter. Neither can function when thus covered by the repressor protein. When lactose molecules become abundantly present, the repressor moves and binds to these molecules instead. This exposes the promoter and operator sites and allows RNA to be transcribed from the three structural genes. The three genes are transcribed as a set and only translated later into three different proteins.

Figure 6.6 Somatostatin production*.

1. **Determine Sequence of Amino Acids**

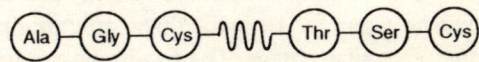

2. **Make Synthetic DNA to Match**

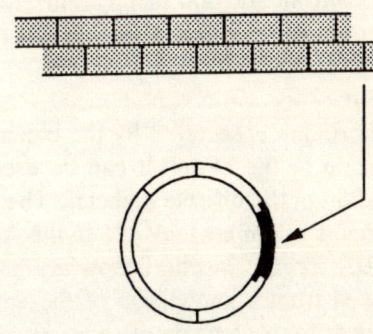

3. **Open up Plasmid and Recombine with Somatostatin Gene**

4. **Transform into E.coli**

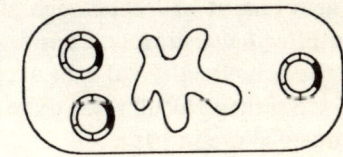

5. **Harvest Somatostatin**

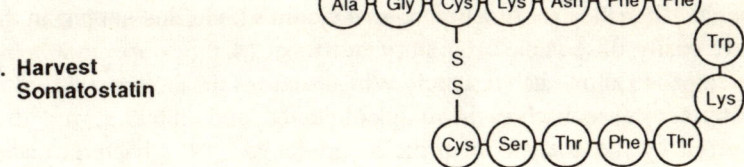

* After (7)

119

In order to produce synthetic somatostatin, *E. coli* containing the plasmid pBR322 is cultured. If the synthetic somatostatin human gene is inserted correctly into the plasmid transcription continues through the *lac* operon and the somatostatin gene. The somatostatin peptide can then be separated from the three structural proteins produced by the *lac* operon at a later stage. The resulting somatostatin is identical to the natural hormone. What is more, instead of a yield of one milligram of hormone from 500,000 sheep brains, the same amount can be extracted from a four-litre culture of recombinant *E. coli* cells.

Insulin

This hormone is secreted by the pancreas and regulates glucose concentration in the blood. It can be used to treat disorders of glucose regulation in the disease diabetes. The insulin molecule is made up of two chains of amino acids: 21 in the A chain and 30 in the B chain. A synthetic form of insulin is now available. Synthetic genes were again produced from a knowledge of the amino acid sequences. The DNA sequences for each chain were inserted into separate pBR322 plasmids and the plasmids were then inserted into *E. coli* cells. After the two amino acid chains had been separately produced they were linked together after harvesting and purification. Before the production of insulin by this method, it had to be extracted from the pancreases of pigs and cows. Synthetic insulin was the first rDNA product to be approved for commercial use in 1982.

Such practical outcomes depended on what was already known about the structure and function of bacterial cells and knowledge continues to accumulate rapidly. Nevertheless, it is important to know how bacteria operate when they are functioning in a victim's body, and not just in the more easily observable laboratory test-tube. Methods are now being developed to allow such research. Whilst some of the factors involved in bacterial disease, such as the toxins of cholera and diptheria, were discovered by the analysis of proteins produced by the bacteria under laboratory conditions, researchers have sought ways of identifying genes which are switched on in the much more complex situation of the host body. Attempts began about a decade ago to approximate to such conditions by mixing host cells with bacteria, but recently more sophisticated means have been developed.[14]

The method, called *in vivo* expression technology, was used with *Salmonella typhimurium*, which causes a typhoid-like disease in the mouse. The first step involved working with a bacterial strain which cannot grow in the mouse because it lacks the gene *pur A* that is required for purine metabolism. Functional *pur A* genes were removed from a related bacterial strain and linked to *lac Z*, a gene which makes an enzyme that is easily detectable by use of a colour assay technique.

The entire *Salmonella* genome was then split up and pieces were inserted in front of the artificial two-gene combination that had been prepared. The researchers assumed that some of the pieces of *Salmonella* DNA would contain genes that would switch on the inserted *pur A* and *lac Z* in the real host conditions. All the constructed lengths of DNA were then put into the strain of bacteria lacking *pur A* which were then used to infect mice. Bacteria that survived for three days were collected from the infected mice. It was assumed that in order to survive in the mice, the bacteria would have had their inserted *pur A* switched on. To discover whether these bacteria also had their *pur A* switched on in the laboratory they were grown on special agar which changed colour in response to the operation of *lac Z*.

Of the bacteria that survived after three days in the mice 95 per cent were shown to be able to operate in the laboratory as well as in the host. However, five per cent were found *not* to operate in the laboratory. These, logically, had to contain gene fragments which were switched on specifically in the mouse-host conditions alone. It was a fair assumption that such genes were necessary only for host infection. The genes were therefore likely candidates as virulence genes. So far, genes necessary for growth of the bacteria in the host have been identified, but if genes necessary for the deadliness of the infection were to be discovered, they would be potential targets for mutation to make attenuated strains of the organism which could perhaps then be used in live vaccines. Another possible line of research that could be followed with such a technique would be to attempt to discover the factors required to switch on the deadly effects of bacteria which are particularly harmful when they migrate to a specific cell type in the host body.

Hepatitis B Virus (HBV)

This virus causes a common form of liver disease and is also associated with the later development of liver cancer. World-wide, almost 300 million people are thought to be chronically infected with HBV, three-quarters of them in Asia. Children are frequently infected via their mother at birth or soon afterwards.[15,16]

The population in some badly affected regions may have 10 per cent of chronic carriers of HBV. In poor parts of the world the disease primarily affects the young. In the rich world there are far fewer carriers and they are primarily adults whose lifestyle brings them into contact with the virus. It appears that a chronic infection goes through a stage of active virus replication with minimal immune reaction from the host individual. After 20 to 30 years the virus seems to get less efficient and an immune response builds up. The infected liver cells are destroyed where active virus replication is evident, but in other cells the virus becomes incorporated into the genome of the cell itself. People may suffer both declining liver function and liver cancer, although it does not appear that the virus is directly responsible for switching on oncogenes, potential inducers of cancer, in the cell in which it is incorporated.

People infected with HBV produce an antibody in their bloodstream which can be used to detect the presence of the virus. This antibody is produced against the HBV surface antigen. The immediate disease may take a variety of forms, ranging from acute hepatitis followed by recovery (with considerable immunity to reinfection), to a fatal disease caused by immune responses resulting from killer T-cells attacking infected liver cells. A proportion of victims recover, as explained above, but become chronic carriers with about 100 times the normal risk of developing hepatocellular carcinoma.

Modern biotechnology has been extremely successful in understanding the HBV virus and the disease it causes and in finding ways of dealing with the disease. Much of the initial work obviously concentrated on finding good vaccines. The HBV genome is packaged inside two coats. The inner of these, called the capsid, is made up of one protein. The outer coat has three proteins and the surface antigen is found in each of these proteins. The HBV genome is the smallest of known animal virus genomes, being a circular DNA molecule of about 3,200 nucleotide sub-units. Unusually, one strand of DNA is longer than the other. Using standard techniques, the HBV genome was cloned in *E. coli*. This allowed the production of large amounts of the virus and its components for detailed study.

The entire sequence of bases was determined and the way in which its proteins are coded worked out. There are only four potential genes and these overlap in an amazingly compact structure which also contains the necessary regulatory sequences that control protein production. Gene S, for example, codes for the major outer coat protein and the surface antigen. About 500 bases which precede the S gene are transcribed along with it. This sequence partly codes for the other two outer-coat proteins and is also involved in the penetration of the virus into liver cells. Using transgenic mice, which have had part or the complete HBV genome added to their DNA, it has been possible to show that gene S is expressed at high levels only in liver cells and this expression is under the control of steroid hormones. This would explain why men, who have higher circulating levels of steroids than women, are at a greater risk of HBV infection and disease.

HBV is a member of a group of similar viruses called hepadnaviruses which have an extraordinary mechanism of replication. Studies of how these viruses function in animals has elucidated this mechanism. Instead of using their DNA as a template to produce new DNA direct, these viruses replicate indirectly via an RNA intermediate. After penetrating the target cell, the hepadnavirus genome enters the cell nucleus where a long RNA molecule is transcribed from its DNA. This is called the pregenome. Pregenome and a viral DNA polymerase are enclosed in a newly-formed capsid and move back into the cytoplasm of the cell. There the RNA is reverse-transcribed by the polymerase into a DNA strand; the RNA pregenome is destroyed and a second DNA strand is made to complement the first. The capsid and the viral DNA are then enclosed in a new outer layer of protein protection prior to leaving the liver cell.

With this level of knowledge, it is not surprising that practical applications have been possible. Diagnostic tests have been developed which rely on the affinity of short strands of cloned DNA for complementary DNA in blood serum containing infectious viruses. The technique is so reliable and sensitive that it may be used to track the level of viruses in the blood following medical treatment. The sensitivity of the test has also been increased by using the polymerase chain reaction to amplify the amount of DNA in the infected sample.

Vaccines were originally produced by inactivating viruses obtained from the blood serum of chronic HBV carriers. The problem was that, although the vaccine had been shown to be reliable, the serum supply was limited, purification was complex and expensive, and all batches had to be tested for safety. Thus a genetically-engineered vaccine was a high-priority target for researchers.

It was found that genetically-engineered bacteria could mass-produce the surface antigen, but its chemical structure was not reproduced accurately enough in these organisms to be properly immunogenic. It was therefore necessary to produce the required material in higher organisms. One vaccine was produced and marketed after genetically-engineered production in yeast, and mammalian cells have also been used to produce antigenic material. Vaccination of very young children against HBV has been shown to be extremely effective. Forty-seven countries now have national vaccination campaigns. In one of the earliest of these, dating from 1984 in Taiwan, the percentage of children carrying evidence of the surface antigen, and therefore evidence of past exposure to HBV infection, has dropped dramatically.

The HBV vaccination works by activating a person's immune system to deal with invading viruses. It has been found that viruses have evolved a variety of strategies to frustrate the immune system. One such was demonstrated by workers researching tumour necrosis factor (TNF), a molecule used by the immune system to increase attack on tumours or virus-infected cells. On searching DNA databases for sequences resembling that for the TNF receptor they found something very similar in a member of the poxvirus family. The viral gene was, however, different from the true TNF receptor gene. For the true gene the protein product is anchored in the membrane of the host cell. When TNF binds to the protein receptor in the correct response, an internal reaction is triggered in the cell. The viral gene appears to have lost the membrane-anchoring aspect, suggesting that its role is to produce a soluble product that exists in the bloodstream rather than being attached to a cell membrane. The investigators guessed that this product would bind and deactivate the TNF. This turned out to be true. Virus-infected cells were shown to secrete a protein that binds to TNF; TNF was bound to the soluble protein in fluids rather than on to the protein anchored in the surface of virus-infected cells. In short, the virus has evolved a decoy system to disable the body's defence by mopping up TNF and preventing it binding to, and activating, virus-infected cells. Other examples were quickly demonstrated of soluble products being used in a similar way against other parts of the immune system.[17]

Another viral strategy involves a more direct interference with the operations of the immune system. A group of plasma proteins called 'complement' is involved in immune responses to infectious agents. When not in use, complement is kept under control by specific proteins. Vaccinia virus (see below) apparently produces a protein with a similar controlling function to help frustrate the host defensive system during infection.[18] More complex strategies have also been described, but the general point is that with the level of understanding we now have major new therapeutic applications are very likely.

Vaccinia Virus

Almost two centuries after Jenner first used vaccination against smallpox this much-feared disease was eradicated. The vaccinia virus which has been used for protection in the modern era is an orthopoxvirus closely related to variola, the cause of smallpox, with cross-reactive antigens sufficient to provide good cross-protection. Research on vaccinia did not cease after the elimination of smallpox in 1977; indeed, there has been major progress of particular interest from our point of view.[19]

One reason for continuing research on vaccinia was that, unlike most viruses, DNA replication takes place in the cytoplasm and not the nucleus of host cells. Instead of being able to use the host nuclear enzymes, the vaccinia virus must carry coding for many of the enzymes necessary to make viral mRNA, and for DNA replication. The virus is therefore a good target in which to study how processes such as transcription actually take place.

The other major reason for the continuing interest in vaccinia research is that it has proved possible to insert DNA into its genome, and to delete sections from its genome, without destroying its infectivity. Thus it is possible to have genes derived from other organisms producing antigenic material when a recombinant virus is replicating in a host. This provides a new route for the production of vaccines in medicine or veterinary work. The vaccinia virus used in this way is called a vector. Other viruses have also now been used in the same way, as live immunogens. These viruses, because they retain their infectivity, are self-replicating and are cheap to manufacture and administer, have many advantages for vaccine production. They also have good resistance to T-cell or hormonal attack by the host immune system.

The orthopoxviruses are a genus of the Poxviridae family. Besides vaccinia, this group includes variola, cowpox, and monkey pox. Whilst all these viruses, and other genera of the Poxviridae, have a common strategy of replication, most is known about vaccinia. The vaccinia virus particle, as mechanically isolated from cells, is a large oval structure about 200 by 300 nm (m^{-9}). The outer surface is covered by tubules. Antibodies directed against the protein of these tubules, or against a surface protein, can neutralise the infectivity of the virus. The core of the virus has a complex structure. Characteristically for this group of viruses, the core carries both the genome and many enzymes derived from its DNA. When naturally released from infected cells, and not mechanically isolated, the virus particle has a further envelope of proteins around it.

The vaccinia genome is a linear, double-stranded DNA molecule of about 185,000 base pairs. The ends of the DNA have variable regions which can be deleted or transposed to the opposite end of the genome without affecting virus replication in many cell cultures. This allows relatively large amounts of foreign DNA to be inserted into the genome, without corresponding deletions, in forming a recombinant virus. The vaccinia vector can therefore be used to construct potential vaccines against more than one pathogen.

In contrast to the ends of the genome, which are so variable, the central portion of about 120,000 base pairs is necessary for the correct functioning of the virus. This is typical of the orthopoxviruses and the central section is therefore said to be highly conserved. The central part of the genome has been analysed with restriction enzymes and much of the DNA sequence has been determined. The genes deduced to be present from knowledge of the DNA sequence appear to be closely packed without intervening non-coding sequences. The viral mRNAs and protein amino acid sequences can thus be readily identified. From this information much has already been deduced about how viruses in general are assembled and operate.

Vaccinia recombinant viruses are assembled in a two-stage process. The foreign DNA is first cloned into a plasmid downstream of a vaccinia promoter, the whole being flanked by vaccinia DNA from a non-essential part of the genome. This plasmid is then transfected (introduced) into cells which are infected with vaccinia. Within such cells recombinant viruses are made by transfers between the inserted vaccinia sequence in the plasmid and corresponding regions of the infecting vaccinia virus. Although some of the viruses so produced in the infected cells will have recombinations resulting from transfers, most will not, so standard techniques have been developed for marking and selecting those that do.

Vaccinia already had major advantages which had favoured its use in the smallpox eradication campaign. It was heat stable, and cheap to manufacture, and easy to administer in the field. Its considerable capacity for carrying foreign DNA and its broad range of potential hosts added to the attraction of this vector system. There is now a long list of examples of protective immunity being established in experimental animals by the use of altered vaccinia virus. Work continues: to improve the amount of antigen expressed, to increase the degree of immune response to the antigens, and to improve the safety of the vaccines.

Many genes have been identified in the vaccinia genome which are implicated in viral pathogenicity in a multicellular host. These can be grouped into genes aiding viral replication within cells; genes which promote cell proliferation and thereby provide host cells with greater activity in which the virus can operate; genes which help viral dissemination; and genes which assist in the evasion of the host immune system. The protein mentioned previously, which interferes with the complement control process, is in this final group.

Transgenic Plants

Humankind has been involved in selectively breeding plants for some 10,000 years. Whilst methods have become more sophisticated during the twentieth century, it is only for about a decade that the techniques of genetic engineering have been employed.[20]

The first and still most widely-used methods relied on the plant pathogen *Agrobacterium tumefaciens* which produces crown gall disease. This bacterium naturally transfers part of its DNA (called transfer or T-DNA) into the DNA of infected plants. There it induces the plant to produce elevated levels of plant hormones. These cause the plant to produce abnormal structures, such as galls, which provide suitable places and nutrients for the particular strain of *Agrobacterium* to thrive.

Researchers first removed the disease-causing elements from the transfer DNA. Such 'disarming' leaves the transfer mechanism intact without the complication of the disease. The first demonstration of the creation of a transgenic plant, in the early 1980s, involved the transfer of resistance against a plant inhibitory chemical by this method. Besides demonstrating that genes could be transferred to plants in this way, the transferred resistance to the inhibitory chemical provided a useful way of distinguishing the cells affected by the treatment, an example of a marker technique.

Since whole plants can be regenerated from very small pieces of tissue, genetic engineering usually concentrates on small groups of cells cut away from plants. The *Agrobacterium* method is now used routinely around the world and applied to such small groups of cells. Many thousands of plants have been modified by this technique, but numerous plant species, including cereals, are not natural hosts for *Agrobacterium* and other methods of modification have therefore had to be developed. One method relies on removing the strong plant cell wall and then moving DNA across the exposed plasma membrane; but, again, this does not work well with the critically important cereal grains. A different method involves very small metal particles coated with DNA being shot into the plant cells. The cell walls rapidly close over the small holes and the metal particles just remain in the cell. Some of the injected DNA can then be incorporated into the plant's own DNA. A much cheaper and easier method of introducing foreign DNA to plant cells has recently been announced.[21] Microscopic crystals of silicon carbide are briefly agitated in water with the DNA to be inserted and the plant cells: the extremely hard crystals perforate the cells and allow the DNA to enter.

Genes that will work in higher organisms need three regions, first the promoter sequences region, which is involved in the timing and location of the expression of the gene, then the structural gene, which specifies the protein to be produced and finally, the polyadenylation (or poly-A) region, which ensures the correct termination of mRNA transcription from the DNA. In plant genetic engineering the structural gene can come from a wide variety of different sources and the promoter can be designed to operate in specific plant organs, such as leaves or roots, or even inside special cell types within such organs.

A major subject of economically important research is obviously the transfer of resistance to viruses into plants. If, for example, the coat protein of tobacco mosaic virus (TMV) is expressed in tobacco or tomato plants by the methods described, the plants are found to be strongly resistant to the virus. It has long been known that infection of a plant with a mild form of a virus gives protection against subsequent infection by a virulent strain. There appears to be an interference with the subsequent infection caused by replication of the mild strain. This method has therefore been used to produce resistance in a number of different crop species.

For three decades farmers have used the bacterium *Bacillus thuringiensis* (Bt) to provide some protection against predation by moth and butterfly caterpillars. If the bacteria are sprayed on to crops the insecticidal proteins they produce disrupt caterpillar feeding. The chemicals do not seem to be toxic to mammals or even other insect species. Unfortunately, the bacteria are easily washed off plants by rain or watering. From the mid-1980s onwards attempts were made to transfer the bacterial genes for the insecticidal proteins into plants. The original efforts led to the Bt protein being poorly expressed and only affecting very susceptible insects in the laboratory. However, the original bacterial gene was redesigned and then achieved much enhanced effects. For example, Bt genes in cotton plants have effectively controlled major pests. Careful screening of strains of the bacterium have uncovered some which attack other insect pests. Very good results have recently been achieved in protecting potato plants from Colorado beetle by the genetic engineering of a toxin gene from *Bacillus thuringiensis tenebronis* into *Agrobacterium* and thence into Russett Burbank potatoes, the most popular US variety.[22]

Other applications of plant genetic engineering have conferred improved resistance to herbicides, delayed ripening and enhanced nutritional properties. While there are limitations to what can be done, biotechnology seems one of the few practical means by which the food required by the world's rapidly expanding human population may be produced. Nowhere is this need for efficient food production more pressing than in China, where 20 per cent of the world's population has only seven per cent of the world's cultivable land. Not surprisingly, great efforts have been made to develop plant biotechnology there.[23] Following the successful work with tobacco mosaic virus described above, Chinese scientists began to test coat protein genes from local pathogenic viruses. This is the most active area of plant biotechnology in China today, where coat proteins for TMV, cucumber mosaic virus (CMV), potato viruses and a number of others have been cloned and characterised. Some have been engineered into plants and tested for antiviral activity in field trials. Other genes from resistant local plants are also being studied.

Most work is understandably being carried out on rice. In August 1992 the Chinese government announced a 15-year 'Rice Genome Project' to sequence the whole rice genome. Other research is directed to increasing the nitrogen-fixing capabilities of the bacterium *Rhizobium* which is symbiotic with legume varieties, and to introducing cloned genes, which produce heavy-metal-binding proteins, into weeds which can be used to help to clear contaminated land.

The preceding sections are intended to convey the reality of a new mechanistic biology in operation around the world. If the revolution in chemistry at the end of the last century allowed the development and use of chemical weapons in the First World War, and the revolution in nuclear physics earlier this century allowed the development and use of nuclear weapons in the Second World War, the inevitable question that must be asked is 'Can we prevent the development and use of new biological weapons in the inevitable conflicts of the next few decades?'

. 7 .

NEW WEAPONS?

During the last decade authors across the political spectrum in the West have warned of the dangers of new biological weapons. Examples are Susan Wright and Robert Sinsheimer's article in the *Bulletin of the Atomic Scientists* in 1983, 'Recombinant DNA and biological warfare';[1] in 1986, Joseph Finder's article in *The Washington Quarterly* entitled 'Biological warfare, genetic engineering, and the treaty that failed';[2] and, in 1992, the article by Joseph Douglass Jr. asking 'Who's holding the psychotoxins and DNA-altering compounds?' in *Armed Forces Journal International*.[3]

Many other articles could be cited where this issue has been discussed, and particular viewpoints argued, in both the specialist and the general open literature. Fortunately also, official government estimates of the problem have been given in papers related to the Review Conferences of the BWC. Before attempting further detailed analysis, it therefore seems sensible to summarise how governments have seen the problem.

Official Positions

The depository governments were asked to prepare a background paper on new scientific and technological developments for the first review in 1980. This paper provides a good baseline against which to set more recent estimates for the 1991 third Review Conference.

1980–1991

The paper produced for the first review[4] had five major sections in addition to a general introduction and final summary. The major central

130

sections were concerned with recombinant DNA techniques, new infectious diseases, chemical synthesis of toxins, the industrial use of fermentation techniques, and the microbial control of pests.

The conclusion of the document was quite sanguine. The paper ended:

> . . . From a scientific and technological standpoint, the developments discussed in this paper, which are directed to peaceful purposes, do not appear to alter substantially capabilities or incentives for the development or production of biological or toxin weapons.

This viewpoint is closely reflected in the individual sections of the paper, for example in regard to recombinant DNA techniques. While these are clearly set out, the possible relevance to biological weapons stated, and the need for continued monitoring noted, the techniques were said to be 'similar in principle' to classical genetics, and it was concluded that any agents produced would be:

> . . . unlikely to have advantages over known agents sufficient to provide compelling new motives for illegal production or military use in the foreseeable future . . .

It might be argued that a separate paper from Sweden had a slightly different tone in stating, for example, that the new genetic techniques 'imply a potential' to change existing biological weapon agents and that the possibility of the construction of new agents could not be excluded.[5]

On the chemical synthesis of toxins, the paper from the depository governments noted that in the future it would probably be possible to synthesise anything, however large or complex, but at the time the syntheses were very difficult. It appeared unlikely that production of militarily-significant quantities of toxins would be achieved by such a route. Similarly, whilst the rapid expansion of capabilities in fermentation technology were described, it was concluded that:

> . . . From a scientific and technological standpoint, growing industrial use of fermentation techniques does not appear to substantially alter capabilities or incentives for biological or toxin warfare.

Finally, in regard to the microbial control of pests, although it was accepted that there were some similarities to biological warfare in such activities, it was concluded that the risks were outweighed by the advantages of the peaceful purposes of such work.

As Sims has commented,[6] there was little consideration of scientific and technical issues at the first Review Conference. He gained the impression that participants were optimistic, if not complacent. Even the Swedish paper, he felt, did not really dissent from the depositories' reassuring assessment. He also noted that, perhaps to avoid the sensationalism and crudity of some popular presentations, the papers prepared by the depositories and other governments for the second review in 1986 were sober and measured.

There is no doubt, however, that the assessment of the impact of biotechnology, as reflected in the papers for the second review, was changing. Sims pointed out that the Swedish paper for this review referred to frequently-voiced concerns over the introduction of resistance to antibiotics, microencapsulation of agents, production of toxins on a large scale, and insertion of genetic material coding for the production of a potent toxin into a virulent organism that can infect human beings. Indeed, he felt that the British paper qualified the judgement made by the depositories in 1980 by suggesting that the pace of change indicated a greater potential to alter capabilities and incentives in regard to biological weapon developments than was evident earlier.

A study prepared in the USA for the Office of the Defense Secretary in March 1986, during the run-up to the second review, detailed some of the reasons for the increasing concerns.[7] Arguing that the previous decade had witnessed impressive advances, and that the distinction between biology and chemistry was becoming blurred, it listed seven technologies which were having an impact in areas of concern. These are listed in Table 7.1. The similarities between this list and the technologies discussed in the previous chapter (see Table 6.1) are apparent.

Table 7.1   Specific technologies impacting on biological agent preparation, production and use[1]

---

1. Recombinant DNA (genetic engineering).

2. Protein engineering.

3. Computer-aided orthomolecular drug design.

4. Fermentation engineering.

5. Mammalian cell culture.

6. Peptide synthesis.

7. Biophysics of cell membranes.

---

[1]Data from reference 7.

132

Within the first topic of genetic engineering, the text went on to discuss plasmid stabilisation by which, instead of bacterial strains tending to lose their drug resistance during fermentation, all the cells would retain the genes for drug resistance. Other aspects of genetic engineering covered were the manufacture of plant toxins, enhancement of the lethality of bacteria and new viral pathogens. Even though protein engineering was seen to be some years away from realisation, computer-aided ortho-molecular drug design applied to short sections of proteins (peptides) was reported to have been used. Considerable attention was given in the report to progress in fermentation engineering. Particular note was taken of the increase in productivity that could be achieved by the use of computers in process control. This is an important issue which has continued to be a focus of attention.

We shall deal with the significant issue of mammalian cell culture later in regard to documents prepared for the third review of the BWC in 1991, but in this 1986 document particular attention was paid to peptide synthesis. Peptides were seen as important substances, active at very low concentrations, which could have startlingly different effects on animals after what appeared to be slight changes of chemical structure. It was pointed out that new means of transferring peptides from the environment into the human bloodstream were being discovered (biophysics of cell membranes) and that these substances could have a wide range of effects from controlling mood, sleep or emotions, to mental processes and consciousness.

Summarising some of the implications of all such technological changes, it was suggested that one outcome might be new, improved strains of drug-resistant bacteria with more poisonous toxins, a reduced lethal dose because of plasmid stability, and a higher production yield through computer control of the process. Indeed, as a further result of such improvements, the size of the production plant needed might be 10 to 50 times smaller, with some pieces of equipment 1,000-fold smaller.

Concerns about the consequences of scientific and technical change were evident in the background document prepared for the third Review Conference in 1991,[8] to which a number of countries contributed. The Australian contribution was brief and to the point. A short introduction stated that there had been major advances in biotechnology since the last review, national capabilities had spread and, whilst this had positive benefits, it also had the potential for misuse. The remainder of the contribution was divided into five sections covering production cell culture, fermentation technology, harvesting, dissemination and delivery, and genetic engineering.

As we discussed in the previous chapter, many biological compounds of commercial interest cannot be produced by fermentation using bacteria, even by means of genetic engineering, because bacteria lack the capabilities of more complex cells to modify products after translation from RNA. Such products, for example some hormones, must be produced in animal cells. As viruses are necessarily parasitic, they must also be grown in appropriate cell systems. It is not surprising, therefore, that many new ways were sought and found to improve animal cell growth systems. The old system was to have a monolayer of cells on a solid surface in roller bottles. The Australian text explained the development of new means of growing cells on the surface of beads and then the use of hollow-fibre perfusion systems where the cells remain within the fibres and nutrients pass to them through pores in the fibres. This allows very high density of cells and in the case of soluble products provides a simultaneous separation of product from cells. The section concluded that:

> These new techniques simplify virus production and allow large yields from relatively small facilities.

The theme of improvement in production technology was stressed strongly in the next section of the Australian contribution. Automation of process control, in-plant cleaning systems and continuous flow fermenters were given as examples of important developments. Improved harvesting techniques also have been necessitated by the improvement of fermenter technology.

In the section on dissemination and delivery it was suggested that reaction against the overuse of chemical pesticides had led to increased interest in biological control methods. Unfortunately, many of the problems in applying such methods are similar to those encountered in biological warfare. Agents in both cases are affected by UV light or desiccation. Means developed to microencapsulate agents for peaceful pest control could clearly also be used to protect warfare agents, and the lessons learned in developing effective spraying systems for agriculture could also be used for biological warfare.

In regard to genetic engineering the crucial impact was seen to be the possibility of the large-scale production of toxins:

> . . . Most potent toxins have formerly been available only in very small quantities, and then only upon isolation from vast amounts of biological material. The cloning of the genes coding for production of toxins into micro-organisms has enabled production of kilogram quantities of these toxins . . .

It was also noted that the advances in fermenter technology referred to previously made it possible to carry out such production in small facilities. Concern over the use of genetic engineering to create bacterial strains resistant to antibiotics was repeated.

The contribution from the UK began by explaining that the term genetic modification (GM) would be used in place of recombinant DNA techniques or genetic engineering in order to reflect current practice in the European Commission Directives. The term biotechnology was defined as 'the application of scientific and technological principles to the processing of materials by micro-organisms'. The text explained that this covered GM techniques, fermentation and downstream (later) processing of products.

The UK argued that there had been no major innovations in GM techniques since the last review, but rather a steady refinement and ever-widening application. Similar trends to those covered in the Australian document were mentioned; for example, it was stated that modification of the characteristics of any microbial species had become increasingly possible. Two specific examples were given:

... Modification (increase) of virulence has been reported for several pathogens: thus, an increase in the virulence of *Yersinia pseudotuberculosis* after a double mutation has been described ...

and:

... baculovirus modified by insertion of the gene for the neurotoxin of the North African scorpion showed increased virulence for some species of insect.

The same illustrative approach was then used to demonstrate that capabilities for vaccine production were spreading:

... several vaccines now at the field trials stage have been developed outside developed nations, including vaccines for leprosy (Venezuela and India), leishmaniasis (Venezuela and Brazil) and dengue haemorrhagic fever (Thailand) ...

and to show that GM techniques were being used for advanced developments:

... Use of GM to produce a live vaccine is one idea being considered for the development of an oral vaccine against anthrax for use with livestock or wildlife, by introducing the gene for the Protective Antigen into a non-anthrax bacterial species ...

135

We shall consider studies of anthrax in more detail later in this chapter. The 1991 UK text also mentioned GM techniques being used to produce a protein from *Brucella* in *E. coli* and the development in the UK of an animal vaccine that used fowl pox virus as a vector for Newcastle disease viral antigens.

The UK paper also covered protein engineering and other techniques using labelled antibodies and the polymerase chain reaction. It was noted that the latter developments could have a positive impact by improving capabilities for identification and diagnosis of possible biological warfare agents. On the other hand, the increasing capabilities for the large-scale production of toxins and agents were seen as potentially open to abuse, and the UK argued that further advances in these capabilities were to be expected.

In line with assessments made by the depository states in 1986, the UK concluded that newly-recognised diseases such as Marburg, Ebola and Lassa had no special relevance in relation to the BWC. However, the point was made that, as knowledge of these new diseases and new arboviruses increased, there was an associated increased potential for its misuse. Considerable attention was then given to toxins and their production. It was argued that since 1986 more toxins had been isolated, they could be more readily produced and much more was understood about the molecular bases of their toxicity. Such understanding allowed the construction of novel toxins not found in nature:

> . . . For example, the A and B sub units of Shiga toxin and Shiga-like toxins have been combined. Such toxins may have altered toxicological or immunological properties . . .

The increased potential for the production of toxins by microbial cloning was recognised, though chemical synthesis was seen as remaining difficult to scale up. Whilst special problems were felt to remain in using micro-organisms to produce some compounds, the possibility of cloning 'cassettes' of genes to produce non-protein toxins was pointed out.

As in the Australian submission, special attention was paid by the UK to industrial microbiology. Similar points were made, for example, relating to the necessity of using higher organisms to produce some proteins, and the gains in productivity that had come from the use of real-time sensors, feedback loops and microprocessor control. The UK concluded that :

> There can thus be no doubt that the proliferation of legitimate civilian industrial microbiology activities, and the continuing development of

136

the underlying theory and equipment, has increased the potential world-wide for developing and producing biological weapons in contravention of the BWC . . .

The paper added that the increasing attention to environmental risks, and thus the use of better containment means, actually made it easier for the necessary equipment and expertise to be gained by countries around the world.

In regard to the microbial control of pests, *Bacillus thuringiensis* was still seen as the most widely used entomopathogen (insect pathogen), but it was noted that some 20 of the several hundred fungal species of entomopathogens were also being studied. Work was also mentioned on making these control methods more efficient, for example by the use of UV protectants. Again the conclusion was significant:

> . . . there has been increased study of factors relevant to effective dissemination. Such knowledge could in principle be misused by an aggressor intending to attack crops. . . . Some aspects of the dissemination technology would also be relevant to the deliberate release of organisms or toxins harmful to humans or animals.

In general, the UK concluded that the increased potential for the misuse of biotechnology noted in the 1986 review was even more evident in 1991. In 1986, it was recognised, there was an increased potential for large-scale production of possible agents with enhanced military utility. In 1991 the world-wide increase in knowledge of pathogenic micro-organisms, toxins and other possible agents had further augmented this potential, as had the continuing pace of developments in civil technology. The continuing evolution of biotechnology, the expansion of industrial activity and of the microbial control of pests, in short, had:

> . . . further increased the capability world-wide for the production and dissemination of micro-organisms, of their products, and of other types of biological agents . . .

This capability could clearly be abused in an offensive biological weapons programme.

The paper produced by the USA covered much the same ground, with sections on altered organisms, toxins, peptides, advances in production, mammalian cell culture, continuous flow fermenters, safety and environmental standards, and hollow fibre technology. The general conclusion of the USA was that:

... The ease and rapidity of genetic manipulation, the ready avail-
ability of a variety of production equipment, the proliferation of safety
and environmental equipment and health procedures to numerous laboratories and production facilities throughout the world, are *signs of
the growing role of biotechnology in the world's economy* ...
[Author's emphasis]

The paper ended by stressing once again that these same signs point to
the possibility of misuse.

Canada contributed only a short note of two paragraphs to the background document, which referred to a study, *Novel Toxins and
Bioregulators: the Emerging Scientific and Technological Issues
Relating to Verification and the Biological and Toxin Weapons
Convention*[9] which it had circulated to state parties. The Canadian contribution noted that although the study, prepared by a contract
organisation, carried a traditional disclaimer, this 'should be understood
to apply only to ... policy issues'. That is to say, the disclaimer did not
apparently apply to the scientific and technical content which, in effect,
was therefore endorsed by the government.

The study, in addition to an introduction and a general conclusion,
had three sections dealing with technological changes, the novel toxins
and bioregulators, and the potential dangers created by changes to the
technology in this general area. The introduction made clear that before
1975 production of militarily-significant quantities of peptides (a peptide was defined as a molecule linking up a chain of between two and 50
amino acids) was not possible. Since 1986, it was stated, progress had
been such that many commercial companies could offer for sale 'quantities of peptides that could have military importance'. There had been
progress across the board in identification, synthesis, modification and
large-scale production. Large-scale production was stated to be possible
through recombinant DNA techniques, enzymatic synthesis or solid-
phase synthesis.

The introduction also explained that toxins, inanimate chemicals as
they are, became incorporated in the BWC largely by historical accident.
At the time the convention was agreed, it was still necessary to extract toxins from biological material, and production methods were therefore
similar to those for biological weapons agents. Thus they became grouped
together. Toxins, though inanimate, generally have a higher specificity for
their living target receptors than do man-made chemicals such as nerve
agents. Bioregulators were defined as small peptides that often control the
release of hormones and 'could be considered master switches of life'.

The technological changes in this area between 1975 and 1990 were felt to have been dramatic, with a thousand-fold increase in capabilities for the synthesis and purification of peptides. The study also briefly reviewed a number of toxins and bioregulators. Examples were conotoxins from marine snails, which are relatively small peptides of 13 to 29 amino acids, and the 14-amino acid-chain somatostatin that was discussed in Chapter 6. It was argued that, although the available evidence showed that the lethality of toxins could not be increased by manipulation of their structure, considerable effects could be produced by changes in the structure of bioregulators. Furthermore, the understanding of the structure and function of bioregulators was said to be at an early but rapidly developing stage.

The study suggested that there were military consequences to all these developments that needed monitoring. In regard to toxins it was suggested that new agents might be developed and produced which had novel sites of action, rapid and specific effects, the ability to penetrate protective filters in masks or the ability to incapacitate. The question of the production of militarily-effective incapacitating agents was discussed also in relation to bioregulators. Given that these substances can affect many different functions, and can be selectively modified by changing their amino acid sequences, it was suggested that:

> . . . this gives rise to the possibility of selectively affecting mental processes and many aspects of health, such as control of mood. . . . Even a small imbalance in these natural substances could have serious consequences, inducing fear, fatigue, depression . . .

Not surprisingly, the study concluded that the possibility of new warfare agents had increased.

It is overwhelmingly obvious from these official reports that a significant change had been detected between 1980 and 1991. There are many aspects of modern biotechnology that give rise to concerns over its misuse in offensive biological weapons programmes. There is not space here to review in detail all the aspects mentioned in these studies, but what may be more useful is to try to illustrate the present state of knowledge, and ideas of future developments, in a few key areas which are well covered in the open literature. As in previous chapters, we shall focus mainly on agents and toxins in our discussion.

Aims of Research

In the late 1980s Professor Harry Smith, who had long experience both in the British biological research programme at Porton Down and later in medical research at the University of Birmingham, published two articles in which he reviewed the development of studies on bacterial[10] and bacterial and viral[11] pathogenicity. He stated that the goal of studies of pathogenicity was 'to explain in molecular terms the various biological aspects of this multifactorial property'. This level of molecular explanation, he argued, required the accomplishment of a series of logical steps which are set out in Table 7.2. Clearly, if it were possible to show that only a virulent strain produced a certain toxin and that this toxin, because of its chemical structure and its target in a host, damaged the host in a very specific way, the kind of explanation required would be achievable.

Table 7.2   Steps required in the molecular-level explanation of pathogenicity[1]

---

1. Comparison of virulence of strains in the host or relevant model.

2. Identification of strains of high and low virulence.

3. Strains compared in biological tests related to the key requirements for pathogenicity: infection and penetration of mucous surfaces; multiplication *in vivo*; interference with host defences; and causation of damage to the host.

4. Identification of the determinants that cause these biological properties.

5. The relevance of a property and its determinant to infection *in vivo* must be proved.

6. The chemical structure of the determinant must be related to its biological action.

---

[1]Data from reference 11.

Smith explained that there have been two periods of rapid development of knowledge in this field of scientific research, first during the 'golden age of medical bacteriology' between the 1870s and the First World War and then again since the 1960s. In his opinion, however:

> . . . Only for a few bacterial toxins and for certain aspects of viral replication have all these steps been achieved . . .

Indeed, in Smith's opinion, studies of bacterial pathogenicity were essentially moribund in the late 1940s and studies on the pathogenicity of viruses had hardly begun.

Smith's views on the impact of genetic manipulation must be seen against that background. As he put it:[11]

To sum up, genetic manipulation has transformed the study of pathogenicity. Difficulties may arise in using a particular method, but now there is such a variety of powerful techniques that if one does not work, another will probably substitute.

Although the study of the effects of mutagens on pathogens has been pursued for decades, the present ability to remove a virulence property from a strain or to add it to a non-virulent strain by removing or inserting specific genes is extraordinarily powerful. Moreover, the gene products causing a particular effect can now be altered down even to the change of single amino acids by altering the nucleotide sequence of the gene. In this way the steps required for a molecular-level explanation can be undertaken. As Smith noted:

. . . Site-directed mutagenesis is even more specific. . . . Two examples among many are single amino acid substitutions in diphtheria toxin fragment A and in the exotoxin of *P. aeruginosa*, which showed that glutamic acid residues at positions 148 and 553, respectively, are crucial for . . . toxicity.

Yet a great deal remains unknown. Smith argued in 1989 that future work should both attempt to achieve a molecular level of explanation in more examples than those at present under study, and certain neglected areas should receive more attention.

For bacteria, Smith identified areas needing more work, such as how small numbers of bacteria initiate the first stage of infection and how long-term survival in the host is assured, in both cases against the forces of the host defence mechanism. However, in his opinion:

. . . The major gap in our understanding of bacterial pathogenicity is lack of knowledge of the nutrients and metabolism that underlie growth *in vivo* . . .

In regard to virus virulence Smith's view was that it had not been analysed in anything like the depth achieved for bacteria. He suggested that whilst viral replication had been well studied:

. . . mucosal invasion, mucosal penetration, and interference with host defence mechanisms have been neglected, and damage to host tissue has been understudied . . .

He thought that such omissions needed remedying. The lag between bacterial and viral research had another consequence, however, which we must examine before turning to the current state of the art in some specific areas of research.

Defensive Research Programmes

We shall discuss the argument about the wisdom of developed countries carrying out defensive biological research programmes in Chapter 9, which is concerned with current policy choices for Western states. Here we need only note one particular characteristic of these programmes which is relevant to the direction of current developments.

David Huxsoll, who was formerly commander of the US Army Medical Research Institute for Infectious Diseases (USAMRIID) at Fort Detrick, pointed out that the technology required for production of large amounts of viral agents in cell culture only became available at the end of the offensive biological research programme in the USA.[12] Had the programme not been terminated, he would have expected to see viral agents which were in the research and development phase in the late 1960s moved forward to classification as standard agent types in the 1970s, to join the predominantly bacterial agents already standardised.

This view fits well with Smith's assessment that studies of bacteria were further advanced than studies of viruses throughout the Cold War period. It would follow that dangerous new advances are now even more likely in regard to potential viral agents than for possible bacterial agents. This point was made strongly by Erhard Geissler in his assessment of new biological weapons carried out as part of the SIPRI study of biological and toxin weapons in the mid-1980s.[13] Geissler listed publicly-available information on military interest in various viral, fungal and bacterial pathogens for different years. He concluded that in 1969 most potential agents (20 out of 31) were bacterial or fungal whereas in 1983 most (19 out of 22) were viral.

Whilst this measure may have been relatively crude, Geissler then gave four good reasons to support his observation. He suggested that the advent of genetic engineering techniques had allowed agents previously very dangerous to handle in the laboratory to be manipulated with relative safety. An example cited was the study of the function of various genes within *E. coli*. Viral diseases were often more attractive to the military planner, Geissler suggested, because they were even more difficult to treat than bacterial diseases. Such viral diseases were often also much more difficult to diagnose. Finally, he argued that an increasing number of anti-viral vaccines were being developed which would allow the protection of an aggressor's own military forces prior to the agents being used.

Geissler covered many of the points made by Smith concerning the lack of knowledge about the mechanisms underlying viral virulence. He indicated that genetic engineering raised the new possibility of increasing such virulence by adding toxin-encoding genes to the viruses. He noted that vaccinia virus had been used to develop vaccines by the addition of genes for antigens (see the previous chapter) and that the same techniques had been applied to other viruses. Thus:

> . . . the same techniques might possibly be used to develop viral vectors carrying genes coding for highly toxic molecules . . .

It will be recalled that the British paper for the 1991 review had mentioned just such an example of a toxin being added to a baculovirus, thereby increasing its virulence against insects.

In a later study Geissler himself expanded on the same theme,[14] stating that:

> . . . Recombinant virus expression vectors have been created as novel vaccination agents, carrying and expressing, for example, genes derived from dengue virus, Hantaan virus, Lassa virus, Rift Valley fever virus, and Russian tick-borne encephalitis virus. These viruses have been considered as putative BW agents . . .

Given that work is also under way to develop means of targeting such viruses, say against cancer cells, very powerful new lethal agents could become available. Increasing knowledge of, and the ability to manipulate, viral genomes are obviously two of the major specific developments that we need to address in considering the current state of the art.

Examples of Current Research

It will be convenient to deal first with some recent examples of work on bacteria and bacterial toxins, then to look at peptides and finally recent studies of viruses.

Bacteria

Recent reviews[15,16] show clearly that studies of bacterial pathogenesis have moved beyond investigations of single genetic factors within species or even of several different genetic factors within a single species. It is now possible to make factually-based broad generalisations about how regulator genes control the operation of several lethal factors in a pathogen and about how evolutionary developments of different pathogens have arisen. Additionally, the complex interactions between hosts and pathogens are becoming clearer and molecular-level explanations are being advanced of how pathogens operate within micro-environments created by these interactions. Discussions of individual cases have to be seen against that broader background of developing knowledge.

One example described recently concerned the species of *Yersinia* which are pathogenic for humans. *Y. enterocolitica* and *Y. pseudotuberculosis* are acquired by ingestion and are not particularly dangerous; *Yersinia pestis*, which is transmitted by the bite of rodent fleas, is the cause of plague. It appears that these species are very closely related; indeed, *Y. pestis* has been classified as a sub-species of *Y. pseudotuberculosis*.[17] The most obvious difference in the genetics of the latter two species is that *Y. pestis* possesses two large plasmids. The smaller of these has been shown to have a definite link to causation of plague.

If mice are infected with *Y. pestis* deeply, by intravenous means, it does not matter whether this plasmid is present or not for plague results because the bacterium is free to multiply all over the body. However, if the bacteria are injected just subcutaneously (as in a flea-bite) and the smaller plasmid is absent, the median lethal dose required to cause infection increases by more than a million-fold because the bacteria are unable to break out of the localised area and reproduce massively. Thus it seems that the acquisition of the smaller plasmid was the crucial factor which led to the evolution of *Y. pestis* from the *Y. pseudotuberculosis* line. The smaller plasmid is required to ensure that the initial flea-bite turns into a widespread massive infection and then uninfected fleas will be infected on biting such an infected animal. As death in humans appears to be caused by over-reaction to the coating of the bacteria if they are present in large numbers rather than to a specific toxin they produce, it would appear that the plasmid is also responsible for the virulence of the species in humans.

In the *Y. pestis* strain KIM-10, isolated from a human plague victim in Iran in the early 1960s, the smaller plasmid was designated pPCP1. A series of strains containing mutants or cloned fragments of pPCP1 was constructed by investigators and it was demonstrated that if the gene for a particular one of the three products known to be produced by the plasmid was missing or inactivated, virulence dropped in the dramatic manner just described for mice. Similarly, if this gene was present, even in the absence of any other gene on the plasmid, the virulence was restored.

This plasmid gene, termed *pla*, encodes for a surface protease. The operation of this enzyme was investigated by growing large amounts of it in *E. coli* after genetic engineering. The investigators thought the most likely mode of operation of the enzyme was in breaching the barriers put around the site of the initial infection by the host body's defence mechanisms. Such an action would then allow the bacteria to spread throughout the body. Genes with strong similarities to *pla* have been found in other bacteria and are thought to probably play a similar role in such species and their pathogenesis.

Another well-understood host-pathogen example is that of anthrax.[18] There appear to be two principle virulence factors which operate in man and animals. *Bacillus anthracis* produces a capsule which protects it from phagocytosis and is therefore crucial in allowing an infection to become established, and a three-component toxin which causes tissue oedema and is the major cause of mortality. The virulent strains of the bacterium contain two large plasmids designated pXO1 and pXO2. The genes for the toxin are on pXO1 and those for the capsule are on pXO2. Virulence requires both genes. Strains without pXO1 do not produce toxin and are therefore not virulent. Strains without pXO2 but *with* pXO1 are at least 10^5 times less virulent than the original wild strain because the bacteria lack the protective capsule and are destroyed more effectively by the host. Although the organism has been shown to secrete other substances, none has been shown to be involved in pathogenesis.

The anthrax toxin components are individually not toxic. The three proteins involved are called the protective antigen (PA), the lethal factor (LF) and the oedema factor (EF). It appears that there are two distinct toxic activities. Combinations of LF and PA are called lethal toxin and combinations of EF and PA are called oedema toxin. The PA protein appears to bond to receptors on suitable cells and promote the entry of LF and EF. PA is the main immunogen for the production of vaccines against anthrax.

Early work between 1940 and 1965 led to methods which allowed the production of anthrax toxin in milligram amounts. However, the genes have now been sequenced and cloned into the related species *B. subtilis*. The PA gene has also been sub-cloned into baculovirus-derived vectors, and expressed in insect cells, and also into vaccinia virus. The mechanism of action of the toxin has been extensively studied as has the evolution of its component parts. Clearly, the role of PA in promoting the entry of LF and EF into cells might be enhanced by the use of other proteins. The damage caused within cells would thereby be increased.

Toxins

Botulinal neurotoxins produced by *Clostridium botulinum* have been the subject of intense research for decades.[19] There are seven different types of botulinal neurotoxin, four of which (A, B, E and F) have been discovered through outbreaks of botulism in human beings. There is just one type of tetanus toxin, produced by a related bacterium of the *Clostridia* group.[20]

Tetanus is safely prevented by immunisation with a formaldehyde-treated toxin. This is the most extensively used vaccine world-wide, but there are still large numbers of people needlessly affected by tetanus in poor parts of the world. Tetanus is initiated through a wound; botulinal toxins are usually ingested and therefore have to survive through the gut. Both toxins, however, then have specific effects on the nervous system. As both toxins rapidly kill, infection leads to an animal corpse of enormous potential infectivity containing vast numbers of infective spores.

For *Clostridium tetani* it was shown in the mid-1970s that toxigenic strains always contained a large plasmid, loss of which correlated with loss of the toxic effect. The complete sequence of nucleotides of the gene for the toxin was worked out in the mid-1980s. Much is also known about the genetics of the botulinal toxins and the gene for the A toxin, although not on a plasmid, was recently completely sequenced.

The amino acid sequences of the tetanus toxin and some of the botulinal toxins have been worked out and detailed comparisons have been made between them and other bacterial toxins. The mechanisms of action of these toxins on the nervous system are still being intensively studied and genetic engineering techniques are being increasingly used. A recent reviewer concluded that it seemed merely a matter of time before the parts of the molecules involved in their binding to nerve cells, entry into nerve cells and toxic effect would be characterised. Then it would be possible to undertake a genetic redesign of the toxins. Similar understanding of the genetics, structure and function of staphylococcal[21] and many other bacterial toxins is also being achieved.

Some toxins (e.g. Saxitoxin) have recently been brought under the direct control of the Chemical Weapons Convention. However, concerns have been expressed about a very wide range of possible new agents such as trichothecenes in yellow rain and new incapacitating agents.[22] While less emphasis has been placed on the possible misuse of trichothecenes in recent years, it may be that new chemical incapacitating agents, such as the US Advanced Riot Control Agent,[23] could escape control if developments are not monitored carefully. Generally, it seems that toxicologists are increasingly seeking molecular explanations for the phenomena they study and, within the larger field of research, *neuro*toxicology is particularly important.[24] An example of what can be done was the response to a disorder which affected some people in Nova Scotia who ate contaminated mussels in 1987. The usual symptoms of food poisoning were followed by continuing problems with short-term memory. The cause was found to be a substance called demoic acid, and several research groups are now studying how it interferes with the formation and storage of memory.

Viruses

The classification of viruses is still being developed and many new ones are being discovered. Standard classifications rely on the morphology, structure, site of replication, mode of transmission and so on of the viruses. One system of classification, advanced by the Nobel Prize-winner David Baltimore, focuses on the mode of replication and expression of the viral genes. This classification is helpful to our present concern with current research on viral diseases at the molecular level.

As protein synthesis takes place in the same way in all cells, messenger RNA (mRNA) is central to the scheme.[25] All viruses are grouped according to the pathway of mRNA synthesis in Baltimore's classification. In order to maintain the unity of the scheme, all mRNA is designated as plus (+) and strands of viral RNA or DNA which are complementary to the mRNA are designated as minus (−). Those which have the same sequence as mRNA are obviously also designated as plus.

The scheme logically leads to seven classes of virus type. These are set out in Table 7.3. Class 2 is split because the Class 2b group of viruses was discovered after Baltimore produced his classification and therefore had to be made a sub-set rather than having a class of their own in the scheme.

As we have seen in Chapter 3, yellow fever virus was investigated as a potential biological warfare agent. Current research on this, and related flaviviruses, can provide a picture of the current state of research on such organisms. It will be recalled that yellow fever was recognised as a disease from the seventeenth century onwards and that it caused great misery until the role of mosquitoes as vectors for transmission of the virus was discovered at the beginning of this century. A safe vaccine

Table 7.3   The Baltimore classification of viruses[1]

1.   Viruses with double-stranded DNA genome.
2a. Viruses with single-stranded DNA genome of the same sequence as mRNA.
2b. Viruses with DNA complementary to mRNA. Before synthesis of mRNA the DNA must be converted to double-stranded form.
3.   Viruses with double-stranded RNA genome. Known viruses of this type have a segmented genome, but mRNA is only synthesised on one strand of each segment.
4.   Viruses with single-stranded RNA genome of the same sequence as mRNA. Synthesis of the complementary strand needed prior to production of mRNA.
5.   Viruses with single-stranded RNA genome of base sequence complementary to mRNA.
6.   Viruses that have a single-stranded RNA genome and which have a DNA intermediate during replication.

[1]Modified from reference 25.

was eventually also developed, but the disease cannot easily be eradicated because it also infects monkeys. The entire genome of yellow fever virus was sequenced in the mid-1980s and the relationship between the genome and the key viral proteins was deduced.[26] A review of what was known of the flavivirus genome in the early 1990s gives an overview of what was known of this group of viruses as a whole.[27]

The Flaviviridae family of viruses takes its name from yellow fever, the Latin for yellow being 'flavus'. The group contained 68 known viruses in 1990, the majority of which are transmitted to vertebrates by mosquitoes or ticks. The life-cycles of the viruses between their very different hosts are therefore complex. The infective virus particles or virions are small, being about 40–70 nm (m^{-9}) in diameter. The single-stranded positive RNA in the genome (Baltimore Class 4) is immediately enclosed by a protein capsid to form the nucleocapsid. This structure is enclosed by another envelope of lipoprotein. Representative examples of the group, besides yellow fever, are tick-borne encephalitis, St. Louis encephalitis and dengue. Yellow fever, dengue and Japanese encephalitis are major world diseases; a number of the other viruses in the group are of regional concern.

The genome RNA is approximately 11,000 bases in length. It is infectious and can thus be used for translation of viral proteins. Following translation, the +mRNA replication involves the production of complementary minus strands of RNA which are then used as templates for the production of more plus strands. These +mRNA strands can then be used for the direct production of proteins, synthesis of more minus strands, or encapsulation into new viruses. The most important feature of the genome is that it has one open-reading frame of over 10,000 bases. That is to say, only one polyprotein is produced which is then cut in various places to produce the virus structural and non-structural proteins. At least ten proteins are produced: three of these are structural and seven are non-structural. Much is known about these proteins throughout the flavivirus group. Figure 7.1 illustrates the genome of yellow fever virus and the relationship of major protein products to the coding regions of the RNA.

The capsid structural protein (C) is small. It forms the structural part of the capsid which together with the genome of the virus constitutes the nucleocapsid. The amino acid sequence of this protein, and thus the RNA sequence coding for it, is quite variable amongst different flaviviruses. The prM protein is a precursor to the M glycoprotein which together with the E protein forms part of the lipid bilayer of the envelope surrounding the nucleocapsid. It seems that inside the infected cell the prM protein is the only form of this protein, but outside the cell the M part predominates as the pr segment is removed. The E protein is the major structural protein of the complete virus particle or virion and is assumed to be important in key activities such as binding to cells and fusing with membranes. It is the main target for antibodies. The protein has been studied in some detail and a model of its structure proposed. This is based on studies of the tick-borne encephalitis virus.

The NS3 non-structural protein is the second largest produced and is very similar (highly conserved) throughout the flavivirus group. NS5 is the largest of the proteins and is again highly conserved. It is thought that the conservation of the NS3 and the NS5 proteins throughout the group indicates that they play a role as enzymes in RNA replication. The strong similarities between the genetics of the group of viruses is thought to be due to the selective pressures exerted by their need to adapt to both their arthropod and mammalian hosts.

More importantly, from our point of view, the complete genome of virulent yellow fever and the avirulent YF 17D vaccine strain have been compared. These differ at 67 nucleotide positions and in 32 amino acids (because of the redundancy of the nucleotide code, not all substitutions change the amino-acids). As it is now possible to produce complementary DNA and clone it to make infectious RNA, rapid progress in understanding the biological basis of virulence should be possible.

As the authors of the 1990 review concluded:[27]

Figure 7.1 Organisation of the yellow fever genome and the processing of proteins*.

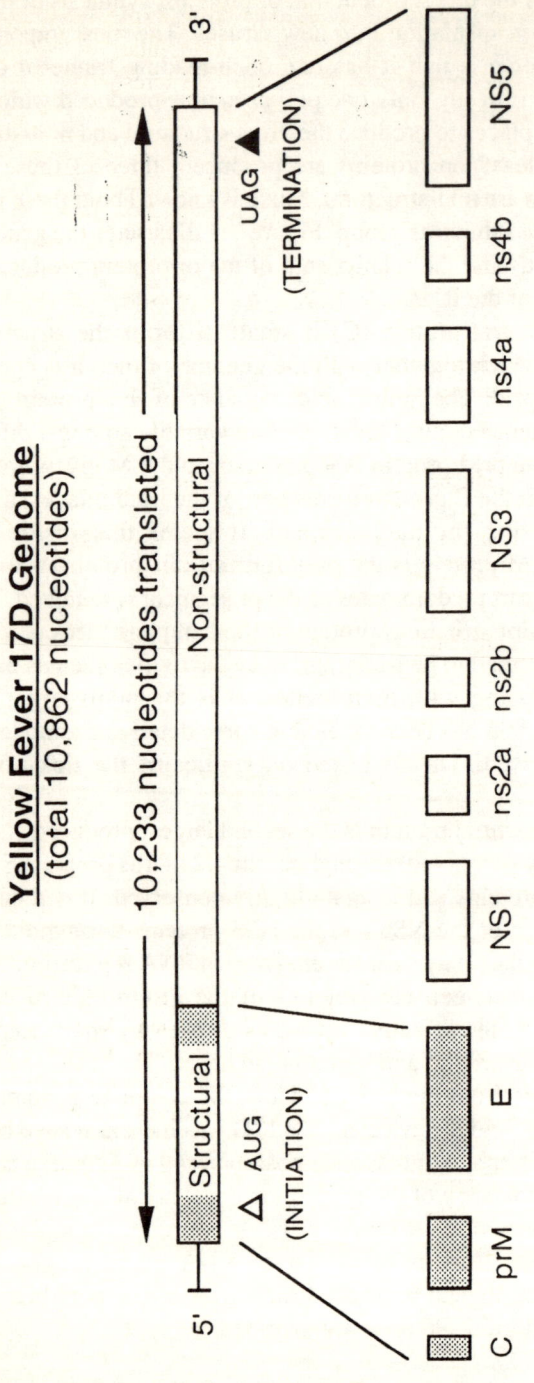

Yellow Fever 17D Genome
(total 10,862 nucleotides)

10,233 nucleotides translated

Structural

Non-structural

5'

3'

AUG (INITIATION)

UAG (TERMINATION)

C prM E

NS1 ns2a ns2b NS3 ns4a ns4b NS5

*After (26)

150

Molecular studies on flaviviruses have entered an explosive phase. The past several years have seen an amazing accumulation of structural information and common as well as distinct features of flavivirus genome RNAs and proteins have begun to emerge . . .

The review ended with hopes that such advances would lead to the discovery of means to control these important pathogens. The reverse side of the coin, clearly, is that the same knowledge could so easily be misused.

The pace of research continues to be swift, as was seen at the IXth

Table 7.4 Examples of current studies of flaviviruses[1]

Paper No.	Institution	Topic	Virus
W77-2	Faculty of Medicine Mahidol University Bangkok, Thailand	Japanese encephalitis in Asia. Description of current incidence of disease, causes and prevention measures	Japanese encephalitis
W77-1	Medical departments in Japan and Pakistan	Detection of viral sequences in cerebro-spinal fluid from encephalitis cases using reverse transcriptase-polymerase chain reaction	West Nile and Japanese encephalitis
W10-5	Department of Microbiology Emory University Atlanta, USA	Proteins involved in flavi-virus virion assembly investigated by expression of gene cassettes in a vaccinia virus expression system	West Nile and Dengue
P10-6	John Curtin School of Medical Research Australian National University, Canberra	Investigation of prM protein cleavage and spike secretion by NS3 proteinase using vaccinia virus recombinants	Murray Valley encephalitis
P10-9	Microbiology/ Molecular and Cell Biology Departments Singapore	Investigation of NS2a and NS2b proteins expressed in *E. coli*	Dengue 1

Paper No.	Institution	Topic	Virus
P10-16	Institute of Virology University of Vienna Austria	Molecular basis of virulence studied by comparison of genomes of virulent and non-virulent strains	Tick-borne encephalitis strains
W51-4	Dept. of Molecular Microbiology Washington Univ. St Louis, USA	Highly neuro-virulent strain for mice compared with less virulent strain in terms of C-prM-E-NS1 nucleotide sequences	Yellow fever
P51-6	Australian National University Canberra	Variants of the E protein tested for cell fusion and virulence in mice. A specific single amino-acid substitution found to increase median lethal dose needed by 10^6-fold	Murray Valley encephalitis
P30-7	Institut Pasteur Paris, France	Investigation of the immunogenicity of E protein expressed in insect cells via baculovirus vector	Dengue 2
W30-5	Army Medical Research Institute of Infectious Diseases; National Institutes of Allergy and Infectious Diseases, USA	Evaluation of alternative vaccines produced via recombinant vaccinia virus, baculovirus expression and construction of a chimeric dengue	Tick-borne encephalitis
P10-18	Centre for Applied Microbiology, Porton Down, UK and Ivanovsky Institute, Moscow	Investigation of antigenic variation in viruses from different sources in Russia by means of monoclonal antibodies against both E and NS1 proteins	Tick-borne encephalitis
W30-6	Institute of Molecular Biology, Novosibirsk Region, Russia	Vaccinia virus containing multiple foreign genome pieces responsible for immune responses produced and tested in preclinical trials	Tick-borne encephalitis (Hepatitis B, Venezuelan equine encephalitis)

[1]Data from reference 28

152

International Congress of Virology held in Glasgow during August 1993. Over 50 papers on flaviviruses were presented at the Congress.[28] Some representative examples have been briefly summarised from the abstracts and are listed in Table 7.4. It will be noticed that investigators are spread across the world; studies of the structure and function of the genome and its immediate protein products are advancing on many fronts; numerous vector and expression systems are in use; and the research is clearly going to pay increasing dividends in medical applications.

From our point of view, perhaps the most significant of the papers was by the group at Washington University, St. Louis, some of whom were individually responsible for the earlier papers on yellow fever virus that have been cited here. Paper W51-4, on the genetic analysis of yellow fever neurovirulence in mice, states that for a strain highly neurovirulent in mice '3 amino-acid changes were consistently observed in the E protein relative to the less virulent [strain]'. These very small changes are now being investigated in greater detail in recombinant viruses. Of course, this example of the detailed knowledge being generated in present studies is not an isolated one. The paper on the E protein of Murray Valley encephalitis (P51-6) shows how a single specific amino acid change can have a dramatic impact on virulence. Again, such a specific change can be subjected to further effective research.

Similar advances in knowledge are being achieved with many viral groups other than just the Flaviviridae, as papers at the Congress demonstrated. Table 7.5 gives examples of current work on some viruses known to be of potential interest to planners of biological warfare programmes. The papers of outstanding interest are obviously those concerned with the elucidation of the nucleotide sequences of the smallpox (variola major) strains (W 20-1, W 20-2). The Congress included a round-table discussion of the current proposals for the final elimination of smallpox stocks. The research on recently discovered viruses like Marburg, Lassa and Ebola is also reaching an advanced stage as full nucleotide sequences become available. In general terms, the papers listed in Table 7.5 again illustrate the widespread ability to manipulate a large number of vector and expression systems for these viral genomes. It is instructive to compare such recent research with the requirements for a molecular level of understanding of viral pathogenicity set out in Table 7.1.

In an article at the end of 1993 on the French research which produced a map of the human genome, the London *Financial Times* suggested that it had been a 'golden year for genetics'. The year had produced more of significance than any since 1953 when Watson and

Table 7.5 Examples of current studies of potential viral agents[1,2]

Paper No.	Institution	Topic	Virus/Group
W6-2	Medical Virology, University of Heidelberg, Germany	Viral proteins expressed in yeast cells after cloning with a shuttle vector	Hantavirus (Bunyavirus)
W6-3	Virology Division, Army Medical Research Institute for Infectious Diseases, and Chemical Engineering, Johns Hopkins University, USA	Viral proteins expressed in a recombinant baculovirus and in recombinant vaccinia virus studied for assembly of virus-like particles and induction of immunity	Hantaan (Bunyavirus)
W20-1	Centre for Disease Control and Prevention, Atlanta, Institute for Genomic Research, Gaithersberg, USA	Complete nucleotide sequence of virulent strain compared with vaccinia virus	Variola major (strain Bangladesh 1975) (Poxvirus)
W20-2	Institute for Molecular Biology, Novosibirsk Region, Russia	Complete nucleotide sequence of virulent strain compared with that of variola minor sequences	Variola major (strain India 1967) (poxvirus)
W32-6	Virus Reference Division, Colindale, and Centre for Applied Microbiology, Porton Down, UK	Use of reverse transcriptase and polymerase chain reaction for a fast and safe diagnostic technique	Lassa fever (Arenavirus)
W38-4	Kenya Agricultural Research Institute, Nairobi; US Universities	Expression of proteins in a recombinant capripoxvirus and determination of immunogenicity for domestic ruminants	Rift Valley (Bunyavirus)
W52-4	Institute for Molecular Biology, Novosibirsk Region, Russia	Complete nucleotide sequence obtained and compared with Ebola virus sequence	Marburg (Popp strain) (Filovirus)

Paper No.	Institution	Topic	Virus/Group
P38-3	Institute for Plant Protection and university departments in Tel-Aviv and Jerusalem, Israel	LqhaIT neurotoxin cDNA cloned into AcMPV insect baculovirus and expressed in extracts of insect cells. Toxin tested effectively on live insects	Yellow scorpion insect-specific neurotoxin
P44-7	Institut für Virologie, Marburg, Germany	Expression of the L gene multifunctional protein enzyme in insect cells	Marburg (Filovirus)
P51-16	Institute for Molecular Biology, Novosibirsk Region, Russia	Computer analysis of complete genome sequence compared with protein data banks to identify clusters of genes important in pathogenicity	Variola major (strain India 1967) (Poxvirus)
P52-2	Institute for Molecular Biology, Novosibirsk Region, Russia	Full nucleotide sequence of genome determined	Ebola (Filovirus)
P65-23	Botanical Institute, Munich	The $Tm-2^2$ resistance gene used in most commercial cultivars shown to be overcome by a ToMV mutant with two specific amino acid substitutions in the movement protein.	Tomato mosaic virus (ToMV)

[1]Papers are included in this list only in order to illustrate the range of topics covered in the Congress which *could* be of interest to military planners.
[2]Data from reference 28.

Crick discovered the structure of DNA, and the precise genetic cause of many inherited diseases had been found.[29]

Dr. Cohen, leader of the French team, was quoted as saying:

. . . In 10 to 20 years most of the diseases caused by single gene defects like cystic fibrosis will be cured . . .

As for the diseases of Western society which have much more complex causes, involving multiple gene interactions and the environment,

Cohen added that 'in 50 years most of these serious diseases will also be cured'. That may give us an appropriate timescale to consider for the issues we are discussing.

It seems most probable that a nation wishing to initiate an offensive biological weapons programme today would attempt to produce well-known agents such as anthrax or botulinal toxins. This was what Iraq attempted. To go beyond that would require a country to have a strong background in biotechnology and the ability to organise a talented research group from currently limited resources. We cannot expect that situation to last long. Maybe for the next decade the capabilities we have just discussed will remain predominantly in the hands of Western countries, but it seems unlikely to be true 20 years from now. Certainly in 50 years' time, the ability to construct many different kinds of new biological weaponry will surely be widespread. What today would require the ingenuity of a Nobel Prize-winner will by then be commonplace.

. 8 .

VEREX – TOWARDS A
VERIFICATION PROTOCOL?

As the arms control and disarmament agreements of a particular historical period largely reflect what the powerful states of that time consider
it in their interests to negotiate, it should not be expected that a particular set of agreements will survive a radical change in the distribution of
power. Thus, although we are probably still too close to the Cold War to
properly discern the radical nature of recent change, we are beginning to
see parts of the old Cold War arms control arrangements falling into dis-
use and new systems beginning to appear.

The radical change in the distribution of power is not, of course,
solely due to the demise of the Soviet Union, but is also the result of the
shift from a predominantly east-west confrontation towards a predominantly north-south antagonism.[1] In such a world, with a more
widespread distribution of power, unless the United States and its allies
wish to rely mainly on a coercive approach to arms control, the multilateral mechanisms which functioned so hesitantly during the Cold War
will have to assume much more of the burden of delivering arms control
agreements.

Now that the Chemical Weapons Convention (CWC) has been agreed
and is moving towards implementation, concerns about the proliferation
of weapons of mass destruction are likely to focus more strongly on the
much less well-known subject of biological weapons.[2] As we have seen,
Western governments have certainly not avoided voicing their concerns
on this issue. Given that earlier worries they expressed over biological
weapons programmes in Iraq and the Soviet Union proved to be well-
founded, the suggestion that ten states have such programmes[3] cannot
easily be dismissed.

Naturally, as we discussed in the two preceding chapters, the very

157

rapid advances being made in the new field of biotechnology have heightened fears about the ease with which biological weapons may be produced. All such concerns are magnified by the widespread recognition that the Biological Weapons Convention, which was agreed without any effective verification conditions in the early 1970s, is not a strong barrier to proliferation today.

Whether the international community is quickly able to modify the BWC to make it a more effective means of control, before much greater proliferation occurs, is thus an important test of the capabilities of modern multilateralism.

VEREX

It was against this background of rapid technological change, concerns over proliferation and unease about the adequacy of the Biological Weapons Convention as a control measure that the third Review Conference was held in Geneva in September 1991. As we saw in Chapter 4, in their consideration of Article V of the convention dealing with consultation and co-operation, the state parties agreed to expand and enhance the confidence-building measures already established as a result of the second Review Conference in 1986.[4]

More importantly perhaps, in order to strengthen the convention, it was also decided to establish an *Ad Hoc* Group of government experts to 'identify and examine potential verification measures from a scientific and technical standpoint'. It was also agreed that the group would meet in Geneva in March-April 1992 under the chairmanship of Ambassador Tibor Tóth of Hungary. Further meetings would be held as necessary with the aim of completing the work by the end of 1993.

In fact, four of what have become known as VEREX meetings have been held: the March-April 1992 opening session being followed by a second meeting in November-December 1992 and then by the third and the fourth meetings in May-June and September 1993. A final report was completed at the last meeting and this was then circulated to state parties.

It is necessary to understand what the participants in the VEREX meetings were instructed to do before we can discuss their findings and the possible consequences of their work. It will be noted, first, that they were *not* asked to attempt to produce any final conclusions on how verification measures might be incorporated into the BWC and this despite the detailed work already in the open literature on the subject.

158

Previous Studies

An ex-diplomat from the Netherlands, Berend ter Haar has attempted to set out what a proper verification protocol to the BWC would be like.[5] His analysis began by pointing out the longer-term problem with confidence-building measures. While they provide welcome information in the short term, without any means of verifying the accuracy of the data submitted they will eventually lead to doubts and suspicions. He then referred to the basic problem of the convention in its present form. He argued that it is almost unverifiable:

> . . . because all its obligations depend on the intentions of a party. In almost all controversial cases, a party could argue that its actions were justified by their non-prohibited purpose . . .

As examples of this he went on to note that:

> . . . A large stockpile of a potential biological warfare agent might, for example, be explained away as a stockpile for several years of vaccine production and large-scale testing of protective equipment . . .

Even though the trust that could be put in such arguments might be low, ter Haar argued that they would be difficult to prove false.

He therefore suggested that a verification protocol based on clear, objective criteria was required. The principles of his approach were a focus on the agents and equipment that present the largest risk, on acceptance by parties of restrictions on the production and use of such agents and equipment, and then on declaration and possible inspection of these items. It is important to note that he did not argue that his scheme would necessarily stop violations or lead to their detection; rather, he expected it to make violations more difficult (and thus less attractive) and increase the chance of their detection. The main elements of ter Haar's suggested protocol are set out in Table 8.1. These elements recur in the discussions of verification which are reviewed in this chapter.

Papers produced for the Federation of American Scientists (FAS) in 1990 and 1991 on the possibility of a verification protocol resulted from the efforts of a special working group on biological and toxin weapons verification chaired by Robert Weinberg, Professor of Biology at MIT. Marie Chevrier of Harvard University compiled the results of the discussions by the core group of distinguished US ex-diplomats and scientists and the reviews of their work carried out by a large international group of experts.

The FAS working group produced two sets of proposals for the third

Table 8.1 Elements for a verification protocol[1]

Article 1. Quantitative constraints

Article 2. Transfer.

Article 3. Declaration of biological agents and toxins.

Article 4. Declaration of relevant facilities.

Article 5. Routine verification.

Article 6. Challenge inspections.

Article 7. Inspection procedures.

Article 8. Organisation.

Annex to Article 1: Lists of agents, toxins, agents capable of producing toxins.

---

[1]Data from reference 5.

review of the BWC: those aimed at short-term changes they thought necessary and possible on such a timescale, and those that they saw as of a longer-term nature. The long-term proposals are of most interest here as they were intended to form the basis of a verification protocol to the convention under Article V. However, one short-term proposal under Article V was that:[6]

> The Review Conference should call a series of meetings of experts from the Parties to draw up a draft proposal for a Protocol to the BWC on verification.

As we shall see, the conference did not move quite that far.

The long-term proposals included the requirement for annual declarations, a technical secretariat/inspectorate to administer the protocol, and inspections. Three types of inspection were specified: routine on declared facilities, challenge on any site, and special monitoring of certain events. In an appendix a list of agents was produced as an example of what would be required in a full protocol.

In their 1991 document the FAS tried to show that a workable verification regime could be implemented.[7] They attempted to specify the information that should be given in annual declarations so that effective assurance of compliance was possible. Additionally, their report:

> . . . lists the documentation that could be maintained at declared sites for access during inspection, and outlines inspection procedures; and it lists and discusses the significance of the information that can be obtained by inspection . . .

The document clearly resulted from detailed work by people conversant with the relevant technology. As an example, Table 8.2 gives the capabilities checklist required to be reported on for declared facilities. The identification of the capabilities set out in this table may be understood by referring to the discussion of biological agents and biotechnology in previous chapters. It should be noted also that the studies of inspection procedures, and particularly the discussion of the significance of the information obtained, foreshadowed the work of government experts at the VEREX meetings.

Table 8.2 Capabilities checklist for declared facilities[1]

Microbial, cell culture or virus production.

Vaccine, toxoid, antitoxin or antiserum production.

Plant or animal (including primates and arthropods) cultivation, breeding or maintenance.

Animal or plant testing.

Germ-free animal work.

Egg incubation.

Tissue culture and non-cellular *in vitro* test systems.

Associated medical, veterinary or public health facilities.

Microencapsulation.

Aerosol generation.

Freeze drying, spray drying.

Sterilisation.

Field work.

Storage of microbial agents, viruses, toxins.

Genetic and protein engineering techniques, including biological active site modelling.

---

[1]From FAS, reference 7.

VEREX Framework

The instructions for the government experts at these VEREX meetings were that they should attempt to:[4]

> . . . identify measures which could determine:-
> – Whether a State Party is developing, producing, stockpiling, acquiring or retaining *microbial or other biological agents or toxins*, of types

and in quantities that have no justification for prophylactic, protective or peaceful purposes; and,

– Whether a State Party is developing, producing, stockpiling, acquiring or retaining *weapons, equipment or means of delivery* designed to use such agents or toxins for hostile purposes or in armed conflict. [Author's emphases]

The measures, which clearly pertained to the restrictions in Article I of the Convention, could be addressed singly or in combination. The Group was instructed finally that it should specifically:

. . . seek to *evaluate potential verification measures*, taking into account the broad range of types and quantities of microbial and other biological agents and toxins, whether naturally occurring or altered, which are capable of being used as means of warfare. [Author's emphasis]

A set of criteria which were to be used to examine the measures was also defined (Table 8.3).

Table 8.3   Main criteria for examination of potential verification measures[1]

Their strengths and weaknesses based on, but not limited to, the amount and quality of information they provide, and fail to provide;

Their ability to differentiate between prohibited and permitted activities;

Their ability to resolve ambiguities about compliance;

Their technology, material, manpower and equipment requirements;

Their financial, legal, safety and organisational implications;

Their impact on scientific research, scientific co-operation, industrial development and other permitted activities, and their implications for the confidentiality of commercial proprietary information.

---

[1]Data from reference 4.

Further restrictions on the nature of the report that could be produced were also evident in their instructions:

The Group shall adopt *by consensus* a report taking into account views expressed in the course of its work. The report of the Group shall be a *description of its work* on the identification and examination of potential verification measures *from a scientific and technical standpoint*, according to this mandate. [Author's emphases]

It appears that this restricted mandate was all that the United States was prepared to accept.[8] This powerful country had long held that the convention was not verifiable. As Michael Moodie of the United States was reported to have told a plenary meeting at the third Review Conference, his 'Government had made it clear at an earlier stage that it believed that the Convention was not effectively verifiable'.

On the other hand, state parties more enthusiastic for enhanced verification measures appear to have been successful in opening up the possibility of further progress after the VEREX meetings, the final document of the third Review Conference stating that:

> The report of the Group shall be circulated to all State Parties for their consideration. *If a majority of State Parties ask for the convening of a conference to examine the report*, by submitting a proposal to this effect to the Depository Governments, *such a conference will be convened. In such a case the conference shall decide on any further action.* The conference shall be preceded by a preparatory committee. [Author's emphases]

This stage had been reached by the end of 1993, with some people hoping for a preparatory committee to meet in the spring of 1994 and the follow-on conference to go ahead in the autumn of 1994. That would allow for more technical work before the fourth Review Conference of the BWC in 1996. These hopes were, in fact, fulfilled.

As is clear from the criteria set for the experts (Table 8.3), there were potential differences at the VEREX meetings, not only between the United States and some of its usual allies, but also between the rich world and the poorer Third World countries. The last two criteria on the list suggest a concern about the potential costs of verification of the BWC and the implications for the potentially important co-operative activities set out in Article X of the convention.

Despite these potential problems, it appears that the VEREX meetings settled down to a pragmatic and well-structured process of completing the mandated work. In broad terms, VEREX 1 identified the potential measures while VEREX 2 examined the measures and began their evaluation. VEREX 3 continued the process of evaluation and VEREX 4 was then concerned with the completion of the final report.

An indication of the seriousness with which the task was undertaken may be gained from the number of working papers produced by the state parties for the VEREX meetings. The summary of the work of the first meeting lists, amongst other documents, 31 working papers by different countries.[9] The summary of the work of the third meeting lists working papers numbered 97 through to 175, amongst a variety of other documents.[10]

Allied Contributions

Given the position of the United States, the actions taken by the West Europeans and other usually allied countries became crucial for the eventual outcome of the VEREX meetings. In an early paper for the first meeting, the French put their view bluntly.[11] France did not sign the BWC in 1972 mainly because it lacked a verification regime. When it joined in 1984, France wanted to work towards the setting up of one and, the paper stated, VEREX represented a real opportunity to pursue that aim. The difficulties were not minimised: the BWC was thought to be uniquely difficult to verify because of the dual-use nature of the technology, the potentially infinite list of agents and the lack of firm knowledge about weapon systems for the delivery of biological agents. Nevertheless, the paper argued:

> Sight must not be lost of the ultimate objective of the Group's work, namely the elaboration of a set of measures resulting in the preparation of a verification protocol . . .

The thrust of the paper was that success would come from breaking the problem down into smaller parts.

Specifically, it was argued that the group of experts should split so that some could deal with 'upstream' questions and others with 'downstream' questions. The first sub-group would thus be concerned with agents and the second with weapon systems. The study of possible verification measures could then home in on specific sub-problems. An illustrative list of agents categorised by hazard level was also provided in an annex.

The Netherlands also argued that the VEREX expert group had a unique opportunity in examining the possibility of establishing an effective verification regime for the BWC. It was further argued that the problem was made more urgent because the increasing effectiveness of other disarmament regimes might indirectly increase temptations to evade the BWC.[12]

As in the paper from France, the clear aim of producing an inspection protocol was identified. The Netherlands saw the VEREX meetings as the first (technical) stage of a four-stage process:

i.   Expert group on technical matters;
ii.   Drafting and signing of an inspection protocol;

iii.   Ratification, establishment of institutions;
iv.   Entry into force, operational phase.

The paper then proceeded to put forward a practical, step-by-step scheme for addressing the first technical stage. This was based on a series of questions. Thus to consider what a 'state of the art' offensive biological weapons programme would look like, a conceptual outline was put forward. There would have to be research and development of agents to begin a programme. The paper noted that:

> . . . Research and development are taken together, because there are no objective criteria to draw a line between those two.

It added in a footnote that the 'much discussed question as to whether Article I of the BWC includes or excludes research' is 'less relevant' and might be discussed informally.

Following research and development there would have to be agent production and storage. In a second stream of activity, research and development would be needed on weapons and means of delivery. This would be followed by production of the means of delivery and weapons filling and storage. Before use, there would also have to be development and implementation of military doctrine.

The paper pointed out that the further along this process a country had proceeded, the better the chances of detection:

> It is the combination of R&D on potential BW agents and on dissemination methods that could yield relevant indications of non-compliance. Production of virulent BW agents and storage, in combination with the production and storage of production facilities, would further enhance suspicions . . .

In answer to another question on what new sources of information could be developed, the paper noted the possibility of establishing 'national profiles' of state parties against which further information might be judged. The overall impression, as in the paper from France, is of a search for means of dividing the problem into practically solvable sub-problems.

Germany argued that, although control of non-compliance could never be 100 per cent, the aim should be to achieve the highest probability of detection.[13] It suggested that a solution might be a regime consisting of several elements (Table 8.4). Although of a more general character, this regime can be recognised as having the same thrust as ter Haar's proposals (Table 8.1). It also provided a comprehensive, ordered checklist of key words which could be used in further detailed discussions.

Table 8.4   Elements of a BW control regime[1]

Transparency of national biological and biotechnological programmes by annual declarations of research and development and production activities.

Exchange of information gained from the monitoring of biological agents and toxins as well as relevant equipment for the production of biological materials.

Inspections at laboratories, production and storage facilities as well as at any other type of facility that is assumed to be engaged in a weaponisation activity.

Inspections at sites where an accidental or deliberate use of BW has taken place.

---

[1]Data from reference 13.

A further example of a practical, West European input can be seen in the UK paper on the lessons that could be learned from the inspections in Iraq by the UN Special Commission.[14] The paper accepted that BW verification is difficult but it added:

> . . . Deterrence of non-compliance is the basic objective, and any verification regime would need to have a significant probability of exposing evidence of non-compliance. . . . All that is necessary is to create a regime in which a potential cheater judges that sufficient information may be available to enable the international community to take political and other action against it.

It will be noticed that this theme – that 100 per cent confidence is not attainable nor required – runs through the West European papers. No doubt this had some connection with the known US position.

The UK paper noted that at the end of 1991 two BW-dedicated inspections had been conducted at 11 sites and a joint CW/BW inspectorate had visited several sites in Iraq. In all cases, the paper stated, the inspectors:

> . . . were able to come up with reasonably definite assessments about the nature of activities seen by them, and their relevance or potential significance in the context of an offensive BW programme . . .

The paper suggested that the key question concerns the factors which allowed such conclusions to be reached.

The general point stressed was that:

... Access to both buildings and personnel was the crucial factor; little, if anything, could have been achieved without it. Such access is essential to gain detailed site knowledge, to take samples, to discuss issues with personnel of all levels, examine documentation 'in context' and to determine the site's purpose ...

Papers produced by the UK for the second VEREX meeting showed the same determined effort to deal practically with specific problems. In one paper[15] an attempt was made to investigate concerns over commercial confidentiality that might arise from the sampling and analysis of specimens during on-site inspections. As the paper stated, it:

... examines the risks to intellectual property rights (IPR) from sampling and identification during inspections, and suggests some measures to reduce the chances of accidental or deliberate loss of IPR.

Clearly, in a commercial area where advances are rapid but where large sums of money may have to be invested over long periods before commercial profits are forthcoming, the loss of specific information could be extremely damaging and thus produce reluctance in the industry to accept inspections.

The UK paper recognised this point quite explicitly:

... Commercial programmes involving new uses of micro-organisms and new products may take 10 years or more from inception to full production, and so the capital investment can be very large.

The paper then went on to discuss a number of potential difficulties and their possible solutions. These ranged from how inspection protocols could prevent deliberate (or inadvertent) attempts by inspectors to remove samples during inspections, through to means by which the information available to inspectors might be limited, say, by random selection techniques so that commercial concerns could be assuaged but inspection needs reasonably met.

In another paper for the second VEREX meeting the UK discussed the philosophy and scope of declarations and notifications.[16] Taking up a point made in the earlier paper by the Netherlands[12] the UK paper pointed to the importance of national patterns of activity:

A verification regime which efficiently addresses compliance with the BWC will need to establish an overview of national approaches to work on micro-organisms and toxins as a baseline for any on-site verification activities ...

After discussing the objectives of declarations and constraints on declarations (for example, in regard to commercial confidentiality) the paper attempted to summarise and analyse all the contributions to the first VEREX meeting that dealt with declarations.

The paper then put forward a conceptual scheme which might be used in further work. Declarations were grouped into four categories concerned with: facility concepts; programme concepts; transfer concepts; and general concepts. An annex provided detailed lists of elements within these categories. It was argued, however, that care should be taken in selecting items for a verification regime:

> . . . It will be necessary both to reduce and refine these elements in order to arrive at a small, focused, and highly informative scheme . . .

Focused declarations of physical resources, micro-organisms and toxins of special concern under the BWC and staff resources were then discussed in some detail. The listing of staff names at facilities was rejected, for example, as an infringement of human rights and a potential risk to the safety of individuals from terrorists or animal rights activists. After more detailed discussion of special facilities and agents, an attempt was made to list what a minimal declaration focused on key patterns of activity might look like (Table 8.5).

The UK continued its practical approach in the third VEREX meeting, reporting there on a trial inspection that had been carried out.[17] This report indicated that a series of inspections was planned in order to test the effectiveness of verification, discover the issues that might arise for industry, and find out whether sufficient access to the plant and documentation could be achieved without unacceptable risks to commercial confidentiality. It was also pointed out that specially-chosen facilities, where most difficulties and concerns might arise, would be used.

The general conclusion from the first inspection of a pharmaceutical pilot plant was that adequate access was possible and that commercial confidentiality could be protected. The paper noted that:

> This practice inspection demonstrated the feasibility of on-site inspection. . . . Given the nature of health, safety, environmental, and other regulatory provisions that govern the pharmaceutical and biotechnology industries in the West, demonstrating compliance with Article 1 of the BWC is comparatively straightforward.

The principal lesson learned was that further work needed to be carried out on *portable* equipment which could be used to assist in verification. It was also stressed that inspections of other kinds of plant (for example,

Table 8.5 The suggested scope of minimal declarations[1]

Facilities with most of the capabilities for misuse
- R&D involving listed agents
- R&D facilities having BL4 or equivalent levels of containment
- Facilities having key aerosol-handling capabilities such as aerosol test chambers suitable for use with pathogens and toxins
- R&D and production of vaccines involving listed agents
- Production of pharmaceuticals by fermentation, above certain scales
- R&D, test and evaluation on biological defence

Key activities, especially those involving micro-organisms and toxins of most concern to the BWC
- National biological defence programmes
- Vaccination programmes for listed agents
- Disease outbreaks involving listed agents
- Import and export of listed agents
- Import and export of certain dual-use production equipment
- Pest/weed control programmes for listed agents, or involving aerosol control technologies with agents

The framework in which microbiology is carried out
- Regulations, legislation, especially related to the provisions of the BWC or to activities with listed agents
- Arrangements for public/animal/crop health, especially involving listed agents

---

[1]Data from reference 16.

a production plant) might throw up different problems. A more detailed paper[18] provided further information on the pharmaceutical pilot plant inspection exercise, for example that the inspection team was able to conclude:

> . . . from the fermenter and containment equipment specifications and the air handling and effluent treatment systems, that the site lacked features needed for safe handling of ACDP Hazard Group 3 or 4 pathogens, and certainly did not meet the ACDP requirements for work on HG3 and HG4 agents in the UK . . .

Other information such as working protocols, health and safety documentation and so on was available to confirm the visual assessment.

VEREX Results

Fifty-three state parties to the BWC participated in the VEREX 1 meeting. In total, 18 meetings and seven informal meetings were held. In the first week there was wide-ranging discussion, covering such topics as the objectives for verification of the BWC. In the second week, however, detailed studies were carried out on the identification of potential measures in relation to the development, acquisition or production, and stockpiling or retention of agents or weapons systems. The chairman integrated the various lists into a 'Compiled List of Potential Verification Measures' (Table 8.6) and the date of the second VEREX session was agreed.[9]

Table 8.6   Compiled list of potential verification measures[1]

Surveillance of publications

Surveillance of legislation

Data on transfers, transfer requests and on production

Multilateral information sharing

Exchange visits (off-site)

Declarations

Surveillance by satellite

Surveillance by aircraft

Ground-based surveillance (off-site)

Sampling and identification (off-site)

Observation (off-site)

Auditing (off-site)

Exchange visits - international arrangements

Interviewing (on-site)

Visual inspection (on-site)

Identification of key equipment (on-site)

Auditing (on-site)

Sampling and identification (on-site)

Medical examination (on-site)

Continuous monitoring by instruments (on-site)

Continuous monitoring by personnel (on-site)

---

[1]Chairman's list as slightly modified at VEREX 2 (see reference 19).

The second session in November-December 1992[19] was attended by 46 state parties. The group held 19 formal meetings and one informal one. The agenda allowed for the examination, the summing-up of the examination and then the beginning of the evaluation of the list of potential verification measures. The chairman made extensive use of national experts both as moderators in the task of examining the potential measures in the three broad areas of development, acquisition or production, and stockpiling or retaining, and as rapporteurs and moderators in the discussion of the individual measures. The high level of expertise available is evident from the national positions held by the experts.

The rapporteurs provided factual summaries of the discussions held according to an agreed format (Table 8.7). As an example, the 'Identification of Key Equipment (On-Site)' lists under 'definitions' nine types of equipment of particular interest in regard to development. In regard to production and acquisition 14 examples are given, and in regard to stockpiling and retention two categories of specific key equipment are listed. The dual-use nature of much of the equipment is stressed. There is obviously a considerable correspondence between this listing of key equipment and the capabilities set out by the FAS group (Table 8.2).

Table 8.7 Summaries of examination of measures to be presented by the rapporteurs (structural elements)[1]

Summaries should provide a factual description (without any value judgement) of the information contained in the oral contributions, national papers and documents available, arranged according to the following structural elements:

1. Definition(s)

2. Characteristics and technologies:
   2.1 State of the art
   2.2 Capabilities (development, production or acquisition, stockpiling or retaining)
   2.3 Limitations (development, production or acquisition, stockpiling or retaining)

3. Potential interaction with other measures

4. List of documents introduced

---

[1]Data from reference 19.

The second VEREX session also considered papers concerned with how the next stage of evaluation might take place, agreed to a certain amount of intersessional work, and arranged the date of the third meeting for May-June 1993.

At the third VEREX session 42 state parties participated. The group held 17 formal and five informal meetings. Additionally, Ambassador Tóth, as chairman, held a series of informal consultations. The same format of moderators and rapporteurs was employed as in the second session and two other experts worked as 'Friends of the Chair' on the evaluation of the measures in combination. A further expert[10] carried out consultations 'with a view to identifying an agreed approach to handling the question of possible determination of *types and quantities of biological agents*'. [Author's emphasis]

The pragmatic and practical process set in train by the third Review Conference began to pay dividends at the third VEREX session. After introduction by the rapporteurs each measure was discussed in detail and an evaluation report on each was agreed by consensus. Furthermore, using an agreed methodology, the group discussed and evaluated an illustrative set of examples of measures in combination. The results of the consultations on types and quantities of agent was included by consensus in the summary of the meeting and informal exchanges of views took place on the results of two trial inspections carried out by the Netherlands and Canada, and by the UK.

Although a possible warning note was sounded in a statement by the non-aligned and other developing countries 'expressing their wish that, in order to arrive at consensus final results, potential verification measures should serve the purpose of strengthening the Biological Weapons Convention', it was agreed by the group 'to prepare and adopt by consensus at its last session a report on its work'. An outline of the form of the intended report was also agreed (Table 8.8) and means arranged for intersessional work before the final meeting.

The reports on the 21 potential verification measures agreed at the third VEREX session show that the experts were able to distinguish those which would be the most valuable. Thus in regard to declarations it was noted that:[10]

> Declarations, if properly structured, could be an important mechanism for building up a picture of the biological activities in a nation . . .
>
> On balance, it would appear from this evaluation that declarations have a high status in terms of potential utility . . .

Table 8.8   The intended VEREX report[1]

---

1. Character of the Report
    1.1 Description of the work from a scientific and technical standpoint
    1.2 To be adopted by consensus, taking into account views expressed
        in the course of its work

2. Elements of the Report
    2.1 Summary Report
    2.2 Annex (VEREX 1–3 summaries)

3. Summary Report
    3.1 Short and readable
    3.2 4–5 pages

4. Structure of the Summary Report
    4.1 Introduction
    4.2 Identification and examination
    4.3 Evaluation of measures singly
    4.4 Evaluation of measures in combination
    4.5 Other aspects (three broad areas, types and quantities. . . .)
    4.6 Conclusion

---

[1]Data from reference 10.

On the other hand, in regard to exchange visits–international agreements the consensus was that:

> . . . It appears that alone, this measure would serve best as an enhanced CBM, expanding openness and transparency . . .

Similarly firm conclusions were reached in regard to measures in combination, the report of the 'Friends of the Chair' stating, for example, that whilst no single measure could effectively distinguish between permitted and prohibited activities:

> . . . the reports of the rapporteurs . . . have identified measures that in combination may give an enhanced effect. Measures in combination may provide enhanced capabilities and thereby enhance the effectiveness of each measure when it is used in combination with others . . .

Specific illustrations of such enhanced effects are given in relation to measures in all three areas of development, production and acquisition, and stockpiling and retention.

In regard to the question of types and quantities of agent, the expert appointed by the chairman reported in part that:

> . . . Taking into account already existing lists, there is no doubt that

173

illustrative lists of agents may be developed to serve particular verification measures.

and:

> . . . an illustrative list of agents is established, it would be possible to
> identify the quantities of each agent which are currently produced for
> justified prophylactic, protective or other peaceful applications . . .

In short, it is hard not to conclude from the findings of the third VEREX
session that the BWC could be made verifiable to a considerable extent.

This viewpoint was clearly reflected in the final report produced at
the fourth VEREX session. The report took the basic form decided at
the third session, but it also included a summary of the complete evaluation of the measures carried out at VEREX 3. It was argued, however,
that the first three criteria (set out in Table 8.3) mainly represented
judgements concerned with the effectiveness of individual measures
whereas the second three criteria were concerned with requirements
and impacts. Thus the capabilities and limitations of each measure were
summarised under these two headings. The summary for 'Identification
of Key Equipment (On-Site)' is given in Table 8.9. The report concluded that:[20]

> . . . potential verification measures as identified and evaluated could
> be useful to varying degrees in enhancing confidence, through
> increased transparency, that States Parties were fulfilling their oblig-
> ations under the BWC . . .

and:

> Based on the examination and evaluation of the measures . . . against
> the criteria given in the mandate, the Group considered, from the sci-
> entific and technical standpoint, that some of the potential verification
> measures would contribute to strengthening the effectiveness and
> improve the implementation of the Convention, also recognizing that
> appropriate and effective verification could reinforce the Convention.

In short, while they considered that more technical work was needed, for
example on the protection of sensitive, commercial, proprietary information, the experts produced a generally positive answer.

Table 8.9 Identification of key equipment (on-site)[1]

Definition

An essential part of identification of key equipment on-site is to confirm a facility's declaration and help to ensure that the equipment is not used for prohibited activities.

Evaluation (Capabilities and Limitations)

Criteria 1-3

Can provide substantial amounts of high-quality information, if carried out by experienced specialists. Properly trained individuals may not be available immediately. Assessment of facilities' capabilities is possible. The vast majority of key equipment in biological facilities is of a dual-use nature. Portable equipment can be moved out of a facility to deceive inspectors. Lack of equipment or combinations of equipment as well as capacity could be used as one important indicator when it comes to differentiate activities, but equipment is mostly of dual-use nature.

Criteria 4-6

There may be legal problems. Safety of inspectors must be considered. Proprietary information may be negatively affected. Financial implications should be taken into consideration. Costs can be high if a large number of inspections is carried out. Legal problems may be connected with on-site inspections as such and with the confidentiality of information obtained.

---

[1]Modified from reference 20.

Verification Possibilities

The experts were not, of course, arguing that a system of verification could be put in place which would give 100 per cent assurance that proliferation was not occurring. Rather, it appears, they believe that a system which would greatly deter cheating, because of the high possibility of detection, is possible. One may envisage, for example, a focused, low-cost operation which concentrates on declarations related to the greatest risk areas, backed up by on-site inspections of declared and non-declared facilities. The inspections could include interviews, visual checks, identification of key equipment, auditing of records, and sampling and identification of biological material. The whole system could be agreed as a protocol to the BWC without opening up discussion of major changes in the convention text itself.

The problem of the verification of the BWC under the pressure of ongoing developments in modern biotechnology was investigated broadly by Zilinskas in the mid-1980s.[21] Following a brief history of chemical and biological weapons disarmament issues, he began his analysis by reviewing the attempt in the 1970s SIPRI study to discover whether verification was feasible.

It will be recalled that the SIPRI study covered many aspects of the problem of CBW. In its study of verification, 26 stages in the development of a chemical or biological offensive capability were identified. These ranged from an initial policy review of the 'pros and cons of an offensive CBW effort' through to troop manoeuvres and exercises with agents. Five main methods of verification were also identified:

> ... (a) administrative and budgetary inspection; (b) literature surveillance; (c) remote observation; (d) economic analysis; and (e) through visiting inspection teams ...

The different methods were then analysed to see what could be discovered assuming various levels of intrusiveness. The work was extensive and involved, among other things, attempts to estimate what kinds and sizes of facilities would be required in an offensive programme and whether the conversion of civilian facilities would be possible. An inspection experiment involving 14 research laboratories in nine countries was also carried out.

In this experiment small teams of microbiologists carried out inspections to see whether it was technically possible to discover if the production of agents on a militarily relevant scale (set at 10 kilograms of microbial paste or spores) could be carried out in a non-secret research or production facility. The microbiologists were asked quite specific questions concerning the degree to which they thought detection would be possible. According to Zilinskas the SIPRI conclusion was positive and he quoted it as follows:

> ... a substantial measure of on-site verification would be possible provided certain conditions were fulfilled: documentation, free access to all facilities and personnel, the possibility of visits at short notice ...

He then analysed the implications, as he saw them, of the new advances in biotechnology for verification of the BWC.

In order to deal with a reasonable number of issues Zilinskas compressed the SIPRI list of stages of an offensive programme into just seven: the design phase; applied research; limited testing; pilot-plant; manufacture; large-scale field testing; and storage and transport. However, he also attempted to deal separately with the possibility of verification in regard to human, animal and plant agents and toxins at each of these stages. The results of his analyses for the agents are summarised in Table 8.10. The importance of P4 containment laboratories/facilities obviously makes the verification problems much easier at earlier stages in regard to human pathogens, but only when larger-scale manufacture and testing get under way did he believe that verification would become realistic for plant and animal pathogens. He was generally even more pessimistic about verification in regard to toxins. The value of Zilinskas' study, nevertheless, is to indicate the considerable further technical work that will be required if the VEREX process is to lead to a verification protocol for the BWC.

Table 8.10 Zilinskas' analysis of verification possibilities[1]

Stage	Target of Weapons		
	Human	Animal	Plant
1. Design (e.g., protein engineering)	Not possible	Not possible	Not possible
2. Applied Research	Possible (P4 containment needed)	Not possible	Not possible
3. Limited Testing	Possible if aerosols used (P4 containment needed)	Not possible	Not possible
4. Pilot-Plant Stage	Possible (P4 facility required)	Not possible	Not possible
5. Manufacture	Possible	Possible	Possible
6. Large-Scale Field Testing	Possible	Possible	Possible
7. Storage and Transport	Difficult	Difficult	Difficult

[1]Data from reference 21.

A Verification Protocol

The fact that government experts have reached a positive conclusion on the possibility of verifying the Biological Weapons Convention from a scientific and technical standpoint does not mean that this multilateral process has had a successful outcome. Great difficulties could lie ahead over the next few years.

One does not have to look hard for potential problems. If only about a third of the state parties attended the VEREX meetings, can a majority be persuaded to support the calling of a follow-on conference and an effective grouping be mobilised to support change at that conference? As many state parties will also be involved with the CWC and the costs of its complex verification, can they be persuaded that the costs involved in verifying the BWC will be worthwhile? Can the state parties be persuaded that the intrusive nature of CWC verification should be duplicated by a similar level of intrusiveness in regard to the BWC? What will be the effect of the potential weakness of one of the depository states (Russia) resulting from disclosure of the Soviet offensive BW programme?

At a more political level, it is clear that the United States has changed its overall stance. President Clinton told the UN General Assembly on 28 September 1993 that:[22]

> We will also seek to strengthen the Biological Weapons Convention by making every nation's biological activities and facilities open to more international scrutiny . . .

and Thomas Graham, acting director of the US Arms Control and Disarmament Agency, told the UN First Committee on 22 October that:[23]

> We support the consensus report of the recently-concluded Ad Hoc Group of Government Experts convened to identify and examine potential BWC verification measures. . . . we support the early convening of such a [follow-on] conference . . .

Yet there has long been opposition in parts of the US establishment to the idea that the BWC can be verified. It is far from clear that the US has now reached a new consensus supporting far-reaching change.

Given the widely-understood difficulties of the verification of the BWC, it could be that, during further examinations of the VEREX conclusions and detailed technical consideration, a process of delay and diminution begins. This is particularly likely if the USA retains its original position, which some have suggested is based on the management, not the prevention, of proliferation, and the retention of that management in its own hands.[8] The apparent change in its position on the VEREX meetings might be an attempt to placate its allies who are much more enthusiastic about the verification of the BWC.

If the USA has not basically changed its position, other countries may also find opportunity to obstruct. China and India, among others, are clearly not yet enthusiastic supporters of the VEREX conclusions. A benign interpretation of their position might be that they wish to see much more co-operation in relevant biotechnology (generally, or specifically through Article X) than is presently on offer. If that is the case, further progress may be possible, but is not assured. A less benign interpretation would suggest that such states might be using concerns over the confidentiality of information as a cover for preventing intrusive inspection systems that they object to for reasons of national security.

The key issue now is whether the international community can agree on a tight verification protocol for the BWC in the next two or three years or whether the BWC will be left in its present inadequate state for a decade or more. If the process of enhancing verification is delayed, the rapid developments in biotechnology are almost certain to be the cause of increasing distrust in some conflict-prone regions of the world. The process of proliferation could then become unstoppable.

At the end of 1993 it was reported that the UN First Committee had agreed on a resolution commending the VEREX work and asking the Secretary General to provide the necessary assistance to the depository states should a majority of the state parties ask for the convening of a special conference.[24] It was later agreed that a special conference would be held in 1994.

.9.

WESTERN POLICY OPTIONS

In mid-1993 Jane's Consultancy Services published a book entitled *Defence Exports: Current Concerns.*[1] Although this was not an official government document, the British Minister of Trade contributed a foreword which stated that its contents would help exporters to understand and support British non-proliferation policy and the control systems that were necessary to implement the policy.

The information in the book is presented country by country. For each, an attempt has been made to assess the status of its nuclear, chemical, biological and missile programmes as part of a general view of each country as a potential recipient of British goods. In Table 9.1A the summary of the estimate in regard to biological weapons is presented for each of the countries assessed. The central column gives the estimate provided by Jane's. It is clear, as many authors have commented previously, that it is very difficult to know exactly what such assessments actually mean.[2] What exactly, for instance, is the difference between a 'probable developer' and a 'potential possessor'? I have, nevertheless, in the right-hand column of the table, attempted a simplification of the data. This leads to the totals of known, probable and possible possessors of biological weapons given in Table 9.1B.

These totals, and the particular countries identified, are not dissimilar to those in the estimates we have referred to previously such as the recent study by the US Office of Technology Assessment.[3] The evidence from the last few chapters also suggests that if we focus solely on such reports we may miss the main point requiring attention. What is abundantly clear is that the biotechnology revolution is spreading and that, at best, we shall not have an effective verification system in place for some years yet. What we must therefore ask is not what the *present*

180

Table 9.1   A UK estimate of the proliferation of biological weapons[1]

A.	Country	Comment	Simplification
	Algeria	No ambition evident	Doubtful
	Belarus	Capable	Possible
	People's Republic of China	Potential possessor	Probable
	Cuba	Remote threat	Doubtful
	Egypt	Unlikely possessor	Possible
	India	Potential possessor	Probable
	Iran	Probable developer	Probable
	Iraq	No report	Known
	Israel	Potential possessor	Probable
	Jordan	Unlikely to seek capability	Doubtful
	Kazakhstan	Unlikely possessor	Doubtful
	Korea (North)	Potential possessor	Probable
	Korea (South)	Possibly capable	Possible
	Libya	Developer	Probable
	Pakistan	Potentially capable	Possible
	Russia	Possessor	Known
	South Africa	Potential possessor	Probable
	Syria	Potential possessor	Probable
	Taiwan	Potential developer	Possible
	Ukraine	Capable (?)/Unlikely possessor	Possible
B.	**Totals**		
	Known	2	
	Probable	8	
	Possible	6	
	Doubtful	4	

[1]Modified from reference 1.

threat is, but what the threat is likely to be in the years ahead. Only on that basis can we sensibly review the policy options available to Western (industrialised) states today.

Rather than considering just some repetition of what was found in Iraq – a relatively small effort to pursue traditional toxins and agents (botulinal toxins and anthrax) – it seems necessary also to take an alternative example of a large effort by a well-equipped country determined to pursue the research, development and production of new toxins, bioregulators and genetically modified agents. The obvious choice alongside Iraq is the acknowledged programme carried out after the signing of the BWC in the former Soviet Union. Between these two examples we can envisage the range of possible future threats.

Information on the Soviet offensive biological weapons programme has come into the public domain since the early 1980s. The 1984 edition of the US Department of Defense's *Soviet Military Power*,[4] for example, stated that:

> The Soviet Union has an active R&D programme to investigate and evaluate the utility of biological weapons and their impact on the combat environment. . . . There are at least seven biological warfare centers in the USSR that have the highest security and are under the strictest military control . . .

Such evidence continues to accumulate but that available to the general public still seemed far from complete at the end of 1993.

In its CBM submission in 1992 Russia stated that it had a national programme of research and development in the field of biological defence.[5] This was financed at a level of about 70 million roubles, and approximately two-thirds of the total was spent on contract work outside defence establishments. The programme was concerned with issues such as the research and development of anti-bacterial and anti-viral preparations for the prevention and cure of diseases caused by probable biological warfare agents, the diagnosis of such illnesses, the detection of the agents, and protective and disinfectant measures.

In the submission under measure F it was admitted that a past offensive programme of biological research and development ran from 1946 to March 1992. Moreover, it was clearly stated that:

> During the nineteen-fifties scientific-experimental bases were established in Sverdlovsk, Kirov and Zagorsk to conduct work on the pathogens of malignant anthrax, tularaemia, brucellosis, plague . . . typhus, Q-fever. . . . botulinal toxin . . .

It was also stated that during the 1960s testing of the production of such agents was carried out in Sverdlovsk and Zagorsk, and testing of such agents and delivery systems was carried out on Vozrozhdenie Island in the Aral Sea.

What happened after the entry into force of the BWC in the 1970s is less clear from the Russian document. It stated that:

> Owing to the USSR's backwardness in the fields of molecular biology, genetics and genetic engineering at the start of the nineteen-seventies, the Soviet government decided to accelerate the

development of these branches of biological science and to use its achievements in the civilian economy . . .

It was also admitted that some of the non-military facilities that were set up (for example, in the Biopreparat Complex) undertook work on dangerous micro-organisms as part of the biological defence programme. However, it was stated that no results of military significance were achieved.

Such reluctance to disclose exactly what had been done in a programme which clearly contravened the obligations undertaken in the BWC was clearly not acceptable in the West.[6] To add to previous suspicions, new information had been received from people involved in the programme (see below) and this appears to have substantially increased the concerns. A series of meetings and visits eventually led to a joint statement being agreed on by the three depository states in September 1992. This aimed to develop further co-operative measures in regard to BWC compliance.[7]

It is hardly surprising in such circumstances that some commentators have continued to suggest that the Soviet programme involved, for example, attempts to produce a deadly agent by putting genes for cobra venom into the genome of an influenza virus.[8] Although such suggestions may be viewed as extreme, it has to be understood that the sophisticated Russian work on viruses such as VEE, Marburg and Ebola noted in Chapter 7 (see Tables 7.4 and 7.5) was carried out at an institute clearly linked to the current defensive biological programme in the Russian CBM declaration.

The general point here concerns the possibility that the West could confront an opponent, not necessarily Russia, of course, equipped with biological weapons. This possibility is growing both quantitatively and qualitatively. The number of states with some form of biological weapons programme is increasing and the nature of these programmes is likely to change and thus produce a more diverse range of possible agents. What then should be the policy of Western industrialised states?

The argument that there would be no problem were the West not involved in interventions in the Third World does not hold. Certainly, Western interventions are not to be undertaken lightly, but in the future, a reformed United Nations could ask for the support of humanitarian interventions with greatly increased legitimacy. Taking part in such operations could then bring Western troops into situations where biological weapons might be used against them. Moreover, to argue that the West should not be concerned over the possible use of biological weapons by other parties, where it was not directly involved, at the least implies a somewhat cavalier attitude to the building of an international regime to prevent the development and use of these weapons. The question of how to formulate an effective policy for Western states therefore remains to be answered.

Western Policy Options

Before we explore the options available to states it is necessary to heed warnings about the dangers of only seeking responses at the state level.[9] Clearly, if a rigid 'realist' position is adopted, there is no room for consideration of what individuals or non-governmental organisations (for example, professional scientific associations) might be able to contribute. Yet given the powerful impact of the oath that physicians take, it is not impossible that the development of ethical codes for scientists will also have an impact in the future.[10] Certainly, as biologists and doctors gain ever-increasing powers to intervene in, for example, embryo manipulation, they are having to take part in debates on the ethics of what they are doing. The days of the 'neutral, distanced, objective' scientist could well be coming to an end in the life sciences. Given the importance of intelligence about what is being done in other countries, and the difficulties of obtaining that intelligence, the enhancement of ethical considerations in the training of scientists has to be considered as part of the process of generating an effective control system for biological weapons.

At the level of state policy, Graham Pearson, head of the UK Chemical and Biological Defence Establishment, has argued for a series of measures additional to the present arms control regime:[11]

> . . . The aim is to achieve a web of deterrence to complement the imperfections of arms control with other measures so that a potential cheater finds obstacles to every possible avenue to cheating . . .

The potential proliferator therefore:

> . . . is led to a judgement that the acquisition of chemical or biological weapons is expensive, of uncertain military value, and politically unacceptable.

Realistically, Pearson views the present arms control regime as inadequate and the acquisition of biological weapons as an option that will be taken seriously by the military in some countries. His suggested 'web of deterrence' is a mechanism designed to slow down the process of deterrence' is a mechanism designed to slow down the process of proliferation at a series of key points.

In addition to a more effective arms control regime, Pearson suggested enhanced monitoring and control of exports in order to make the acquisition of materials more expensive and difficult; development of more effective defensive and protective measures to make the use of biological weapons less attractive; and determined international responses to any development or use of biological weapons. We shall examine these options in some detail and also briefly consider the crucial question of intelligence.

Before dealing with the individual policies we should note two points about Pearson's suggested policies as a whole. He stressed that it is the *risk* of detection that deters, not the inevitability of detection. Thus the imposition of some finite risk is sufficient, rather than an effort to impose so much control that detection of non-compliance would be automatic. This is a vital point because of the need to convince states that the costs of control are acceptable. As Pearson noted:

> ... The aim is to strike the right balance so that the resources required to achieve the degrees of deterrence and detection are commensurate with the security gains achieved.

We shall return to the important issue of balancing costs and benefits in order to gain acceptance by states with different interests later.

Intelligence

Current accounts of the discovery of the Soviet offensive biological weapons programme necessarily stress the role of Western intelligence agencies and their allegations throughout the 1980s. Despite the difficulties involved, it will clearly be necessary to try to follow what is happening in some closed countries by means of satellite imagery and the co-ordinated tracking of exports and key scientists.

We need not add much more on this issue other than to say that the accounts of the revelation of the Soviet programme stressed the importance of individual scientists, at least in the later stages. A US Congressional report in 1993[12] referred particularly to:

> ... a Soviet biochemist, Vladimir Pasechnik, who defected in 1990 and revealed to British intelligence the existence of secret biological weapons research in the ostensibly civilian 'Biopreparat' pharmaceutical and medical complex in then Leningrad.

This once again points to the need for international emphasis on the importance of the responsibility of individual scientists.

Defensive Research

According to the same Congressional study[12] there has been relatively high investment in the US chemical and biological defence programme in recent years, and continuing emphasis on the need for appropriate training. Yet in the war against Iraq, 'the readiness of US armed forces to fight in a chemical and biological environment was unsatisfactory'. At one level this criticism could be taken to include the inability to detect and identify biological agents properly, the difficulties of using standard protective suits in very hot conditions, and so on. Some criticisms of the US defensive programme went far deeper than this and suggested a cause of the lack of preparedness.

In 1991 a General Accounting Office report was cited by US Senator John Glenn when stating that the chemical and biological defence programme had spent too much money researching potential agents which the intelligence agencies had not assessed as threats and too little on agents *known* to be threats. He suggested, as a particular example, that there had been a failure to produce an effective vaccine against anthrax.[13] More recently, in April 1993, the Washington-based Center for Public Integrity, whilst supporting a biological defence programme, argued further that this concentration on 'exotic diseases not recognised as threats' would lead potential adversaries to suspect US motives in carrying out its research.[14]

Such criticisms of the US defensive biological weapons programme and, by implication, other similar programmes in advanced industrial countries have been made since the US programme began to expand in the early 1980s. A general argument was put forward by King and Strauss to the effect that support for the programme was based on two fallacious assumptions: that the programme was designed to protect civilians, and that it was possible to differentiate between a defensive and an offensive biological weapons programme.[15] In regard to the first assumption, it seems clear that the programme is fundamentally designed to protect servicemen and also that there are huge obstacles to producing an appropriate defence for the civilian population; in regard to the second, numerous authors have argued that it is, in fact, extremely difficult for an unbiased observer to distinguish between offensive and defensive programmes, at least until the process of weaponisation is undertaken.

The development of vaccines against agents, King and Strauss argued, would generally require the growth of large amounts of the organism in order to provide the thousands of doses required. The development of a vaccine against an exotic agent would also require considerable research on the agent and then substantial testing of the efficacy of the vaccine against the agent. To go beyond the development of vaccines and attempt to provide a more comprehensive defence against the agent would require further research on its behaviour in the environment and on the adequacy of protective measures, things which would be even closer to what would happen in an offensive programme. Even the development of effective detector systems and methods of decontamination which are widely regarded as quintessentially defensive, they suggested, would be required in an offensive programme in order to be able to know when to move into an attacked area or to be able to decontaminate equipment. In short, they suggested that only the stated intent distinguished effectively between the two types of programme. Whether that stated intent is believed is another matter.

This argument was taken further in studies of specific pieces of research carried out in the defensive programme during the 1980s.[16] Piller and Yamamoto studied over 300 separate projects carried out between 1980 and 1986. They separated them into three categories and concentrated their detailed investigations on the 86 they thought had obvious potential for offensive applications. They noted that these projects appeared to involve efforts, among other things, to create novel agents, to prevent diagnosis and avoid the protective effects of vaccines, and to increase the production of toxins with enhanced effects. They suggested further that these would appear to be intelligent aims for an *offensive* programme and that the stated *defensive* aims of projects could not be easily proved to someone harbouring suspicions that an offensive programme was operative. Thus a stated aim of vaccine development could be interpreted as an aim actually concerned with defeating or compromising vaccines.

This point, they suggested, becomes particularly evident if projects being carried out for a programme under contracts at a number of institutions are considered together by an outside investigator. They pointed to one study of the production of monoclonal antibodies against surface antigens of *Bacillus anthracis* and to a second on the reactivity of certain chemicals called lectins to specific molecules on the surfaces of microbes. The second project showed that the anthrax agent was selectively bound by certain lectins. Could the bound lectins block the access of the monoclonal antibodies, they wondered? If they did, might that finding not have offensive applications in preventing diagnosis? Thus:

> ... even research that may seem harmless or even scientifically meritorious in isolation must be viewed warily considering the possibility that Pentagon planners are combining the fruits of labor from a broad array of work it supports.

These authors had other concerns that led them to be suspicious of the defensive explanation of the US programme. One point they made was that the ongoing changes in US Army doctrine in the 1980s may have led to a reconsideration of the value of biological weapons. As the new doctrine of AirLand Battle enhanced tactical considerations connected with large-scale manoeuvre warfare, a result could have been a perceived operational value for biological weapons.[17] The need for rapid advance rather than destructive capability could be seen to favour the use of such weapons. In addition, Piller and Yamamato suggested that the US Army was actually far less open about what it was doing than it suggested.

Not surprisingly, those who support a defensive biological research programme reacted strongly to these and other criticisms. Pearson in the UK, as we have seen, argued that defensive programmes within an overall web of deterrence served to reduce the range of materials that might be developed and used by an aggressive nation. A similar point was made by Thomas Dashiell, of the US Arms Control and Disarmament Agency, in a long article supporting the US programme[18]. He believed that the programme was designed to improve the protection available to US troops and to provide a highly visible deterrent. Dashiell also felt that the US programme had been well explained to the public during the debates of the 1980s. He thought the programme was largely concerned with medical matters and that both in-house and outside contract work was extensively published in the open literature. The programme covered detection equipment, physical protection and specifically medical matters. These were explained in some detail by staff of the US Army Medical Research Institute of Infectious Diseases at Fort Detrick in 1989.[19]

The emphasis of the programme was said to be on the protection of personnel prior to exposure, hence the development of vaccines for agents such as tularemia, Q-fever and Venezuelan equine encephalitis. Similarly, it was argued that this was the reason for attempts to develop anti-viral drugs and therapeutic agents against toxins. The threat of aerosol attack had to be kept at the top of the list in developing vaccines because this posed the severest threat, and a 'generic' approach was taken towards product development in order to try to be able to cover numerous agents with the same protective measure. Critics of the programme have argued, on the contrary, that given the vast range of natural or modifiable organisms that might be encountered, the approach is fundamentally flawed.

The staff at Fort Detrick, on the other hand, believed that it was quite possible to distinguish between defensive and offensive programmes:

> The only similarities between defensive and offensive research are that common laboratory techniques are used in each at the outset: but even at the outset, the experimental hypotheses are diametrically opposed. Thus, the data that are generated and compiled are different . . .

Moreover, they argued that there are many other differences:

> . . . An offensive program would include research programs on mass producing or storing large quantities of micro-organisms, on stabilisation in an aerosol, on improving virulence or persistence, or on methods for dissemination and weapon development . . .

In contrast, they stated:

> . . . defensive research comprises development of biological agent detection methods, treatment and protection, and decontamination capability . . .

They also believed that the US programme was a model of openness.

Nevertheless, suspicions about the US programme persist. The widely-read journal *Scientific American* carried an article in November 1993 in which suggestions were aired that deaths caused earlier that year by a hantavirus were, in fact, due to release of the virus after its testing by the Army.[20] Relying on the views of an unnamed source, it was suggested that missiles fired from Dugway Proving Ground had landed at Fort Wingate in New Mexico and contaminated it many years previously: the epidemic was then triggered by demolition work when the Fort was decommissioned. This explanation does appear somewhat far-fetched and, in fact, the US Army Institute of Infectious Diseases, having studied the Hantaan virus in detail during the 1980s and sequenced its genome in 1986, was able to provide significant assistance in dealing with the outbreak of disease in 1993.[21]

Similarly in the UK, there could be concerns about the fact that the Chemical and Biological Defence Establishment at Porton Down has been studying genetically modified organisms for nine years,[22] but, on the other hand, the Centre for Applied Microbiology and Research there clearly played an important role in supplying anthrax vaccine to the US Army during the Gulf War.[23]

Looked at dispassionately, there are clearly some areas of a defensive programme which will be retained under the control of the military. Intelligence data on other countries' programmes, specific vulnerabilities and the range of vaccines rapidly available are obvious examples where secrecy would be advisable. There does, however, seem to be some justice in the argument that the funding of biological research became unbalanced in the USA (and obviously in the USSR) during the 1980s and work that could have been under open civilian control passed to the military. The net result has been a great increase in knowledge – and suspicion – about possible new viral agents. Therefore the arguments advanced by some critics, that military funding should be restricted as far as possible in order that openness is believed in as well as operating and that, in military programmes, greater emphasis should be given to generally accepted threats and generally accepted, defensively-orientated projects, such as protective systems and new sensors, seem sensible.

In that regard, there certainly appear to be major opportunities to use new techniques in biotechnology to overcome the critical problem of the effective field detection of biological agents. There have also been some interesting suggestions, to which we shall return, for coping with the lack of rapid-response capabilities for vaccine production in the US by regularly using such facilities to produce free vaccines for the billions of people in the world vulnerable to vaccine-preventable diseases.[12] Imaginative, joint, co-operative ventures of this kind may be of great importance in securing world-wide co-operation in the development of a regime to control the proliferation of biological weapons.

Export Controls

The intention in this section is to outline the work of the Australia Group in relation to biological weapons and then to detail how the UK and the USA have proceeded to implement export controls. The debate over the relationship between export controls and verifiable arms control agreements is taken up in the next section in connection with the case of the ongoing implementation of the Chemical Weapons Convention. The general issue of the use of export controls in respect of dual-use technology is considered in the final chapter.

In June 1990 the UK Foreign and Commonwealth Office issued a pamphlet, *Biological and Toxin Weapons*.[24] This succinctly explained the nature of biological weapons and the dangers of proliferation. It then suggested that, as leading exponents of the new biotechnology, Western scientists and companies could be the targets of attempts to obtain this technology. A number of questions were listed to help in identifying potentially suspicious enquiries. An annex summarised agents and equipment suitable for the production of biological or toxin weapons (Table 9.2).

Table 9.2 Agents and equipment suitable for production of biological and toxin weapons[1]

---

1. Biological agents:
   (a) Pathological organisms
   (b) Certain toxins, organisms producing them, products containing them or plasmids coding for them.

2. Technology to develop or modify a strain of a BW agent.

3. Equipment for containment, especially equipment that facilitates work at containment levels 3 and 4.

4. Fermentation vessels of a capacity exceeding 20 litres.

5. Media for cultivating agents especially when ordered in unusually large quantities.

6. Equipment for harvesting agents, for example:
   – continuous flow centrifuges
   – extraction columns
   – filtration techniques.

7. Equipment for conserving and stockpiling agents, for example:
   – equipment for freeze-drying
   – equipment for micro-encapsulation.

8. Equipment for dissemination of biological agents, for example:
   – aerosol generators.

---

[1]Data from reference 24.

The items listed in this table will be familiar and make sense in view of what has been discussed in previous chapters (see, for example, the capabilities identified in Table 8.2). One point that needs further elaboration concerns containment levels (item 3 of the table list). Physical containment (P) or biosafety levels (BL) are defined at four levels (1–4) which increase in stringency the more dangerous the work. The standard system of categorising levels of containment has been described in great

Table 9.3   High hazard containment levels[1]

P1 Level	Standard microbiological practices Decontamination of infectious wastes
P2	Level 1 plus – laboratory coat – limited access – protective gloves – safety cabinets to contain 'high aerosol potential' procedures
P3	Level 2 plus – change room, street clothing removed, lab clothing put on, shower on exit – controlled access – partial containment equipment used for all manipulation of infectious material – filter-exhaust system – negative pressure differential maintained on laboratory suite
P4	Level 3 plus – double autoclaving of all wastes – Class III safety cabinets or positive-pressure personnel suits/chemical shower – two sets of HEPA filters in series or incineration of exhaust air

[1]From reference 26.

detail (for example, see reference[25]) and is summarised in Table 9.3 from a mid-1980s US official report.[26]

In early 1993 the UK issued a more detailed awareness-raising booklet, *Export Control Legislation*,[27] which briefly explained the UK's obligations under the BWC, and the 1974 Biological Weapons Act which translated them into the necessary national legislation. The nature of British export control legislation was then set out. The 1939 Import, Export and Customs Powers (Defence) Act allowed the Secretary of State for Trade and Industry to make orders by statutory instrument. In 1993 the instrument controlling exports was the Export of Goods (Control) Order, 1992 which listed items under specific control.

The order put controls on micro-organisms capable of causing harm, certain toxins, certain containment equipment and other specified dual-use equipment. A particular feature of the order was a 'catch-all' provision which clearly put the onus on the exporter to satisfy himself that dual-use goods were not going to be misused. A set of guidelines was supplied for items that did not require a specific licence but which the exporter might regard as likely to infringe the 'catch-all' provision. Vaccines were exempted from control, except in so far as the 'catch-all' provision might apply. Appendix 2 of this book sets out the annexes to the document which listed agents and toxins requiring licences, equipment similarly controlled and the warning guidelines. Other annexes specified countries requiring special procedures, listed members of the Australia Group and gave detailed information on the 'catch-all' clause. The document explained that its controls were part of a harmonised approach being taken by the like-minded countries of the Australia Group and that plant pathogens were likely to be similarly controlled when agreement was reached within the Group. The Group subsequently agreed on a list of plant pathogens at its June 1993 meeting.[28]

The Australia Group was set up in 1985, by 15 countries in the first instance, in an effort to prevent inadvertent supply of materials required for the manufacture of chemical weapons, as had clearly happened in the case of Iraq. Membership of the Group had grown to 25 (plus the European Commission) by June 1993. Export controls connected with biological weapons proliferation were formally incorporated into the Group's remit in 1992.

The United States had begun to increase control over biological materials earlier in the 1990s than other countries and took a leading role in the evolution of the Australia Group controls. A review of the US experience with such controls, in a report from the General Accounting Office, drew attention to some of the difficulties of implementation.[29]

The report suggested that exporters might lack knowledge of the controls, that there was room for improvement in the inter-agency mechanisms for handling licence applications and, in particular, that the Department of Defense had expertise that could be brought to bear more effectively. More fundamentally – though the view was taken that the Australia Group controls formed a good basis for a better international system – for as long as many countries remained outside the Group its effectiveness would be limited. A state interested in acquiring biological weapons could still obtain many of the necessary materials from outside the Australia Group. It was suggested that more members should be recruited or non-group members encouraged to adopt similar controls on their own exports.

With the best will in the world towards the agencies charged with implementing export controls in the Western world, their track record can hardly be said to inspire great confidence in their ability to stem proliferation. The number of staff at these agencies relative to the number of applications handled and the amounts of money involved for those breaking the law have ensured a sorry record, for example in regard to supplies to Iraq before the 1991 war. Thus while export controls have to be attempted as part of a general control mechanism at the present time, we should not expect too much from them. The potentially vexed question of what should happen to such export controls if an effective verification protocol for the BWC is agreed upon is best taken up in the next section where current experience with the CWC is reviewed.

Arms Control

From a Western perspective, arms control after the Cold War may perhaps be viewed in three categories: issues remaining from the Cold War period; certain regional issues; and global arms control. An example from the first category would be ensuring that the START agreements are implemented; de-escalating the arms build-up in the Middle East would be a prime concern in the second; and controlling the proliferation of weapons of mass destruction and missiles would be seen as vital in the third. From this perspective, the old difficult days of competitive arms control between East and West might be considered as largely replaced by a co-operative effort to reduce arms expenditures amongst former antagonists. Similarly, reducing regional arms build-ups and the proliferation of weapons of mass destruction could be viewed as part of the general de-escalation of tension following the end of hostilities engendered by the Cold War. Naturally there are complications caused by the re-surfacing of long-suppressed hostilities and difficulties in reorientating arms industries and their exports, but the general trend is positive.

With such an improved prospect, it may be difficult to understand some Third World concerns, but, as we have seen, such understanding will be necessary in order to make progress on the crucial issue of verification of the BWC. Fortunately, we can use recent experience with the Chemical Weapons Convention (CWC) to explore this issue further. The CWC, unlike the Nuclear Non-Proliferation Treaty (NPT), is genuinely non-discriminatory in its objective. *All* states are to destroy their chemical weapons and be subject to control; there are to be no special categories of possessor states. However, some Third World participants have argued that, nevertheless, in its implementation the CWC is giving every appearance of being discriminatory.

The issue was the cause of problems in the UN First Committee in late 1993. A resolution from the Netherlands, encouraging states to sign and ratify the CWC, was subject to an amendment from Iran suggesting, in effect, that export controls should be removed when the convention came into force. A consensus could not be agreed; indeed 36 co-sponsors of the Netherlands resolution said they would withdraw were the amendment to be accepted.[30] On the face of it, the position of Third World states in regard to export controls and membership of a verifiable convention would seem to be sound. Why should both be needed, particularly if controls might hinder technology transfer and economic development? Unfortunately, the problem is more complex than that.

The CWC involves the verified destruction of chemical weapons and production facilities and tight control of the dangerous (Schedule 1) chemicals, including the nerve gases and other chemical weapons agents. What is of interest to us is the attempt to control less dangerous (Schedule 2 and 3) chemicals which are dual-use because they have applications in peaceful productive processes as well as in chemical weapons production. It has to be understood that the world-wide chemical industry is very large and continues to expand in Third World countries. The volumes of production of some of the chemicals subject to CWC verification may be several hundred thousand tonnes.[31]

Ralf Trapp, an adviser to the German delegation to the CWC Preparatory Commission, has recently published an analysis for SIPRI of the trial inspections carried out by several parties in the final stages of the negotiation of the convention. He concentrated his analysis on inspections of chemical industry facilities and considered both routine and challenge inspections.[32]

For Schedule 2 chemicals, one of the verification aims under the CWC was to check non-diversion of these chemicals for prohibited purposes. Schedule 3 chemicals, which are regularly produced in large amounts, are subject to notification and inspection of facilities, though at much higher threshold levels. An option for routine inspection of Schedule 2 chemicals was to carry out an analysis of material balances at all facilities, as is done for nuclear materials in the Non-Proliferation Treaty inspections by the IAEA. The aim was to have the means of checking where all relevant material had been located. However, Trapp concluded that this was not possible to do at a national level, given the complexity of what was being attempted. He stated:

> The regime as it stands will not, as negotiators originally wanted, be able to detect deliberate diversions on the national level unless rather large quantities are involved. Neither will it make it possible to detect diversions of material by a facility or a trader via the market (i.e. proliferation attempts).

Thus he argued:

> MBV [material balances verification] can consequently not be applied as the basic concept for CWC verification as it is in nuclear safeguarding . . .

His conclusion was that the work of the CWC International Inspectorate would have to be backed up by national measures such as export controls.

Trapp did not argue that material balances were impossible to obtain at a facility level if sufficient time and effort were applied. The problems were rather with, for example, identification of the facilities to be included in the inspection system and diversion in the market after production. There are thus strong reasons for the retention of export controls by Western countries concerned about proliferation.

The difference between verification procedures required for the Non-Proliferation Treaty and the CWC and the complexity revealed by trial inspections should alert us to the need to take great care in the development of a verification protocol for the BWC. Any description of the biotechnology industry worldwide emphasises its difference from the mature chemical industry. In the world of biotechnology there are many more small entrepreneurial firms driving the high rate of technological change in the pursuit of new products and large profits.[33] Thus even the attempt to impose a minimal verification regime could produce difficult new problems. The US Pharmaceutical Manufacturers' Association was reported in the autumn of 1993 to have expressed 'grave concern' over the protection of confidential proprietary information in efforts to strengthen the BWC.[34]

Concerning this, we should note that Roberts, in a recent balanced attempt to assess Western policy options following consideration of a range of expert opinions on the future of biological weapons,[35] concluded that challenge inspections would be even more important under the BWC than under other regimes. Certainly, challenge inspections modelled on those of the CWC were important elements of the proposals from the Federation of American Scientists discussed in Chapter 8. While challenge inspections of industrial facilities may be infrequent under the CWC and while the original 'anytime-anywhere' concept has been moderated by the idea of managed access, inspectors have the right of access after 120 hours (or even less in some circumstances). Though it may be argued that this could, on the one hand, give sufficient time to clean up a small biological facility which was undertaking *illegal* activity, it could on the other hand, given the power of modern identification techniques, raise concerns for a company carrying out *legal* activities involving massive investment. They might fear for the safety of their commercial information if samples were taken, even inadvertently.

As we have noted previously in this chapter, there might be ways to make more co-operative activities an integral part of the BWC by the joint development and production of vaccines. We have also noted the need for work on vaccines for diseases such as measles and TB in Chapter 2. A specific need in the Americas at present is for a cholera vaccine.[36] Erhard Geissler and others have generalised the idea and suggested a 'vaccines for peace' programme. Identifying viruses such as dengue, Hantaan and Japanese encephalitis as dual-threat agents which cause high morbidity and/or mortality rates in developing countries and are recognised as emerging dangers in industrial countries, a joint effort administered by WHO is suggested.[37] This would help to banish suspicions engendered by the exclusive study of such viruses by the military and help to close the technology gap between rich and poor countries. Similarly, if a focused verification scheme were to evolve out of the VEREX meetings, it might be possible to transfer some Western expertise on control of the health and safety aspects of industrial biotechnology as part of the process.

The fact remains, nevertheless, that Article X has been honoured more in the breach than the observance,[35] and this is likely to remain predominantly the case. Western states see the BWC mainly as an arms control measure, not an economic development agreement. Yet this will surely continue to raise questions in some Third World states of whether they should become enthusiastic supporters of such a dominantly Western concern. That question will be addressed from a wider perspective in the next chapter.

Interventions

The Charter of the United Nations gives the Security Council very wide powers to deal with a threat to or breach of the peace, as the military and other action taken against Iraq very clearly demonstrated.[38] The Secretary General is also empowered to investigate the alleged use of biological weapons under General Assembly Resolution 42/37C of November 30, 1987 and Resolution 44/115B of 4 October 1989.[39] Moreover, very detailed studies have been made on how such official investigations can be carried out in order to best ensure an authoritative result.[40]

There is, nevertheless, a major problem in regard to hopes for united international action against states which are thought to be developing or using biological weapons. The action taken against Iraq since 1990 has to be seen as a quite exceptional case which is unlikely to be easily repeated. A different example – the lack of an international response to the use of chemical weapons by the same state, both against Iran and against its own citizens at Halabja – should always be kept in mind as the more likely response. It is simply very difficult to envisage circumstances arising, as they did when Iraq invaded Kuwait in 1990, in which the international community will be easily mobilised to take united action. The Iraqi attack on Kuwait, after all, posed a direct threat to oil supplies – the lifeblood of Western industrial economies.

In order to envisage strong international responses to the many potential examples of biological weapons proliferation in the future, a much stronger and more widely-recognised norm of non-development and non-use must be present in the international community and amongst the general public. This demands a major change from the present situation in which there is widespread ignorance of the whole subject.

Terrorism

While there are indications that terrorist groups have considered the use of biological and toxin weapons seriously, there have as yet been no attempts to use such means against Western societies. Given the ease with which, say, anthrax or botulinal toxin could be obtained and the simplicity of using such material in an attack against unprotected citizens, it cannot be assumed that terrorists will continue to eschew biological weapons in the future.[41]

Examples of hypothetical attacks put forward in the open literature include a ship attacking New York with aerosolized anthrax and perhaps causing 400,000 deaths, and the deliberate contamination of milk supplies with botulinal toxin at a commercial processing plant. Moreover, though it is possible to think of policy responses which would help to alleviate the danger, for instance organisations analagous to the Nuclear Emergency Search Teams which have dealt successfully with attempts to use the alleged possession of nuclear weapons for extortion, it would be very difficult to prevent a determined terrorist group from using biological weapons effectively.

On the other hand, terrorism is concerned with influencing policy through public display.[42] Terrorists are unlikely to use means that will effectively lose them support from sympathisers and potential sympathisers. Thus the more deep and widespread is the abhorrence of this form of weapon, the less likely that terrorists will use it. Again, there seems every reason to maintain and enhance the widely acknowledged norm which considers the use of biological weapons to be an unacceptable means of waging warfare.

The extent to which that idea, which runs through much of this consideration of policy options for Western states, survives and flourishes depends largely on the type of international society we manage to create in the transitional period following the long east-west Cold War. It is to such wider issues that we now turn.

. 10 .

FUTURE PROSPECTS:
PROLIFERATION OR CONTROL?

Paul DeForest, writing in the journal *Politics and the Life Sciences* in 1990, suggested the relationship between weapons proliferation and arms control involved strategy, law and technology.[1] These factors have generally, under the control of national leaders who believed that military strength was the primary requirement for serving national interests, led to an escalating arms race (Table 10.1).

Table 10.1 Weapons proliferation versus arms control[1]

1. *Strategy*	–	dominance of national interest over international co-operation in an anarchic global system
2. *Law*	–	legitimacy of war as a policy with ineffective constraints
3. *Technology*	–	dynamic weapons system innovation and improvement fuelled by defence research and development

[1]Data from reference 1

Throughout most of the Cold War period horizontal and vertical proliferation predominated over arms control for the key nuclear weapons of mass destruction but for biological weapons, DeForest suggested, the factors have actually operated in favour of control (Table 10.2).

Now it might be objected, on the basis of what we have discussed, that effective strategies for biological weapons use *were developed*, and that they were dismissed by the West only because nuclear weapons were available. Thus, lacking nuclear weapons, biological weapons could be perceived as militarily useful. Nevertheless, we can accept DeForest's basic formulation for the period before the biotechnology

Table 10.2   The predominance of biological arms control in the cold war period[1]

1. Strategies for biological warfare not satisfactorily formulated
2. Customary international law severely restrained use of biological weapons
3. Advances in technology insufficient to overcome tactical and moral reasons for not using such weapons

[1]Data from reference 1.

revolution began in the 1970s: factors for control tended to outweigh factors for proliferation.

One of the main reasons for undertaking the present study was the mounting evidence that in the minds of many people in official positions the balance has now changed. Advances in technology are seen to be favouring the proliferation of biological weapons to a much greater extent than before 1970. Given the information available in the public domain that we have been able to review, this viewpoint would appear to be reasonable. It follows that in order to prevent proliferation from taking place a strengthening of legal restraints will be required.

In this final chapter we shall discuss how greater control might be exerted in this almost classic example of dual-use (civilian and military) technology. In order to change the law it may also be necessary to modify concepts of individual states' interests and co-operative possibilities. We shall therefore end the chapter by discussing how co-operation might be further enhanced – if not directly in relation to the BWC then at least in relation to biotechnology as a whole.

Routes to a Future

It is widely accepted that the bipolar system of states that characterised the post-Second World War era has been destroyed and that we are now in a transitional period. We know something of how this transitional phase of relationships will be affected by technological developments (see Chapter 5), but we do not know what the resulting system will look like. Writers on biological weapons refer to the present time as a 'window of opportunity'.[2] The literature on the management of conflict can help us to see why, and to see what routes we may take into the future.

Geoffrey Vickers argued that we use the word 'conflict' in two different senses: both to describe situations in which parties have different aims, and to describe the hostilities that break out when such differences

201

cannot be resolved.[3] Given the constant change affecting the world, conflicts in the first sense are inevitable. Technology in regard to the life sciences, for example, is constantly presenting us with difficult new issues over which we may genuinely and deeply disagree: such as the extent to which human embryos should be used for research. The important point to make is that conflicts in the first sense need not necessarily degenerate into conflicts in the second sense.

The bonds of membership, the feelings of trust which arise from believing that we are part of the same social system are, according to Vickers, crucial resources for the resolution of conflicts. On the other hand, when hostilities do break out it is these very bonds and feelings of trust, and therefore the resources that we shall need to resolve other (inevitable) disputes in the future, that are destroyed.

Translating that thinking back to the question of the development of a stronger regime for the control of biological weapons, we can see how crucial the present window of opportunity actually is. So far, in the post-Second World War period, the general abhorrence of biological weapons has persisted despite the increasing pressures generated by new technology. If a stronger control system can be put in place that repugnance may, one hopes, continue and be strengthened. On the other hand, should the proliferation of offensive biological weapons programmes become acceptable in one, two, three or four more countries then will the near-neighbours of the proliferators feel secure enough not to respond in kind? And if a response is made with new offensive programmes by two, three, four or five more states, *who* will feel secure?

So we can see from this framework of understanding that the opportunity to strengthen the BWC has to be taken as quickly as possible. If compliance and trust are built up, more can be developed, but if mistrust sets in, a spiral of action and reaction is the more likely result. But is that all we are discussing when we talk of a window of opportunity? It will be recalled that before the negotiation of the BWC in the early 1970s it had been hoped that biological and chemical weapons control would be dealt with together. Only now, after two more decades, is the promise of a Chemical Weapons Convention to be achieved. In one sense then, the window of opportunity now available is to bring the BWC in line with the new CWC as an effective, modern, verifiable, international agreement.

To stop at that point, however, would be to allow ourselves to be blinkered by the past 30 years of fragmentary arms control since the idea of General and Complete Disarmament (GCD) was abandoned. For the last 30 years our efforts at arms control have been predominantly piecemeal and ineffective efforts to prevent the dramatic vertical and horizontal proliferation of ever more advanced weaponry. The limited aims of arms control in the long period of East/West dispute were perhaps all that was possible. To *manage* the most dangerous and excessive aspects of arms escalation may have been the only realistic goal. However, it has left us with a mountain of weaponry and, despite the cuts in defence budgets, an extensive infrastructure devoted to the continued development of new forms of armament. Despite the immediate successes at the end of the Cold War, it is clear that the aims and methods of arms control as practised over the last three decades are inadequate for dealing with our problems as we move into the next century.

It is important to understand that General and Complete Disarmament was considered a realistic objective in the decades following the Second World War. In 1961 the Soviet Union and the United States agreed a joint statement of principles on further negotiations which read, in part:[4]

1. The goal of negotiations is to achieve agreement on a programme which will ensure:
(a) that disarmament is general and complete and war is no longer an instrument for settling international problems . . .

In regard to weapons of mass destruction the statement read:

3. . . . The programme for general and complete disarmament shall contain the necessary provisions . . . for:
(b) the elimination of all stockpiles of nuclear, chemical, bactcriolog-ical and other weapons of mass destruction, and the cessation of the production of such weapons.

In 1962 both superpowers produced detailed draft treaties designed to achieve such objectives. The elimination of chemical and biological weapons was to be accomplished in the second stage of the Soviet plan under Article 23 of the draft treaty. Elimination of these weapons would also have begun in the second stage of the US plan under clause II/A/5 of the draft outline. In the conditions of mistrust which prevailed at that time agreement proved impossible to achieve and fragmentary arms control set in. This process left us where we are today, with an unverifiable BWC and a modern CWC waiting to come into force.

It is vital to grasp that the evolution of ideas, particularly about the use of military force in a stable world order, has brought us back again to the question of achieving General and Complete Disarmament. Biological disarmament is seen as having a leading role to play in that process. A group of experts set out this idea in a recent report for the Secretary General of the United Nations.[5]

After careful consideration of the defensive security concepts and policies which have been put forward in recent years, the experts introduced the idea of 'defensive security' (Table 10.3) which they defined as:

> . . . a condition of peace and security attained step-by-step and sustained through effective and concrete measures in the political and military fields . . .

The report stressed that defensive security goes well beyond ideas such as 'non-offensive defence' and 'reasonable sufficiency' (which arose immediately after the end of the Cold War) in encompassing both military and political elements aimed at ensuring that states' behaviour conforms to the Charter of the United Nations and that their military forces do not pose a threat to others.

Table 10.3 Conditions of defensive security[1]

1. Friendly relations among states are established and maintained;
2. Disputes are settled in a peaceful and equitable manner and the resort to force is consequently excluded;
3. The capacity for launching a surprise attack and for initiating large-scale offensive action is eliminated through verifiable arms control and disarmament, confidence- and security-building measures and a restructuring of armed forces towards a defensive direction.

[1]Data from reference 5.

Regarding weapons of mass destruction it was suggested that, while not necessarily part of an offensive policy, such weapons must pose a severe threat to a general defensive orientation amongst states. It was argued further that there is widespread agreement within the international community on this point and certainly, from the data we have reviewed in Chapter 1, it is clear that biological weapons as well as nuclear weapons could be used in a massive, pre-emptive, first-strike operation. The report concluded:

> . . . the international community is in agreement on the urgency of eliminating chemical and biological weapons. As such, their possession and use is inconsistent with the concept of 'defensive security'.

Given this view of weapons of mass destruction, the report logically concluded that agreed reductions in such weaponry contributed directly to defensive security and that eventually all weapons of mass destruction would have to be eliminated.

The report suggested that it will be easier to eliminate some categories of weapon – such as biological weapons which have already been banned – than others. Thus:

> A strengthened bacteriological (biological) and toxin weapons convention and the rapid conclusion of a chemical weapons convention (both of which now seem to be within reach) represent crucial steps towards the promotion of 'defensive security'.

Our window of opportunity in this field is thus much greater than just the chance to eliminate biological weapons of mass destruction. By successfully doing this – for which there is every reason in its own right – we may also be contributing a crucial element in the building of a more peaceful world in the next century.

That progress *can* be made in ridding the world of weapons of mass destruction is demonstrated by the growing rejection of such means of military force in the countries of Latin America. The Mendoza Declaration by Argentina, Brazil and Chile was complemented in December 1991 by the declaration of five Andean countries made at Cartagena de Indias, Colombia. In the Cartagena declaration the Heads of State proclaimed:[6]

> ... the commitment of their Governments to renounce the possession, production, development, use, testing and transfer of all weapons of mass destruction, whether nuclear, bacteriological (biological), toxin or chemical weapons, and to refrain from storing, acquiring or holding such categories of weapons, in any circumstances.

Yet as we have seen, further progress on this front will require co-operation between the industrialised countries of the North and the developing countries of the South.

In any reasonably unbiased view, export controls on dual-use technology must be seen as having a discriminatory aspect towards the South.[7] Despite the fact that the pivotal Nuclear Non-Proliferation Treaty has a co-operative aspect built into it through the operations of the IAEA to promote civil nuclear energy usage, it seems very unlikely that Article X of the BWC will be activated in any way which is satisfactory to many in the South. Such discrimination is deeply resented. As the former director of the Institute for Defence Studies and Analyses in Delhi put it, in *The Washington Quarterly*:[8]

... Above all, export controls divide the world into North and South, project a racist bias, and have proved to be inefficient instruments for pursuing global nonproliferation objectives.

In practical terms, he added:

... With regard to the chemical weapons treaty, although India is an enthusiastic supporter of the treaty, it opposes the perpetuation of the white nations' club (the Australia Group) after the treaty comes into operation. As we approach the end of the 20th century this apartheid on international security management appears anomalous and counterproductive.

In order to avoid an impasse, we need to ask whether the meagre means of direct co-operation within the BWC can be supplemented by much wider co-operation over the whole range of modern biotechnology. If really effective help were given to developing countries in crucial aspects of biotechnology, which would help with their many problems of peaceful development, would it not be a much simpler matter to agree on effective control of potential proliferation?

Co-operation in Biotechnology

The link between disarmament and development has been a constant theme in writings on arms control. The point was reinforced by the Secretary General of the United Nations in his detailed discussion document, *New Dimensions of Arms Regulation and Disarmament in the Post-Cold War Era*. Reporting in October 1992, Boutros Boutros-Ghali[9] stated that there was a real opportunity to initiate a process of global disarmament, but disarmament had to be integrated with other efforts in order to achieve success:

... Disarmament, the structuring of a new system of international relations and improving economic conditions should be regarded as complementary measures and as far as possible should be implemented in a co-ordinated manner ...

The link between disarmament and the kind of world society we construct was made with great clarity by Maurice Bertrand, a former UN expert, when he discussed 'The difficult transformation from "arms control" to a "world security system"' in 1991.[10]

Bertrand stressed that security problems have always been linked to institutional and ideological questions, and it is therefore no surprise to find that the present changes, following the end of the Cold War, are having repercussions across all three issues. He indicated some of the areas where new ideas will be required (Table 10.4). He argued that if the world system adopts certain forms of society it will not be possible to have certain types of institutional and arms control regimes. Thus if we in the West continue to give every appearance of believing that our security finally rests on our ability to use force for our own ends, we can hardly expect major states in the South necessarily to go along with arms control restrictions on their weapon systems which we consider desirable.

Table 10.4 Linked problems of arms control and societal organisation[1]

---

1. The minimum level of armaments.

2. The kinds of verification and control to fit with the level of armaments.

3. The types of threat that will have to be faced in the future and the means that will be used to deal with these threats.

4. The kinds of institutional arrangements and regimes which will best allow a new system of international security to be organised.

5. The type of society which would fit with these institutions and regimes.

---

[1]Data from reference 10.

The choices, in Bertrand's view, may boil down to two:

> The first will attempt to preserve the main aspects of the structures and the trends in development of the existing military apparatus . . .

It will attempt to continue a qualitative arms race (for example, in the new intelligent weapons systems described in Chapter 5) even if concessions are made on quantity, and it will attempt to limit the impact of arms regulation and disarmament. The second choice described by Bertrand has many similarities to the ideas of defensive security that we have just discussed in this chapter. Because of the links that he saw in the process of change he argued that:

> . . . The question whether the North will be capable of getting the countries of the South to adopt an arms control regime covering all kinds of weapons amounts in the last resort to asking whether the North is capable of producing a homogeneous world society . . .

In short, is the North capable of transferring to the South its ability to sustain a higher standard of living? Bertrand fears the answer may be

'No', but suggested that a race is on between our ability to change our attitudes and actions and the catastrophic consequences that could result from a failure to reach an accommodation with the South.

How such an accommodation may be facilitated is receiving intense consideration in the science and technology community world-wide. A conference held by the Forecasting and Assessment in Science and Technology (FAST) programme of the European Community in mid-1993 reviewed the results of major studies carried out in Europe, Canada, India, Japan and the United States.[11] The European study[12] was based on numerous reports prepared for the FAST programme.

The main conclusion of the study was that it was necessary to reorientate science and technology to meet the basic needs of the eight billion people who will live on the planet in 2020. Clearly, the basic needs which are not being met are those of the 80 per cent of people who live outside the industrialised North. The main possible future scenarios were identified and an analysis was made of how science and technology might be deployed to achieve the most desirable of these possible futures. It is apparent that the obstacles to success lie both with the international financial and economic system[13] and the maldistribution of scientific and technological resources. Both will require major reorientation.

In regard to biotechnology, it was suggested that it had enormous potential to improve the quality of life and to contribute to the solution of global problems and economic inequalities. However, it was argued that biotechnology is highly research-intensive and dependent on research funds for the life sciences. At present, almost the whole of such funding is located in the developed countries and the pattern of private investment looks set to consolidate and enhance that trend. There is little interest among commercial companies for investing in biotechnology in less-developed countries. Worse still, some of the research ongoing in the rich world could lead to the development of substitutes for crops on which less-developed countries traditionally rely. This could then cause them severe economic problems through loss of export earnings.

Mechanisms were therefore considered to be necessary to help such countries participate in the benefits of biotechnology. Suggestions included an International Technology Agency which could help to strengthen Third World scientific and technological resources by subsidising access to technology, by operating data banks, and by assisting them with the making of informed choices.[11]

The Canadian contribution was rather different from the other national papers, being a reflection on over 20 years of experience at their International Development Research Center (IDRC) rather than an analysis of potential futures.[14] Written by Geoffrey Oldham, who had been involved in the design of the centre before heading the policy programme and then directing the widely-known and well-respected Science Policy Research Unit at the University of Sussex, the paper supported public as well as private initiatives in developing science in Third World countries and suggested that the idea of an International Technology Transfer Agency was timely.

On the basis of IDRC's experience, Oldham concluded that developing countries do have the capacity to accept external research funding and, though many of their problems cannot be solved by such means, investment in these indigenous scientific and technological capabilities can make a significant difference to economic and social well-being. He also stressed the need for long-term funding and cited as a successful example IDRC's 17-year support for Dr Gursoran Talwar of the National Institute of Immunology in New Delhi. In Oldham's view, Talwar's development of an anti-pregnancy vaccine was 'potentially the most significant' of all the research supported. This affordable vaccine, with reversible action, is effective for a year, does not interfere with a woman's menstrual cycle, and is currently being tested in five major countries from both the developed and the developing world.

Given that over 23 years IDRC has spent more than 1.5 billion Canadian dollars, supported work in more than 100 countries, and supported 1,000 institutions and 20,000 researchers mainly in developing countries, its experience cannot be discounted. Effective co-operation is possible in building research capabilities in developing countries. So what specifically can be done in regard to co-operation in biotechnology?

As we have seen, there are major opportunities for co-operation between the North and the South in medicine. The development of vaccines is an urgent priority that can be addressed jointly. However, there are also potential dangers for the Third World because their economies may suffer severe adverse effects as a result of developments in biotechnology in the industrialised countries. An example of such an adverse impact was the use of the enzymatic biotransformation of starch into high-fructose corn syrup, which led to a dramatic decline in the international trade in sugar after 1975.[15]

Yet the major threat confronting Third World countries is surely the shortfall in food production. The benefits of the green revolution of the 1960s have been pushed to their limits, and it will clearly be some years before population growth levels off. The short-term solution is therefore to find means of producing more food and, fortunately, it is here that biotechnology can have a significant impact in the Third World if resources are made available.[16] With something in the order of 20–40 per cent of the world's agricultural production still being lost due to pests, weeds and diseases, and with increasing insect resistance to pesticides, there is clearly much that can be done with new techniques. The introduction of genes to increase the resistance of crops to pests and diseases could increase food production significantly. Similarly, the genetic alteration of crops to increase productivity in marginal lands could have major impacts in areas untouched by the green revolution (which was confined to good-quality land). Finally, it should be possible to use new techniques to improve some food and cash crops difficult to change by standard plant-breeding methods.

One expert study of farming in the Third World suggested that although early progress would be largely confined to plants of interest in the industrial world such as tobacco and tomato, biotechnology would increasingly open up other avenues:[17]

> ... Substantial progress may be expected for potato, rapeseed and rice in the short term, for bananas and plantains, cassava and coffee in the medium term, and for coconut, oilpalm and wheat in the long term.

But as the study reiterates, all of this is greatly dependent on help from the North.

Conclusion

We began this book with the question 'Will there be biological warfare in the 21st century?' The answer to that question, at one level, is almost certainly 'Yes'. It was reported that in 1991 the US market in new biotechnology products was £1.1 billion and that this was expected to reach £28 billion by 2000 AD.[15] This represented 'a growth rate of nearly 40 per cent per annum compound'. With such commercial opportunities available the technology is certain to develop much further and it will then spread. What would require the skills of a Nobel Prize winner in one decade will become common laboratory practice in the next. So the chances of biological weapons being used somewhere in the world during the next century – in overt warfare, terrorism, or economic sabotage – must be rated rather high. It would be quite extraordinary if a major new development in science was *not* applied in warfare, and there is probably little that we can do to prevent it at this level.

At another and much more important level, however, the answer is different and more hopeful. The crucial question is whether the present norm of international behaviour based on a general abhorrence of this terrible form of weaponry is to be reinforced or destroyed. While it is perfectly possible that the current norm and the regime of control centred on the 1925 Geneva Protocol and the BWC will be destroyed, and that large-scale preparation, and use, of biological weapons will occur in the next century, it is far from inevitable. The breakdown of the international norm of rejection of these weapons will only happen if we allow it to happen. It really does come down to the military, politicians and, above all, the general public keeping up the pressure for civilised behaviour. As we have seen, there are practical means available to reinforce the regime of control in regard to biological weapons. It is our joint responsibility to ensure that these are implemented successfully.

Yet it has to be stressed that we in the rich industrialised world cannot expect to achieve long-term success without the help of the vast majority of people who live in poorer parts of the world. The habits of seeking to achieve what we want by domination and force are deeply ingrained in our ways of thought[17], but these habits will have to change. A much more co-operative attitude to development will be required if we wish to rid ourselves of the threat of warfare, including our particular concern here – biological warfare.

NOTES

Preface

1 Dando, M. R. (1994), 'Biological weapons: curbing the test tube danger', *New Zealand International Review*, **XIX**(1), pp. 10–15.

Chapter 1: The Spectre of Biological Warfare Returns

1 Rogers, P. and Dando, M. R. (1992), *A Violent Peace: Global Security after the Cold War*, Brassey's, London.
2 Pearson, G. S. (1992), 'Talking Point: Preventing biological warfare', *New Scientist*, 21 March, p. 8.
3 Roos, J. G. (1992), 'Chem-Bio Defence Agency will tackle "last major threat to a deployed force"', *Armed Forces Journal International*, December, p. 10.
4 President Clinton (1993), *Address to UN General Assembly* (Clinton warns of perils ahead despite Cold War's end), Official Text, United States Information Service, London, 28 September.
5 *Arms Control Reporter* (1992), 'Update on Russian/USSR BW development', 701.B. 88–90, February–April.
6 Harris, E. D. (1987), 'Sverdlovsk and yellow rain: two cases of Soviet noncompliance?'. *International Security*, **11**,(4), pp. 41–95.
7 Perry Robinson, J., *et al.* (1990), 'Yellow rain in southeast Asia: the story collapses', In: Wright, S. (ed.) *Preventing a Biological Arms Race*. MIT Press, Cambridge, Mass.
8 Abramova, R. A., *et al.* (1993), 'Pathology of inhalation anthrax in 42 cases from the Sverdlovsk outbreak of 1979', *Proc. Natl. Acad. Sci.* (USA), **90**, pp. 2291–94.

212

9 Department of External Affairs and International Trade (1991), *Novel Toxins and Bioregulators,* Ottawa, Canada.

10 Office of Technology Assessment (1993), *Proliferation of Weapons of Mass Destruction: Assessing the Risks*, OTA-ISC-559, Washington, DC.

11 SIPRI (1973), *CB Weapons Today*, Almqvist & Wiksell, Stockholm.

12 SIPRI (1971), *The Prevention of CBW*, Almqvist & Wiksell, Stockholm.

13 United Nations (1969), *Chemical and Bacteriological (Biological) Weapons and the Effects of Their Possible Use*, E.69.1.24, New York.

14 Fetter, S. (1991), 'Ballistic missiles and weapons of mass destruction: What is the threat? What should be done?', *International Security*, **16**(1), pp. 5–42.

15 Grim, B. S. and Rose, W. H. (1983), *Biological Vulnerability Assessment: The US East Coast*, DPG-S-84-503, US Army, Dugway Proving Ground, Utah.

16 Proceedings of the Conference on Airborne Infection (1961), *Bacteriol. Rev.*, **25**, pp. 173–382.

17 Dowling, H. F. (1966), 'Airborne infections: the past and the future', *Bacteriol. Rev.*, **30**, pp. 485–87.

18 Perry Robinson, J. (1991), 'Adherence to the 1972 Biological Weapons Convention', Paper presented at the Quaker Residential Conference, 'Strengthening the Biological Weapons Convention', Chateau de Bossey, Switzerland, 31 May–2 June.

19 Meselson, M. (1989), Prepared Statement, Hearings on *Global Spread of Chemical and Biological Weapons*, before the Committee on Governmental Affairs and its Permanent Subcommittee on Investigations. US Senate, Washington, DC, 17 May.

20 See, for example, *Arms Control Reporter* 701.E.5 (2.93); 701.E.5 (3.91); 701.E.2 (9.89); 701.E.1 (5.86).

21 Carter, G. B. (1992), 'Biological warfare and biological defence in the United Kingdom 1940–79', *Royal United Services Institute Journal*, December, pp. 67–74.

22 Rose, Commander S. (1989), 'The coming explosion of silent weapons', *Naval War College Review*, **XLII**(3), pp. 6–30.

23 Zilinskas, R. A. (1990), 'Biological warfare and the Third World', *Politics and the Life Sciences*, **9**(1), pp. 59–76.

24 Hereim, A. T. (1975), *Covert Biological Weapons Literature Review*, Final Report, DPG 75–294. US Army, Dugway Proving Ground, Utah.

25 Stricklett, R. D. (1986), *Current Factors Affecting the Possible Use of Biological Weapons by Terrorists*, Technical Note, DPG-TA-86-03, US Army, Dugway Proving Ground, Utah.

Chapter 2: Potential Agents for Biological Weapons

1 Rennie, J. (1992), 'Living together: trends in parasitology', *Scientific American*, January, pp. 105–13; Ewald, P. W. (1993), 'The evolution of virulence', *Scientific American*, April, pp. 56–62.

2 Pelczar, M. J., Chan, E. C. S. and Krieg, N. R. (1993), *Microbiology: Concepts and Applications*, McGraw–Hill, New York.

3 Nossal, J. V. (1993), 'Life, death and the immune system', *Scientific American*, September, pp. 21–30.

4 For a straightforward account which has provided a basic source for the summaries presented here, see Kiple, K. F. (1993) (ed.), *The Cambridge History of Human Disease*, Cambridge University Press, Cambridge.

5 McNeill, W. H. (1976), *Plagues and Peoples*, Blackwell, Oxford.

6 Mitchison, A. (1993), 'Will we survive?', *Scientific American*, September, pp. 102–8.

7 Anderson, R. M. and May, R. M. (1991), *Infectious Diseases of Humans: Dynamics and Control*, Oxford University Press, Oxford.

8 Mercer, A. (1992), *Disease, Mortality and Population in Transition*, Leicester University Press, for Pinter Publications, London.

9 Prescott, L. M., Harley, J. P., and Klein, D. A. (1990), *Microbiology*, W. C. Brown, Indiana.

10 Weiss, R. (1992), 'Measles battle loses potent weapon', *Science*, **258**, pp. 546–47.

11 Cohen, M. L. (1992), 'Epidemiology of drug resistance: implications for a post-antimicrobial era', *Science*, **257**, pp. 1050–55.

12 Vicary, Colonel, A. G. and Wilson, Wing Commander, J. (1981), 'Nuclear, biological and chemical defence', *Royal United Services Institute Journal*, **126**, pp. 7–12.

13 United Nations (1969), *Chemical and Bacteriological (Biological) Weapons and the Effects of Their Possible Use*, (Annex IV), E.69.1.24, New York.

14 SIPRI (1973), *CB Weapons Today*, Almqvist and Wiksell, Stockholm.

15 Parry, D. (1990), *Plant Pathology in Agriculture*, Cambridge University Press, Cambridge.

16 Agrios, G. N. (1978), *Plant Pathology*, Academic Press, New York.
17 Singh, U. S., *et al.* (1992), *Plant Diseases of International Importance*, Volume 1: *Diseases of Cereals and Pulses*, Prentice Hall, New Jersey.
18 Geering, W. A. and Forman, A. J. (1987), *Animal Health in Australia*, Volume 9: *Exotic Diseases*, Australian Government Publishing Service, Canberra.
19 See, for examples of recent studies, Stephen, J. and Pietrowski, R. A. (1986), *Bacterial Toxins* (2nd edn.), Van Nostrand Reinhold, UK.

Chapter 3: Offensive Biological Weapons Programmes Before1969

1 *Report from the United Kingdom of Great Britain and Northern Ireland* (1992), DDA/4-92/BW111 [pp. 213–51], Office of Disarmament Affairs, United Nations, New York.
2 *Report from the United States of America* (1992), DDA/4-92/BW111 [pp. 252–428], Office of Disarmament Affairs, United Nations, New York.
3 Carter, G. B. (1992), 'Biological warfare and biological defence in the United Kingdom 1940–1979', *Royal United Services Institute Journal*, December, pp. 67–74.
4 Hugh–Jones, M. (1992), 'Wickham Steed and German biological warfare research', *Intelligence and National Security*, 7(4), pp. 379–402.
5 Carter, G. B. (1991), 'The Microbiological Research Establishment and its precursors at Porton Down: 1940–1979', *ASA Newsletter* (Applied Science and Analysis, Inc.), 11 December, pp. 91–6.
6 United States Army Chemical Corps Historical Office (1960), *Summary of Major Events and Problems, Fiscal Year 1959*, Army Chemical Center, Maryland.
7 Murphy, S., Hay, A. and Rose, S. (1986), *No Fire No Thunder: The Threat of Chemical and Biological Weapons*, Pluto Press, London.
8 Hersh, S. M. (1968), *Chemical and Biological Warfare: America's Hidden Arsenal*. MacGibbon & Kee, London.
9 Clarke, R. (1968), *We All Fall Down: The Prospects of Biological and Chemical Warfare*, Penguin Books, London.
10 Bernstein, B. (1990), 'Origins of the biological warfare program', In Wright, S. (ed.) *Preventing a Biological Arms Race*, MIT Press, Cambridge, Mass.
11 Wright, S. (1990), 'Evolution of biological warfare policy,

1945–1990'. In Wright, S. (ed.), *Preventing a Biological Arms Race*, MIT Press, Cambridge, Mass.

12 Williams, P. and Wallace, D. (1989), *Unit 731: The Japanese Army's Secret of Secrets*, Hodder & Stoughton, London.

13 United States (1949), *Report of the Secretary of Defense's Ad Hoc Committee on Biological Warfare*, 11 July, JCS, 2C934.

14 Perry Robinson, J. (1991), 'Adherence to the 1972 Biological Weapons Convention', Paper presented at the Quaker Residential Conference, 'Strengthening the Biological Weapons Convention', Chateau de Bossey, Switzerland, 31 May–2 June.

15 Rose, W. H. (1981), *An Evaluation of Entomological Warfare as a Potential Danger to the United States and European Nato Nations*, DPG 81–41, US Army, Dugway Proving Ground, Utah.

16 SIPRI (1973), *CB Weapons Today*, Almqvist & Wiksell, Stockholm.

17 US Army (1973), *Joint CB Technical Data Source Book VIII: Bacterial Diseases, Part Two: Anthrax*, DTC-TR-73-517, Fort Douglas, Utah.

18 US Army (1973), *Joint CB Technical Data Source Book VI: Toxin Agents, Part Two: Agent PG*, DTC-TR-J400P, Fort Douglas, Utah.

19 Manchee, R. J. and Stewart, W. D. P. (1988), 'The decontamination of Gruinard Island', *Chemistry in Britain*, July, pp. 690–1.

20 Martin, D. (1993), *The Use of Poison and Biological Weapons in the Rhodesian War*, Southern African Research and Documentation Centre, Harare.

Chapter 4: Efforts at Control to 1991

1 Rogers, P. and Dando, M. R. (1990), *NBC 90: the Directory of Nuclear, Biological and Chemical Arms and Disarmament 1990*, Tri-Service Press, London.

2 Smith, E. A. (1984), 'International regulation of chemical and biological weapons: "yellow rain" and arms control', *University of Illinois Law Review*, (4), pp. 1011–73.

3 Lang, W. (1990), 'The role of international law in preventing military misuse of the biosciences and biotechology', *Politics and the Life Sciences*, 9(1), pp. 37–45.

4 United Nations (1980), *The United Nations and Disarmament 1945–1970*, Department of Political and Security Council Affairs, New York. (Chapter 16 deals with efforts to ban biological weapons.)

5 United Nations (1969), *Chemical and Bacteriological (Biological)*

Weapons and the Effects of Their Possible Use, E.69.1.24., New York.

6 Sims, N. A. (1986), 'Banning germ weapons: can the treaty be strengthened?', *ADIU Report*, **8**(5), pp. 1–4.

7 Sims, N. A (1971), 'Biological disarmament: Britain's new posture', *New Scientist*, 2 December, pp. 18–20.

8 Sauerwein, B. (1992), 'Chemical Weapons Convention: belling the cat', *International Defense Review*, **11**, pp. 1065–66.

9 Texts of the final declarations of the first and second review conferences are given as appendices in: Sims, N. A. (1992), 'Biological and toxin weapons: the 1972 Convention and the reinforcement of its Disarmament Treaty Regime (DTR) through the Review Conferences of 1980, 1986 and 1991', *Vredesonderzoek*, **6**, March.

10 Final Document (1992), *Third Review Conference of the Parties to the Convention on the Prohibition of the Development, Production and Stockpiling of Bacteriological (Biological) and Toxin Weapons and on their Destruction*, BWC/CONF.III/23, Geneva.

11 Levin, A. L. (1990), 'Historical outline', In: Geissler, E. (ed.), *Strengthening the Biological Weapons Convention by Confidence–Building Measures*, Oxford University Press, Oxford (for SIPRI).

12 Geissler, E. (1990), 'The first three rounds of information exchanges', In: Geissler, E. (ed.), *Strengthening the Biological Weapons Convention by Confidence–Building Measures*, Oxford University Press, Oxford (for SIPRI).

13 Geissler, E. (1991), 'The first four rounds of information exchange', In: Geissler, E. and Haynes, R. H. (eds.), *Prevention of a Biological and Toxin Arms Race and the Responsibility of Scientists*, Akademie–Verlag, Berlin.

14 *Report from the United Kingdom of Great Britain and Northern Ireland* (1992), DDA/4-92/BW111 [pp. 213–51], Office for Disarmament Affairs, United Nations, New York.

15 Goldblat, J. and Bernauer, T. (1991), *The Third Review of the Biological Weapons Convention: Issues and Proposals*, UNIDIR Research Paper No. 9, United Nations, New York.

16 Goldblat, J. and Bernauer, T. (1991), 'Proposals for strengthening the Biological Weapons Convention', *Bulletin of Peace Proposals*, **22**(2), pp. 235–40.

17 Goldblat, J. and Bernauer, T. (1992), 'Towards a more effective ban on biological weapons', *Bulletin of Peace Proposals*, **23**(1), pp. 35–41.

18 Stock, T. (1993), 'Chemical and biological weapons: developments and proliferation', *SIPRI Yearbook*, Oxford University Press, Oxford, pp. 259–305.

19 Sims, N. A. (1991), 'Organisational arrangements for supporting the BWC', Paper presented at the Quaker Residential Conference, 'Strengthening the Biological Weapons Convention', Chateau de Bossey, Switzerland, 31 May–2 June.

Chapter 5: Science, Technology and Warfare

1 McNeill, W. H. (1982), *The Pursuit of Power: Technology, Armed Force, and Society since A. D. 1000*, University of Chicago Press, Chicago.

2 Roland, A. (1993), 'Technology and war: the historiographical revolution of the 1980s', *Technology and Culture*, **31**(1), pp. 117–35.

3 Bodnar, Captain J. W. (1993), 'The military technical revolution: from hardware to information', *Naval War College Review*, **XLVI**(3), pp. 7–22.

4 Arquilla, J. and Ronfeldt, D. (1993), 'Cyberwar is coming', *Comparative Strategy*, **12**, pp. 141–65.

5 Emmett, Fl. Lt. P. C. (1992), 'Software warfare: the emerging future', *Royal United Services Institute Journal*, December, pp. 56–60.

6 Anson, Sir P. and Cummings, D. (1991), 'The first space war: the contribution of satellites to the Gulf War', *Royal United Services Institute Journal*, December, pp. 45–53.

7 FitzGerald, M. C. (1991), 'The Soviet military and the new "technological operation" in the Gulf', *Naval War College Review*, **XLIV**(4), pp. 16–45.

8 FitzGerald, M. C. (1991), 'The Soviet image of future war: "through the prism of the Persian Gulf"', *Comparative Strategy*, **10**, pp. 393–435.

9 Herspring, D. R. (1986), 'The Soviet military in the aftermath of the 27th Party Congress', *Orbis*, **30**(2), pp. 297–317.

10 Herspring, D. R. (1987), 'Nikolay Ogarkov and the scientific–technical revolution in Soviet military affairs', *Comparative Strategy*, **6**(1), pp. 29–61.

11 FitzGerald, M. C. (1987), 'Marshall Ogarkov and the new revolution in Soviet military affairs', *Defense Analyses*, **3**(1), pp. 3–19.

12 Smith, D. L. and Meier, A. L. (1987), 'Ogarkov's revolution: Soviet

military doctrine for the 1990s', *International Defense Review*, **7**, pp. 869–73.

13 Pilat, J. F. and White, P. C. (1990), 'Technology and strategy in a changing world', *Washington Quarterly*, Spring, pp. 79–91.

14 Knox, P. and Agnew, J. (1989), *The Geography of the World Economy*, Edward Arnold, London.

15 Freeman, C. and Perez, C. (1988), 'Structural crises of adjustment, business cycles and investment behaviour', In: Dosi, G. *et al.* (eds.), *Technical Change and Economic Theory*, Pinter, London.

16 Nakamura, H. and Dando, M. R. (1993), 'Japan's military research and development: a high technology deterrent', *Pacific Review*, **6**(2), pp. 177–90.

17 Subcommittee on Defense Industry and Technology (1990), *Department of Defense Authorisation FY 1992 and 1993. Part 5: Defense Industry and Technology,* Committee on Armed Services, US Senate.

18 Brodsky, M. (1990), 'Progress in gallium arsenide semiconductors', *Scientific American*, February, pp. 56–63.

19 Stix, G. (1992), 'Trends in micromechanics: micron machinations', *Scientific American,* November, pp. 72–80.

20 Hill, A. (1993), 'R&D in a tussle over EC funding', *Financial Times*, 26 October.

21 Blundell, T. (1993), 'Biological wealth creation', *Times Higher Education Supplement*, 29 October.

22 Welch, T. J. (1990), 'Technology change and security', *Washington Quarterly*, Spring, pp. 111–20.

23 Hewish, M. (1993), 'DoD studies impact of "military revolution"', *Jane's Defence Weekly*, 12 June, p. 25.

Chapter 6: The New Biology

1 Freeland, P. (1991), *Micro-organisms in Action*, Hodder and Stoughton, London.

2 Advisory Council on Science and Technology (1990), *Developments in Biotechnology*, HMSO, London.

3 Thomas, S. M. (1992), *Global Perspective 2010: The Case of Biotechnology*, Science Policy Research Unit, University of Sussex, Falmer.

4 Peacock, J. (1986), *Biotechnology*, CSIRO, Canberra.

5 Smith, H. (1989), 'The development of studies on the determinants of bacterial pathogenicity', *J. Comp. Path.*, **98**, pp. 253–73.

6 Weatherall, D. J. (1991), *The New Genetics and Clinical Practice* (3rd edn.), Oxford University Press, Oxford.

7 Stine, G. J. (1989), *The New Human Genetics*, Wm. C. Brown, Iowa.

8 Luzio, J. P. and Thompson, R. J. (1990), *Molecular Medical Biochemistry*, Cambridge University Press, Cambridge.

9 Euromonitor (1988), *International Biotechnology Handbook* (1st edn.), Euromonitor Publications, London.

10 Kinoshita, J. (1993), 'Biotechnology: is Japan a boon or a burden to US industry's leadership?', *Science*, **259**, 29 January, pp. 596–8.

11 McKie, R. (1993), 'Gene therapy storms frontiers of disease', *Observer*, 21 March.

12 Krause, R. M. (1992), 'The origin of plagues: old and new', *Science*, **257**, 21 August, pp. 1073–78.

13 Miller, S. K. (1993), 'Irish scourge stalks the world', *New Scientist*, 6 November, p.7.

14 Barinaga, M. (1993), 'Bacteriology: new technique offers a window on bacteria's secret weapons', *Science*, **259**, 29 January, p. 595.

15 Tiollais, P. and Buendia, M–A. (1991), 'Hepatitis B virus', *Scientific American*, April, pp. 48–54.

16 Chen, D–S. (1993), 'From hepatitis to hepatoma: lessons from Type B viral hepatitis', *Science*, **262**, 15 October, pp. 369–70.

17 Barinaga, M. (1992), 'Viruses launch their own Star Wars', *Science*, **258**, 11 December, pp. 1730–31.

18 Kotwal, G. J. (1990), 'Inhibition of the complement cascade by the major secretory protein of vaccinia virus', *Science*, **250**, 9 November, pp. 827–30.

19 Smith, G. L. (1990), 'Vaccinia: virus, vector and vaccine', In: Dimmock, N. J., *et al.* (eds.) *Control of Viral Diseases* (45th Symposium of the Society for General Microbiology), Cambridge University Press, Cambridge.

20 Gasser, C. S. and Fraley, R. T. (1992), 'Transgenic crops', *Scientific American*, June, p. 34–9.

21 Anon. (1994), 'Silicon carbide pokes into DNA', *New Scientist*, 22 January, p. 19.

22 Coghlan, A. (1992), 'Spiked spuds keep beetles at bay', *New Scientist*, 22 August, p.10.

23 Chen, Z. and Gu, H. (1993), 'Plant biotechnology in China.', Science, **262**, 15 October, pp. 377–8.

Chapter 7: New Weapons?

1 Wright, S. and Sinsheimer, R. L. (1983), 'Recombinant DNA and biological warfare', *Bulletin of the Atomic Scientists*, November, pp. 20–6.

2 Finder, J. (1986), 'Biological warfare, genetic engineering, and the treaty that failed', *Washington Quarterly*, Spring, pp. 5–14.

3 Douglas, J. D. (1992), 'Who's holding the psychotoxins and DNA–altering compounds?', *Armed Forces Journal International*, September, pp. 50–2.

4 Depository Governments (1980), *New Scientific and Technological Developments Relevant to the Convention on the Prohibition of the Development, Production and Stockpiling of Bacteriological (Biological) and Toxin Weapons and on their Destruction*, BWC/CONF.I/5, 6 February.

5. Preparatory Committee for the Review Conference (1980), *Views of States Parties on New Scientific and Technological Developments Relevant to the Convention: Submission by Sweden*, BWC/CONF.1/3, 29 February.

6 Sims, N. A. (1989), 'Diplomatic responses to changing assessments of scientific and technological developments relevant to a disarmament regime: the Second Review Conference of the 1972 Convention on Biological and Toxin Weapons, Geneva 1986', In Brauch, H. G. (ed.), *Military Technology, Armaments Dynamics and Disarmament*, Macmillan, London, pp. 92–111.

7 Karpetsky, T. (ed.) (1986), *Technologic Changes Since 1972: Implications for a Biological Warfare Convention*, CRDC-CR-86017, US Army Chemical Research and Development Center, Aberdeen Proving Ground, Maryland.

8 Preparatory Committee for the Review Conference (1991), *Background Document on New Scientific and Technological Developments Relevant to the Convention on the Prohibition of the Development, Production and Stockpiling of Bacteriological (Biological) and Toxin Weapons and on their Destruction*, BWC/CONF.III/4, 26 August.

9 Canada (1991), *Novel Toxins and Bioregulators: The Emerging Scientific and Technological Issues Relating to Verification and the Biological and Toxin Weapons Convention*, Ottawa, September.

10 Smith, H. (1988), 'The development of studies on the determinants of bacterial pathogenicity', *J. Comp. Pathol.*, **98**, pp. 253–73.

11 Smith, H. (1989), 'The mounting interest in bacterial and viral path-

ogenicity', *Ann. Rev. Microbiol.*, **43**, pp. 1–22.

12 Huxsoll, D.L. (1993), 'The US Biological Defence Program', In: Roberts, B. (ed.), *Biological Weapons: Weapons of the Future*, Significant Issues Series, **XV**(1), Center for Strategic and International Studies, Washington, DC.

13 Geissler, E. (1986), 'A new generation of biological weapons', In: Geissler, E. (ed.), *Biological and Toxin Weapons Today*, Oxford University Press, Oxford (for SIPRI).

14 Geissler, E. (1990), 'New assessments of the potential value of BW and TW agents', In Geissler, E. (ed.), *Strengthening the BW Convention by CBMs*, Oxford University Press, Oxford (for SIPRI).

15 Finlay, B. B. (1992), 'Molecular genetic approaches to understanding bacterial pathogenesis', In: Hormaeche, C. E., *et al.* (eds.), *Molecular Biology of Bacterial Infection: Current Status and Future Prospects* (49th Symposium of the Society for General Microbiology), Cambridge University Press, Cambridge.

16 Foster, T. J. (1992), 'The use of mutants for defining the role of virulence factors in vivo', In: Hormaeche, C. E., *et al.* (eds.), *Molecular Biology of Bacterial Infection: Current Status and Future Prospects* (49th Symposium of the Society for General Microbiology), Cambridge University Press, Cambridge.

17 Sodeinde, O. A., *et al.* (1992), 'A surface invasive protease and the invasive character of plague', *Science*, **258**, 6 November, pp. 1004–7.

18 Leppla, S. H. (1991), 'The anthrax toxin complex', In: Alouf, J. E. and Freer, J. H. (eds.), *Sourcebook of Bacterial Protein Toxins*, Academic Press, London.

19 Lamanna, C. (1959), 'The most poisonous poison', *Science*, **130**, 25 September, pp. 763–72.

20 Niemann, H. (1991), 'Molecular biology of clostridial neurotoxins', In: Alouf, J. E. and Freer, J. H. (eds.), *Sourcebook of Bacterial Protein Toxins*, Academic Press, London.

21 Iandolo, J. J. (1989), 'Genetic analysis of extracellular toxins of *Staphylococcus aureus*', *Ann. Rev. Microbiol.*, **43**, p. 375–402.

22 Foreign Science and Technology Center (1986), *Incapacitating Agents, European Communist Countries: Neurotoxins, Psychotropics and Organofluorines*, Army Intelligence Agency, US Army, 24 March.

23 Harvard Sussex Program on CBW Armament and Arms Limitation (1992), 'News Chronology (Notes on FY 1993 Arms Control Impact Statements)', *Chemical Weapons Convention Bulletin*, 3

Impact Statements)', *Chemical Weapons Convention Bulletin*, 3 June.

24 Special Report (1993), 'Toxicology goes molecular' (especially the article entitled 'Hot field: neurotoxicology'), *Science*, **259**, 5 March, pp. 1394–9.

25 Dimmock, N. J. and Primrose, S. B. (1987), *Introduction to Modern Virology*, Blackwell Scientific Publications, Oxford.

26 Rice, C. M. *et al.* (1985), 'Nucleotide sequence of yellow fever virus: implications for flavivirus gene expression and evolution', *Science*, **229**, 23 August, pp. 726–35.

27 Chambers, T. J., *et al.* (1990), 'Flavivirus genome organisation, expression and replication', *Ann. Rev. Microbiol.*, **44**, pp. 649–88.

28 IXth International Congress of Virology (1993), *Abstracts*, Glasgow, Scotland, 8–13 August.

29 Cookson, C. (1993), 'A spur for the gene hunters', *Financial Times*, 20 December.

Chapter 8: VEREX – Towards a Verification Protocol?

1 Rogers, P. and Dando, M. R. (1992), *A Violent Peace: Global Security after the Cold War*, Brassey's, London.

2 Dando, M. R. (1994), 'Biological weapons: curbing the test tube danger', *New Zealand International Review*, **XIX**(1), pp. 10–15.

3 Secretary of State for Defence (1992), *Statement on the Defence Estimates*, HMSO, London.

4 Final Document (1992), *Third Review Conference of the Parties to the Convention on the Prohibition of the Development, Production and Stockpiling of Bacteriological (Biological) and Toxin Weapons and on their Destruction*, BWC/CONF.III/23, Geneva.

5 ter Haar, B. (1991), *The Future of Biological Weapons*, Washington Papers, No. 151, Center for Strategic and International Studies, Washington, DC.

6 Working Group on Biological and Toxin Weapons Verification (1990), *Proposals for the Third Review Conference of the Biological Weapons Convention*, Federation of American Scientists, Washington, DC.

7 Working Group on Biological and Toxin Weapons Verification (1991), *Implementation of the Proposals for a Verification Protocol to the Biological Weapons Convention*, Federation of American Scientists, Washington, DC.

8 Rosenberg, B. H. (1993), 'North v South: politics and the

Biological Weapons Convention, *Politics and the Life Sciences*, February, pp. 69–77.

9 *Ad Hoc* Group of Governmental Experts (1992), *Summary of the work of the* Ad Hoc *Group for the period 30 March to 10 April 1992*, BWC/CONF.III/VEREX/2.

10 *Ad Hoc* Group of Governmental Experts (1993), *Draft summary of the work of the* Ad Hoc *Group for the period 24 May to 4 June 1993*, BWC/ CONF.III/ VEREX/ CRP.28/ Rev.1.

11 France (1992), *Group of Experts on the Verification of the Biological Weapons Convention*, BWC/CONF.III/VEREX/WP.2.

12 Netherlands (1992), *Discussion Paper*, BWC/CONF.III/VEREX/ WP.3.

13 Germany (1992), *Options for the verification of the BWC*, BWC/ CONF.III/ VEREX/ WP.4.

14 UK (1992), *UN Special Commission BW inspections in Iraq: lessons for the* Ad Hoc *Experts' Group on verification*, BWC/CONF.III/VEREX/WP.5.

15 UK (1992), *Commercial confidentiality concerns associated with sampling and analyses during on-site inspections under the BWC*, BWC/ CONF.III/ VEREX/ NON.28.

16 UK (1992), *Data exchange as a potential verification measure under the BWC: the philosophy and scope of declarations and notifications*, BWC/ CONF.III/ VEREX/ WP.36.

17 UK (1992), *UK practice inspection: pharmaceutical pilot plant*, BWC/ CONF.III/ VEREX/ WP.141.

18 UK (1993), *UK practice inspection: pharmaceutical pilot plant*, BWC/ CONF.III/ VEREX/ WP.142.

19 *Ad Hoc* Group of Governmental Experts (1992), *Summary of the work of the* Ad Hoc *Group for the period 23 November to 4 December 1992*, BWC/ CONF.III/ VEREX/ 4.

20 *Ad Hoc* Group of Governmental Experts (1993), *Final Report*, BWC/ CONF.III/ VEREX/ 8.

21 Zilinskas, R. A. (1986), 'Verification of the Biological Weapons Convention', In: Geissler, E. (ed.), *Biological and Toxin Weapons Today*, Oxford University Press, Oxford (for SIPRI).

22 President Clinton (1993), *Address to UN General Assembly* (Clinton warns of perils ahead despite Cold War's end), Official Text, United States Information Service, London, 28 September.

23 Thomas Graham (1993), *Address of ACDA Head Thomas Graham to UN Committee* (US outlines disarmament goals), Official Text, United States Information Service, London, 22 October.

24 Harvard Sussex Program on CBW Armament and Arms Limitation (1993), 'News chronology, 19 November', *Chemical Weapons Convention Bulletin*, December.

Chapter 9: Western Policy Options

1 Reed, J. (1993), *Defence Exports: Current Concerns*, Jane's Consultancy Services, London.

2 Wright, S. (1992), 'Prospects for biological disarmament in the 1990s', Paper given at a seminar, 'Arms Control in the Post-Cold War World', Peace Research Centre, Australian National University, Canberra.

3 Office of Technology Assessment (1993), *Proliferation of Weapons of Mass Destruction: Assessing the Risks*, OTA–ISC–559, Washington, DC.

4 Department of Defense (1984), *Soviet Military Power,* Washington, DC.

5 Report from the Russian Federation (1992), DDA/ 4–92/ BWIII/ Add.3, United Nations, New York.

6 Harvard Sussex Programme on CBW Armament and Arms Limitation (1993), 'Russia and the Biological Weapons Convention', Excerpts from the *SHIB Rolling Chronology*, 29 April.

7 US Department of State (1992), 'Joint US/UK/Russian statement on biological weapons (14.9.92)', *Arms Control Reporter*, 701.D.1, October.

8 Douglass, J. D. Jr. (1990), 'Beyond nuclear war', *Journal of Social, Political and Economic Studies*, **15**, pp. 141–56.

9 Russell, A. M. (1990), 'International relations theory, biotechnology and war', *Politics and the Life Sciences*, **9**(1), pp. 3–19.

10 Rice, M. (1991), 'The personal power of scientists', In: Geissler, E. and Haynes, R. H. (eds.), *Prevention of a Biological and Toxin Arms Race and the Responsibility of Scientists*, Akademie-Verlag, Berlin.

11 Pearson, G. S. (1993), 'Prospects for chemical and biological arms control: the web of deterrence', *Washington Quarterly*, Spring, pp. 145–62.

12 Special Inquiry into the Chemical and Biological Threat (1993), *Countering the Chemical and Biological Weapons Threat in the Post-Soviet World*, Committee on Armed Services, House of Representatives, 102nd Congress, Washington, DC (February).

programme was looking at the wrong BW agents', 701.B.68, 28 January.

14 *Arms Control Reporter* (1993), 'The US Army's biological defense research program had "failed to uphold the public trust"', 701.B.113, 1 April.

15 King, J. and Strauss, H. (1990), 'The hazards of defensive biological warfare programs', In: Wright, S. (ed.) *Preventing a Biological Arms Race*, MIT Press, Cambridge, Mass.

16 Piller, C. and Yamamoto, K. R. (1990), 'The US biological defense research program in the 1980s: a critique', In: Wright, S. (ed.), *Preventing a Biological Arms Race*, MIT Press, Cambridge, Mass.

17 Mechtersheimer, A. (1986), 'US military strategy and chemical and biological weapons. In: Geissler, E. (ed.) *Biological and Toxin Weapons Today*, Oxford University Press, Oxford (for SIPRI).

18 Dashiell, T.R. (1990), 'The need for a defensive biological research programme', *Politics and the Life Sciences*, 9(1), pp. 85–92.

19 Huxsoll, D. L. (1989), 'Medicine in defence against biological warfare', *Journal of the American Medical Association*, 4 August, pp. 677–9.

20 Anon. (1993), 'Were four corner victims biowar casualties?', *Scientific American*, November, p. 8.

21 Anon. (1993), 'Hantavirus outbreak yields to PCR', *Science*, **262**, pp. 832–6 (see also detailed articles in same issue), 5 November.

22 House of Commons *Hansard* (1993), Written Answers: Genetically modified organisms, col. 268–70, 20 May.

23 Harvard Sussex Program on CBW Armament and Arms Limitation (1993), 'News chronology, 27 September', *Chemical Weapons Convention Bulletin*, December.

24 Foreign and Commonwealth Office (1990), *Biological and Toxin Weapons*, London, June.

25 US Army Test and Evaluation Command (1984), *Microbiological Safety*, TECOM Reg 385–2, US Army, Aberdeen Proving Ground, Maryland, 13 March.

26 Patrick, W. C. (1984), *Biological Defense: Functional Area Assessment*, Army Medical Research Institute of Infectious Diseases, US Army, Aberdeen Proving Ground, Maryland, November.

27 Foreign and Commonwealth Office (1993), *Biological Weapons Awareness Raising Booklet: United Kingdom Export Control Legislation*, London, March.

28 Department of Foreign Affairs and Trade (1993), 'Australia Group:

June 1993 Meeting', *Peace and Disarmament News*, Canberra, July, p. 12.

29 General Accounting Office (1992), *Arms Control: U.S. and International Efforts to Ban Biological Weapons*, Report to the Hon. Albert Gore Jr., US Senate, National Security and International Affairs Division, B-251336, December.

30 Harvard Sussex Program on CBW Armament and Arms Limitation (1993), 'News Chronology, 19 November', *Chemical Weapons Convention Bulletin*, December.

31 Trapp, R. (1991), 'Applicable verification lessons from negotiations on the Chemical Weapons Convention', In: Lundin, S. J. (ed.), *Views on Possible Verification Measures for the Biological Weapons Convention*, Oxford University Press, Oxford (for SIPRI).

32 Trapp, R. (1993), *Verification under the Chemical Weapons Convention: On-Site Inspection in Chemical Industry Facilities*, Oxford University Press, Oxford (for SIPRI).

33 International Scientific Committee for Biotechnology (1990), *Biotechnology Worldwide*, Cpl Press, Newbury, UK.

34 Harvard Sussex Program on CBW Armament and Arms Limitation (1993), 'News chronology, 24 September', *Chemical Weapons Convention Bulletin*, December.

35 Roberts, B. (1993), 'New challenges and new policy priorities for the 1990s', In: Roberts, B. (ed.), *Biological Weapons: Weapons of the Future*, Significant Issues Series, **XV**(1), Center for Strategic and International Studies, Washington, DC.

36 Glass, R. I. *et al.* (1992), 'Epidemic cholera in the Americas', *Science*, **256**, pp. 1524–5, 12 June.

37 Geissler, E. (1993), 'Vaccines for peace (VFP): An international programme of development and use of vaccines against dual-threat agents (DTAs)', P77–16, IXth International Congress of Virology, Glasgow, 8–13 August.

38 Lewis, W. H. (1991), 'Proliferation of unconventional weapons: the case for coercive arms control', *Comparative Strategy*, **10**, pp. 299–309.

39 Borass, P. (1992), 'Epidemic field investigations as applied to allegations of chemical, biological or toxin warfare', *Politics and the Life Sciences*, **11**(1), pp. 5–22.

40 Canada (1985), *Handbook for the Investigation of Allegations of the Use of Chemical or Biological Weapons*, Department of External Affairs, Ottawa.

41 Kupperman, R. H. and Smith, D. M. (1993), 'Coping with biologi-

cal terrorism', In: Roberts, B. (ed.), *Biological Weapons: Weapons of the Future*, Significant Issues Series, **XV**(1), Center for Strategic and International Studies, Washington DC.

42 Hurwitz, E. (1982), 'Terrorists and chemical/biological weapons', *US Naval War College Review*, **35**, pp. 36–40.

Chapter 10: Future Prospects: Proliferation or Control?

1 DeForest, P. (1990), 'The matrix of biological disarmament: strategy, law and technology', *Politics and the Life Sciences*, **9**(1), pp. 21–35.

2 Pearson, G. S. (1993), 'Prospects for chemical and biological arms control: the web of deterrence', *Washington Quarterly*, Spring, pp. 145–62.

3 Vickers, G. (1972), 'The management of conflict', *Futures*, **4**, pp. 35–52.

4 United Nations (1980), *The United Nations and Disarmament 1945–1970*, Department of Political and Security Council Affairs, United Nations, New York.

5 United Nations (1993), *Study on Defensive Security Concepts and Policies*, Study Series No. 26, Office for Disarmament Affairs, United Nations, New York.

6 Letter from the Representatives of Bolivia, Colombia, Ecuador, Peru and Venezuela to the Secretary General of the Conference on Disarmament (1992), *Text of the Cartagena Declaration of Renunciation of Weapons of Mass Destruction signed at Cartagena de Indias, Colombia on 4 December 1991*, CD/1114, 9 January.

7 Eavis, P. (1992), *Arms and Dual-use Exports from the EC: A Common Policy for Regulation and Control*, Saferworld, Bristol, December.

8 Subrahmanyan, K. (1993), 'Export controls and the North–South controversy', *Washington Quarterly*, Spring, pp. 135–43.

9 Boutros-Ghali, B. (1992), *New Dimensions of Arms Regulation and Disarmament in the Post-Cold War Era*, United Nations, A/C.1/47/7, 27 October.

10 Bertrand, M. (1991), 'The difficult transformation from "arms control" into a "world security system"', *International Social Science Journal*, **127**, February, pp. 87–103.

11 Europrospective III: Third European Long-Range Forecasting Conference (1993), *Executive Summary*, Wiesbaden, Germany, 3–5

June.

12 Petrella, R. and de la Saussay, P. (1993), *Science and Technology for the Eight Billion People of the Planet by 2020*, Basic Report No. 1, Living Together. Paper given at Europrospective III, Wiesbaden, Germany.

13 Holland, S. (1993), 'Summary: Towards a new Bretton Woods – imperatives for the global economy', Paper given at Europrospective III, Wiesbaden, Germany.

14 Oldham, G. (1993), *Science and Technology for the Eight Billion People of the Planet by 2020*, Basic Report No. 2, Global Development Cooperation: Science for Development, Paper given at Europrospective III, Wiesbaden, Germany.

15 Barnes, D. (1991), *New Life for Industry: Biotechnology, Industry and the Community in the 1990s and Beyond*, NEDC, London.

16 Walgate, R. (1990), *Miracle or Menace? Biotechnology and the Third World*, The Panos Institute, London.

17 Persley, G. (1990), 'Harnessing biotechnology for the Third World', *Partners in Research and Development,* **3**, pp. 7–11, Australian Centre for Agricultural Research.

18 Parker, G. (1991), 'Continuity and change in Western geopolitical thought during the twentieth century', *International Social Science Journal*, **127**, February, pp. 21–33.

GUIDE TO THE LITERATURE

In each chapter references have been given in order that the reader may track down specific points of interest. Where possible I have used literature which is accessible through the library system of a medium-sized city: thus I have tried to quote from a well-known journal rather than a specialist report of limited circulation.

Despite such efforts to ensure that the reader can check my sources and conclusions, and follow these issues in the future, it has to be admitted that the sources used are diverse. Thus keeping an eye on this subject is no easy task. What follows is an attempt to present the literature in a different way. Instead of starting from specific sources I have tried, first, to identify the general areas of interest in the literature and to point out some of the sources which provide an overview of these areas. I have then added some lists of the most important books, reports and journals in each area.

This book has drawn information from the literature on arms control, strategic studies and international politics; from the literature in biology and biotechnology; and finally, from some military literature, for example, in relation to aerobiology and protective medicine. For ease of reference we may term these three areas arms control, biology and the military.

Arms Control

In order to follow arms control negotiations regularly in some detail *The Arms Control Reporter: A Chronicle of Treaties, Negotiations, Proposals* is probably the best single source for anyone outside government. It is produced by the Institute for Defense and Disarmament

Studies in Boston, USA and consists of a monthly update on all currently important negotiations. It is available either as a set of papers for insertion in an annual binder, or as a computer disc. The computer version can easily be used to update a searchable database.

As will have been noticed in the reference lists to some chapters, the Biological Weapons Convention is covered in section 701. As in all other sections, part A gives an outline of the current status of the convention, B gives a chronological update for the year, C reproduces useful public commentary, D official statements, and E is concerned with stockpiles, weapons systems, etc. Altogether, the 701 section allows a reader to keep both up to date on the BWC and associated issues such as proliferation, and to track back through the development of important aspects of the problem. Of course, this is more easily done with the data on disc and with the use of a good search programme.

A more popular monthly journal which carries a range of articles on arms control is *Arms Control Today*, produced by the US Arms Control Association in Washington, DC. Some of the standard international politics/strategic studies journals such as *Arms Control, Comparative Strategy, Defense Analyses, Foreign Policy, Journal of Peace Research, International Defense Review, International Security, Journal of the Royal United Services Institute, Security Dialogue, Survival, The Washington Quarterly* and *US Naval War College Review* frequently carry articles on arms control which can be of interest in regard to the general problem of proliferation, even if biological weapons and biological arms control are not often the specific subject. The journal *Politics and the Life Sciences* has published papers on the subject of biological arms control in a number of issues. A good number of other journals, for example some of the UN journals such as *Disarmament*, also carry arms control articles regularly.

One particular issue of the United Nations Institute for Disarmament Research (UNIDIR) *Newsletter* was devoted to biological weapons. The issue, No. 2 of June 1991, carried a number of articles relating to the third Review Conference of the BWC which was to take place that September. It also listed research projects being carried out on biological weapons and arms control in institutes around the world and, more interestingly for the general reader, it had a consolidated list of references on these issues for the period 1986 to 1991. That set of references would provide a good starting point for anyone generally interested in the subject.

Two specialist publications would also be helpful. The *Chemical Weapons Convention Bulletin*, published by the Harvard

University/Sussex University joint programme, covers biological as well as chemical weapons. This is a quarterly publication which carries articles, a chronological account of important issues and a very helpful listing of 'Recent Publications'.

The *ASA Newsletter*, published bi-monthly by Applied Science and Analysis Inc. of Delaware, USA, is similarly primarily concerned with 'the interface of chemistry and defense' but also carries detailed and useful articles and reports related to biological weapons and arms control.

Biology

To keep abreast of current developments a regular scan of the standard general sources *Science* and *Nature* is by far the best approach. Less technical articles may be found in good popular journals such as *Scientific American* and *New Scientist*. Biotechnology in all its aspects is a large subject and there are many articles of interest being written.

It is useful to have a modern textbook which deals with microbiology and molecular biology in a way that the reader finds interesting. There are many possibilities and it is really a question of personal taste. I liked *Microbiology: Concepts and Applications* by M. J. Pelczar, *et al.* and used it regularly to cross-check what I was reading elsewhere. Similarly, I found *Modern Biotechnology* by S. B. Primrose useful in regard to more industrial matters.

There are numerous specialist biological and medical journals. All carry important articles, but are often too technical for the general reader. It is much better to look for review articles which analyse and summarise work on important themes. Such review articles may be found in journals such as those in the *Annual Review* series or *Microbiological Reviews*. As will be obvious from the reference list of Chapter 6, I found the symposia of the UK Society for General Microbiology particularly helpful as they had recently concentrated on topics of especial interest in regard to this book.

Military

The 1992 British submission on Confidence-Building Measure C, *Encouragement of Publication of Results and Promotion of Knowledge*, lists a formidable set of specialist journals in which the results of government-funded research may be found. Many of these overlap with the specialist journals noted in regard to biology. The list includes the

British Medical Journal, the *British Veterinary Journal, Immunology, Journal of General Microbiology, Journal of General Virology, The Lancet* and so on. It also refers to such directly relevant journals as *Journal of Aerosol Science*. Clearly, no general reader can hope to cover such a wide range of publications and other specialist sources. The same obviously holds true for US material which may be released under the Freedom of Information Act.

Fortunately, however, hearings in the US Congress often bring specialists together to give short summary presentations, and official organisations such as the US Office of Technology Assessment sometimes publish analyses and summaries such as *Proliferation of Weapons of Mass Destruction: Assessing the Risks*. Hearings of the US Congress are obtainable through depository libraries for such material like that at the London School of Economics in the UK. A good starter list of such hearings is given in the Pentagon Library Selective Bibliography on *Chemical and Biological Warfare* of July 1991.

APPENDIX 1

THE 1972 BIOLOGICAL WEAPONS CONVENTION

CONVENTION ON THE PROHIBITION OF THE DEVELOP-
MENT, PRODUCTION AND STOCKPILING OF
BACTERIOLOGICAL (BIOLOGICAL) AND TOXIN WEAPONS
AND ON THEIR DESTRUCTION

Signed at London, Moscow and Washington on 10 April 1972
Entered into force on 26 March 1975
Depositaries: UK, US and Soviet governments

The States Parties to this Convention, Determined to act with a view to achieving effective progress towards general and complete disarmament, including the prohibition and elimination of all types of weapons of mass destruction, and convinced that the prohibition of the development, production and stockpiling of chemical and bacteriological (biological) weapons and their elimination, through effective measures, will facilitate the achievement of general and complete disarmament under strict and effective international control,

Recognizing the important significance of the Protocol for the Prohibition of the Use in War of Asphyxiating, Poisonous or Other Gases, and of Bacteriological Methods of Warfare, signed at Geneva on June 17, 1925, and conscious also of the contribution which the said Protocol has already made, and continues to make, to mitigating the horrors of war,

Reaffirming their adherence to the principles and objectives of that Protocol and calling upon all States to comply strictly with them,

Recalling that the General Assembly of the United Nations has repeatedly condemned all actions contrary to the principles and objectives of the Geneva Protocol of June 17, 1925,

Desiring to contribute to the strengthening of confidence between peoples and the general improvement of the international atmosphere,

Desiring also to contribute to the realization of the purposes and principles of the Charter of the United Nations,

Convinced of the importance and urgency of eliminating from the arsenal of States, through effective measures, such dangerous weapons of mass destruction as those using chemical or bacteriological (biological) agents,

Recognizing that an agreement on the prohibition of bacteriological (biological) and toxin weapons represents a first possible step towards the achievement of agreement on effective measures also for the prohibition of the development, production and stockpiling of chemical weapons, and determined to continue negotiations to that end,

Determined, for the sake of all mankind, to exclude completely the possibility of bacteriological (biological) agents and toxins being used as weapons,

Convinced that such use would be repugnant to the conscience of mankind and that no effort should be spared to minimize this risk,

Have agreed as follows:

Article I
Each State Party to this Convention undertakes never in any circumstances to develop, produce, stockpile or otherwise acquire or retain:
1. Microbial or other biological agents, or toxins whatever their origin or method of production, of types and in quantities that have no justification for prophylactic, protective or other peaceful purposes;
2. Weapons, equipment or means of delivery designed to use such agents or toxins for hostile purposes or in armed conflict.

Article II
Each State Party to this Convention undertakes to destroy, or to divert to peaceful purposes, as soon as possible but not later than nine months after the entry into force of the Convention, all agents, toxins, weapons, equipment and means of delivery specified in article I of the Convention, which are in its possession or under its jurisdiction or control. In implementing the provisions of this article all necessary safety precautions shall be observed to protect populations and the environment.

Article III

Each State Party to this Convention undertakes not to transfer to any recipient whatsoever, directly or indirectly, and not in any way to assist, encourage, or induce any State, group of States or international organizations to manufacture or otherwise acquire any of the agents, toxins, weapons, equipment or means of delivery specified in article I of the Convention.

Article IV

Each State Party to this Convention shall, in accordance with its constitutional processes, take any necessary measures to prohibit and prevent the development, production, stockpiling, acquisition or retention of the agents, toxins, weapons, equipment and means of delivery specified in article I of the Convention, within the territory of such State, under its jurisdiction or under its control anywhere.

Article V

The States Parties to this Convention undertake to consult one another and to cooperate in solving any problems which may arise in relation to the objective of, or in the application of the provisions of, the Convention. Consultation and cooperation pursuant to this article may also be undertaken through appropriate international procedures within the framework of the United Nations and in accordance with its Charter.

Article VI

1. Any State Party to this Convention which finds that any other State Party is acting in breach of obligations deriving from the provisions of the Convention may lodge a complaint with the Security Council of the United Nations. Such a complaint should include all possible evidence confirming its validity, as well as a request for its consideration by the Security Council.

2. Each State Party to this Convention undertakes to cooperate in carrying out any investigation which the Security Council may initiate, in accordance with the provisions of the Charter of the United Nations, on the basis of the complaint received by the Council. The Security Council shall inform the States Parties to the Convention of the results of the investigation.

Article VII

Each State Party to this Convention undertakes to provide or support assistance, in accordance with the United Nations Charter, to any Party to the Convention which so requests, if the Security Council decides that such Party has been exposed to danger as a result of violation of the Convention.

Article VIII

Nothing in this Convention shall be interpreted as in any way limiting or detracting from the obligations assumed by any State under the protocol for the Prohibition of the Use in War of Asphyxiating, Poisonous or Other Gases, and of Bacteriological Methods of Warfare signed at Geneva on June 17, 1925.

Article IX

Each State Party to this Convention affirms the recognized objective of effective prohibition of chemical weapons and, to this end, undertakes to continue negotiations in good faith with a view to reaching early agreement on effective measures for the prohibition of their development, production and stockpiling and for their destruction, and on appropriate measures concerning equipment and means of delivery specifically designed for the production or use of chemical agents for weapons purposes.

Article X

1. The States Parties to this Convention undertake to facilitate, and have the right to participate in, the fullest possible exchange of equipment, materials and scientific and technological information for the use of bacteriological (biological) agents and toxins for peaceful purposes. Parties to the Convention in a position to do so shall also cooperate in contributing individually or together with other States or international organizations to the further development and application of scientific discoveries in the field of bacteriology (biology) for prevention of disease, or for other peaceful purposes.
2. This Convention shall be implemented in a manner designed to avoid hampering the economic or technological development of States Parties to the Convention or international cooperation in the field of peaceful bacteriological (biological) activities, including the international exchange of bacteriological (biological) agents and toxins and equipment for the processing, use or production of bacteriological (biological) agents and toxins for peaceful purposes in accordance with the provisions of the Convention.

Article XI

Any State Party may propose amendments to this Convention. Amendments shall enter into force for each State Party accepting the amendments upon their acceptance by a majority of the States Parties to the Convention and thereafter for each remaining State Party on the date of acceptance by it.

Article XII

Five years after the entry into force of this Convention, or earlier if it is requested by a majority of Parties to the Convention by submitting a proposal to this effect to the Depositary Governments, a conference of States Parties to the Convention shall be held at Geneva, Switzerland, to review the operation of the Convention, with a view to assuring that the purposes of the preamble and the provisions of the Convention, including the provisions concerning negotiations on chemical weapons, are being realized. Such review shall take into account any new scientific and technological developments relevant to the Convention.

Article XIII

1. This Convention shall be of unlimited duration.
2. Each State Party to this Convention shall in exercising its national sovereignty have the right to withdraw from the Convention if it decides that extraordinary events, related to the subject matter of the Convention, have jeopardized the supreme interests of its country. It shall give notice of such withdrawal to all other States Parties to the Convention and to the United Nations Security Council three months in advance. Such notice shall include a statement of the extraordinary events it regards as having jeopardized its supreme interests.

Article XIV

1. This Convention shall be open to all States for signature. Any State which does not sign the Convention before its entry into force in accordance with paragraph (3) of this Article may accede to it at any time.
2. This Convention shall be subject to ratification by signatory States. Instruments of ratification and instruments of accession shall be deposited with the Governments of the United States of America, the United Kingdom of Great Britain and Northern Ireland and the Union of Soviet Socialist Republics, which are hereby designated the Depositary Governments.

3. This Convention shall enter into force after the deposit of instruments of ratification by twenty-two Governments, including the Governments designated as Depositaries of the Convention.

4. For States whose instruments of ratification or accession are deposited subsequent to the entry into force of this Convention, it shall enter into force on the date of the deposit of their instruments of ratification or accession.

5. The Depositary Governments shall promptly inform all signatory and acceding States of the date of each signature, the date of deposit of each instrument of ratification or of accession and the date of the entry into force of this Convention, and of the receipt of other notices.

6. This Convention shall be registered by the Depositary Governments pursuant to Article 102 of the Charter of the United Nations.

Article XV
This Convention, the English, Russian, French, Spanish and Chinese texts of which are equally authentic, shall be deposited in the archives of the Depositary Governments. Duly certified copies of the Convention shall be transmitted by the Depositary Governments to the Governments of the signatory and acceding States.

APPENDIX 2

AUSTRALIA GROUP EXPORT CONTROLS IN THE UK*

I   New entries in the Export of Goods (Control) Order 1992 covering biological materials as follows:
1C351   Human pathogens, zoonoses and toxins
1C352   Animal pathogens
1 C353   Genetically-modified micro-organisms

II   New entry in the EG(C)O 1992 covering biological equipment as follows:
2B352 Equipment capable of use in biological manufacturing

III   Warning guidelines

I

1C351 Human pathogens, zoonoses and toxins

a. Viruses, whether natural, enhanced or modified, either in the form of isolated live cultures or as material including living material which has been deliberately inoculated or contaminated with such cultures, as follows:
1. Chikungunya virus;
2. Congo-Crimean haemorrhagic fever virus;
3. Dengue fever virus;
4. Eastern equine encephalitis virus;
5. Ebola virus;
6. Hantaan virus;
7. Junin virus;
8. Lassa fever virus;

---

*Extracts from reference 27 of Chapter 9.

    9. Lymphocytic choriomeningitis virus;
    10. Machupo virus;
    11. Marburg virus;
    12. Monkey pox virus;
    13. Rift Valley fever virus;
    14. Russian Spring-Summer encephalitis virus;
    15. Variola virus;
    16. Venezuelan equine encephalitis virus;
    17. Western equine encephalitis virus;
    18. White pox;
    19. Yellow fever virus;
    20. Japanese encephalitis virus;
  b. Rickettsiae, whether natural, enhanced or modified, either in the form of isolated live cultures or as material including living material which has been deliberately inoculated or contaminated with such cultures, as follows:
    1. Coxiella burnetii;
    2. Rickettsia quintana;
    3. Rickettsia prowasecki;
    4. Rickettsia rickettsii;
  c. Bacteria, whether natural, enhanced or modified, either in the form of isolated live cultures or as material including living material which has been deliberately inoculated or contaminated with such cultures, as follows:
    1. Bacillus anthracis;
    2. Brucella abortus;
    3. Brucella melitensis;
    4. Brucella suis;
    5. Chlamydia psittaci;
    6. Clostridium botulinum;
    7. Francisella tularensis;
    8. Pseudomonas mallei;
    9. Pseudomonas pseudomallei;
    10. Salmonella typhi;
    11. Shigella dysenteriae;
    12. Vibrio cholerae;
    13. Pasteurella pseudotuberculosis var pestis (Yersinia pestis);
  d. Toxins, as follows:
    1. Botulinum toxins;
    2. Clostridium perfringens toxins;

3. Conotoxin;
4. Ricin;
5. Saxitoxin;
6. Shigatoxin;
7. Staphylococcus aureus toxins;
8. Tetrodotoxin;
9. Verotoxin;
10. Microcystins (Cyanginosins).

1C352 Animal Pathogens as follows:
a. Viruses, whether natural, enhanced or modified, either in the form of isolated live cultures or as material including living material which has been deliberately inoculated or contaminated with such cultures, as follows:
  1. African swine fever virus;
  2. Avian influenza virus, which are:
    a. Uncharacterised; or
    b. Those defined in EC Directive 92/40/EC, as having high pathogenicity, as follows:
      1. Type A viruses with an IVPI (intravenous pathogenicity index) in 6 week old chickens of greater than 1.2; or
      2. Type A viruses H5 or H7 subtype for which nucleotide sequencing has demonstrated multiple basic amino acids at the cleavage site of haemagglutinin.
  3. Bluetongue virus;
  4. Foot and mouth disease virus;
  5. Goat pox virus;
  6. Porcine herpes virus (Aujeszky's disease);
  7. Swine fever virus (Hog cholera virus);
  8. Lyssa virus;
  9. Newcastle disease virus;
  10. Peste des petits ruminants virus;
  11. Swine vesicular disease (Porcine enterovirus type 9);
  12. Rinderpest virus;
  13. Sheep pox virus;
  14. Teschen disease virus;
  15. Vesicular stomatitis virus;

b. Bacteria, whether natural, enhanced or modified, either in the form of isolated live cultures or as material including living material which has been deliberately inoculated or contaminated with such cultures, as follows:
1. Mycoplasma mycoides.

I C353 Genetically-modified micro-organisms, as follows:

a. Genetically-modified micro-organisms or genetic elements that contain nucleic acid sequences associated with pathogenicity and are derived from organisms specified in heads a. to c. of entry 1C351 or heads a. or b. of entry 1C352: Genetically-modified micro-organisms or genetic elements that contain nucleic acid sequences coding for any of the toxins specified in head d. of entry 1C351.

II
2B352 Equipment capable of use in biological manufacturing, as follows:

a. Containment facilities at Containment Level (ACDP) 3 or 4, and related equipment, as follows:
1. Facilities that meet the criteria for Containment Level 3 or 4 as specified in guidance from the Advisory Committee on Dangerous Pathogens approved by the Health and Safety Commission (published by HMSO, Second Edition 1990);
   Note:The criteria for Containment Level 3 or 4 in head a. of this entry are equivalent to the criteria for P3 or P4, BL3 or BL4, L3 or L4 containment as specified in the WHO Laboratory Biosafety manual (Geneva, 1983).
2. Independently ventilated protective full or half suits;
3. Biological safety cabinets or isolators, which allow manual operations to be performed within whilst providing an environment equivalent to Class III biological protection;
   Note:In this entry, isolators include flexible isolators, dry boxes, anaerobic chambers and glove boxes.

b. Fermenters, bioreactors, chemostats and continuous-flow systems capable of operation without the propagation of aerosols, having all the following characteristics:
1. Capacity of 300 litres or more;

    2. Double or multiple sealing joints within the steam
       containment area; and

    3. Capable of *in-situ* sterilisation in a closed state;

 c. Centrifugal separators or decanters, capable of continuous
separation without the propagation of aerosols, having all the
following characteristics:

    1. Flow rate exceeding 100 litres per hour;

    2. Components of polished stainless steel or titanium;

    3. Double or multiple sealing joints within the steam
       containment area; and

    4. Capable of *in-situ* sterilisation in a closed state;

 d. Cross-flow filtration equipment, designed for continuous
separation without the propagation of aerosols, having both of
the following characteristics:

    1. Equal to or greater than 5 square meters; and

    2. Capable of *in-situ* sterilisation;

 e. Steam sterilisable freeze drying equipment with a condenser
capacity exceeding 50 kg of ice in 24 hours and less than
1,000 kg of ice in 24 hours;

 f. Chambers designed for aerosol challenge testing with
pathogenic micro-organisms or toxins and having a capacity
of 1 m^3 or greater.

III

Warning Guidelines

Although items in the categories listed below have not been brought
under export control, it is possible that these items could be used in
BW proliferation programmes and thus enquiries or orders relating to
such items should be carefully assessed.

   (a) ACDP (Advisory Committee on Dangerous Pathogens)
      Hazard Group 4 and Group 3 micro-organisms not controlled
      and some Hazard Group 2 micro-organisms, such as the
      following:
      Clostridium perfringens
      Clostridium tetani
      Enterohaemorrhagic Escherichia coli serotype 0157 and other
      verotoxin producing serotypes
      Legionella pneumophila
      Yersinia pseudotuberculosis
      Absettarov virus

Hanzalova virus
Hypr virus
Kyesanur Forest virus
Louping ill virus
Mopeia virus
Murray Valley encephalitis virus
Omsk haemorrhagic fever virus
Oropouche virus
Powassan virus
Rocio virus
St Louis encephalitis virus

(b) Toxogenic micro-organisms not controlled, such as species of Clostridia and Corynebacteria.

(c) Pathogens harmful to plants, fish or bees, and capable of causing serious economic or environmental damage.

(d) Genetically modified micro-organisms (GMOs) other than those controlled, which cause disease in man, animals, or plants, or harm to the environment, or which contain genes associated with pathogenicity; but excluding pesticides and herbicides active against weed plants.

(e) GMOs having enhanced expression of innate toxins or of other toxic organic chemicals of biological origin, or expression of heterologous toxins or other chemicals. For this purpose an organic chemical is considered to be one containing at least one carbon-carbon bond.

(f) Some types of genetic material, such as genomic libraries from toxogenic or pathogenic micro-organisms, potential host organisms for genetic modification, and nucleic acid factors relevant to expression.

(g) Toxins not controlled, including the following:
Abrin
Cholera toxin
Tetanus toxin
Trichothecene mycotoxin

(h) Media for cultivating agents, especially when ordered in unusually large quantities.

(i) Tissue culture cell lines suitable for large scale growth of viruses, rickettsiae, or chlamydiae.

(j) Equipment other than controlled, on pilot scale or larger, suitable for use in the production, harvesting, drying, or micro-encapsulation of pathogenic micro-organisms, or for the purification of toxins or of other organic chemicals of biological origin.

(k) Equipment suitable for the dissemination of biological agents, such as aerosol generators.

INDEX

247